The Pharisees in Matthew 23
Reconsidered

Layang Seng Ja

© 2018 Layang Seng Ja

Published 2018 by Langham Monographs
An imprint of Langham Publishing

Langham Partnership
PO Box 296, Carlisle, Cumbria CA3 9WZ, UK
www.langham.org

ISBNs:
978-1-78368-438-0 Print
978-1-78368-439-7 ePub
978-1-78368-440-3 Mobi
978-1-78368-441-0 PDF

Layang Seng Ja has asserted her right under the Copyright, Designs and Patents Act, 1988 to be identified as the Author of this work.

All rights reserved. No part of this publication may be reproduced, stored in a retrieval system or transmitted, in any form or by any means, electronic, mechanical, photocopying, recording or otherwise, without the prior written permission of the publisher or the Copyright Licensing Agency.

Greek/English Bible text from: Novum Testamentum Graece, 28th revised edition, edited by Barbara Aland and others, © 2012 Deutsche Bibelgesellschaft, Stuttgart.

British Library Cataloguing-in-Publication Data
A catalogue record for this book is available from the British Library

ISBN: 978-1-78368-438-0

Cover & Book Design: projectluz.com

Langham Partnership actively supports theological dialogue and an author's right to publish but does not necessarily endorse the views and opinions set forth here or in works referenced within this publication, nor can we guarantee technical and grammatical correctness. Langham Partnership does not accept any responsibility or liability to persons or property as a consequence of the reading, use or interpretation of its published content.

It has been a crux in New Testament studies whether the audience of the woes against the Pharisees in Matthew 23 is not traditional but is created by Matthew reflecting only the conflict between the Matthean community and Judaism of his time. In this book, Seng Ja, equipped with advance study in the Jewish and Rabbinic literatures, logical thinking and skillful exegesis, makes a thorough investigation of the issue and suggests that the Pharisees in Matthew 23 is historical. Her case is a strong one and nobody who would like to study the issue can overlook her contribution.

Simon Chow, DTh
Professor of New Testament Exegesis,
Lutheran Theological Seminary, Hong Kong

The twenty-third chapter in Matthew's gospel is notorious for its polemic directed at "the Pharisees." But who were these Pharisees and why are they so severely attacked in this text? Reading Matthew within Judaism and taking into account the diversity that existed within the Pharisaic group itself, especially the conflicts between the houses of Hillel and Shammai, Seng Ja takes on the difficult task of deciding whether these Matthean traditions reflect pre-Matthean realities or were designed to address the situation after the fall of the Jerusalem temple, or both: that Matthew was using traditional material to address contemporary concerns. Concluding the latter, Seng Ja's study contributes further nuance to the conversation about the role of the Pharisees in the Gospel of Matthew. *The Pharisees in Matthew 23 Reconsidered* is a welcome addition to Matthean studies and will be of interest especially to those who seek to understand the relationship of this text to other forms of Judaism.

Anders Runesson, PhD
Professor of New Testament, University of Oslo, Norway

The Pharisees are probably Jesus's most prominent opponents, prompting vicious debates on various occasions during his ministry. Most people think of them as "hypocrites" and "blind guides." But is this a historically accurate picture? Is Matthew 23 in fact reflecting the time of Jesus or a much later time? In this extensive historical and literary study, Seng Ja competently argues that Matthew 23 provides an authentic portrayal of the Pharisees in Jesus's time, but also reflects the turbulent post-70 period where Matthew's

Jewish-Christian community faced conflict from Pharisaic-Rabbinic Judaism. The study contains a wealth of historical information and literary insights, and presents a valuable voice from the Majority World. I warmly recommend this monograph.

Cornelis Bennema, PhD
Senior Lecturer in New Testament,
Union School of Theology, Oxford, UK

Contents

Introduction 1

Chapter 1 5
The Plan of the Study
    1.1. Literature Reviews 5
    1.2. Identifying the Concern of the Study 11
    1.3. The Purpose of the Study 13
    1.4. Methodology 14
        1.4.1 Historical Analysis 14
        1.4.2. Literary Analysis 15
        1.4.3. The Procedure of the Study 16

Chapter 2 17
The Historical Pharisees from the Second Temple Period to the First Century
    Introduction 17
    2.1 The Origin of the Pharisees 19
    2.2 The Pharisees in the Hasmonean Period (140–63 BCE) 27
        The Pharisees and John Hyrcanus 28
        The Jews Executed by Alexander Jannaeus (103–76 BCE) 30
        Salome Alexandra (76–67 BCE) 33
    2.3 The Pharisees under the Herodians 34
        2.3.1 The Pharisees and Herod the Great 34
        2.3.2. The Two Pharisaic Leaders – Hillel and Shammai 43
        2.3.3 The Teachings and Practices of Hillel and Shammai 48
        2.3.4 The Hillelites and the Shammaites 55
    2.4 The Pharisees in Post-70 CE 59
    Chapter Findings 65

Chapter 3 67
The Pharisees in Matthew
    Introduction 67
    3.1. The Pharisees in Matthew 68
        The Pharisees and John the Baptist (3:1, 5–9) 68
        The Pharisees in Galilee 68
        The Pharisees in Jerusalem 72
    3.2. Matthew's Redaction 74
        3.2.1. Matthew's Redaction on Mark 75
        3.2.2. Matthew's Redaction on Q 82

    3.3. The Characteristic of the Matthean Pharisees 89
    Chapter Findings 92

Chapter 4 93
The Literary Analyses of Matthew 23
    Introduction 93
    4.1. The Setting, Literary Context and Structure of Matthew 23 94
    4.2 General Exegesis of Matthew 23 96
        Matthew 23:2–3a 97
        Matthew 23:3b–12 100
        Matthew 23:13–36 106
    4.3. The Traditional Materials in Matthew 23 114
        4.3.1. The Seat of Moses 114
        4.3.2. Phylacteries 117
        4.3.3. Tassels 119
        4.3.4. Proselytes 120
        4.3.5. Oaths and Vows 121
        4.3.6. Utensils Cleaning 124
        4.3.7. Tithing 126
        4.3.8. The House-Criticism Languages 127
    4.4. The Pharisees and Jesus as Reflected in Matthew 23 131
    Chapter Findings 140

Chapter 5 143
Understanding Matthew 23 in the Historical Context of the Relationship between the Matthean Community and Judaism
    Introduction 143
    5.1 The Suggested Community 143
        5.1.1 Jewish or Gentile Community? 143
        5.1.2. Extra-Muros Community 146
        5.1.3. Intra-Muros Community 149
    5.2 The Matthean Community 152
        5.2.1. Intra-Jewish Community 152
        5.2.2. Palestine Located Community 157
    5.3 The Function of Matthew 23 159
    Chapter Findings 162

Chapter 6 165
Conclusion

Bibliography 169

Introduction

This book is entitled *The Pharisees in Matthew 23 Reconsidered*. As Cook states, Matthew 23 seems to constitute "the most systematic and sustained attack against the sects of Judaism in general and the Pharisees in particular."[1] When we look at the gospels, the Jewish leaders from various sects appear aggressive, constantly looking for opportunities to denigrate Jesus. The various Jewish groups depicted there as Jesus's opponents are the Pharisees, the scribes, the Herodians, the chief priests, and the Sadducees. In turn, Jesus denounces and challenges some of these groups. Very often, the gospel writers will pair off Jesus's opponents – the Pharisees and Sadducees or the Pharisees and scribes. At times, it is the Pharisees alone. They thus emerge as playing an important role in Jesus's time.[2] The gospels also portray Jesus calmly rebutting their attacks. Although he is always alone in such situations, the Gospels make it clear that he is the one who always emerges as the final victor.

Jesus criticizes his opponents, the Pharisees in particular. In Matthew 23 they are paired off with the scribes,[3] where Jesus denounces them as blind hypocrites. In the seven woes Jesus charges them as leaders who teach

---

1. D. E. Cook, "A Gospel Portrait of the Pharisees," *Review & Expositor* 84, no. 2 (Spring 1987): 226.

2. B. Repschinski, *The Controversy Stories in the Gospel of Matthew* (Gottingen: Vandenhoeck & Ruprecht, 2000), 323.

3. I agree that most scribes belong to the Pharisaic group. In that sense there are scribal Pharisees in Matthew. In the New Testament, the scribes are associated with the Pharisees and some scribes also worked with the high priests. Josephus does not mention the scribes as a distinct group. For the purpose of this study, only the name Pharisees will be used from now on. See further discussion on this matter in E. Rivkin, *A Hidden Revolution* (Nashville: Abingdon, 1978), 104–124; "Scribes, Pharisees, Lawyers, Hypocrites: A Study in Synonymity," *HUCA* 49 (1978): 135–142; E. Lohse , *The NT Environment* (Nashville, TN: Abingdon, 1976): 115–120 ; J. Jeremias, *Jerusalem in the Time of Jesus* (Philadelphia, PA: Fortress Press,1969), 233–245; M. J. Cook, *Mark's Treatment of the Jewish Leaders* (Leiden:

correctly but act irresponsibly in society. The seven woes denouncement of the Pharisees is unique to Matthew, though Luke does contain a trace of this (Luke 12:1–3). Matthew 23 describes the Pharisees in such a way that they become figures of hate.

This is why I grew up hearing that all the Pharisees were hypocrites and enemies of Jesus. I assume most of our Asian understanding of the Pharisees is the same. Our understanding of the Pharisees comes exclusively from the Gospels. Despite the negative picture given of them in the Gospels, in Matthew in particular, the Pharisees seem to have contributed enormously to Judaism and the history of the Jews. Even though scholars' opinions of the Pharisees vary, it appears that not all of them merited the charges of blindness and hypocrisy. For instance, experts variously describe them as a group of uncertain origin and as a powerful religious leadership group;[4] a learned scholarly group;[5] a group who were not concerned so much about ritual purity and actually mingled with the common Jews and also played an important role in Judaism as well as for the continuation and survival of the Jewish community after the disaster of 70 CE.[6] Others consider that, they were a political force before; after that under the leadership of Hillel and Shammai, they transformed themselves into a group concerned with maintaining purity. The two houses used to argue against one another;[7] still others believe that the Pharisees did not withdraw from public life before 70 CE but they were powerless in all aspects;[8] while some believe that they were a lay movement of middle class urban artisans or even retainers[9] in competition with an elite priesthood. Even from this brief glance, we know

---

Brill, 1978), 85–97; D. A. Carson, "The Jewish Leaders in Matthew's Gospel: Reappraisal," *JETS* 25, no. 2 (June 1982): 161–174.

4. S. Mason, "Pharisaic Dominance before 70 CE and the Gospels' Hypocrisy Charge (Matthew 23:2–3)," *HTR* 83, no. 4 (1990): 363–381, 371.

5. Carson, "Jewish Leaders in Matthew's Gospel," 166.

6. E. Rivkin, "Defining the Pharisees: The Tannatic Sources," in *Origins of Judaism*, vol. 2, part 2, ed. Jacob Neusner (New York & London: Garland, 1990), 173–217; *A Hidden Revolution*, 104–124; "Scribes, Pharisees, Lawyers, Hypocrites," 135–142.

7. J. Neusner, *From Politics to Piety: The Emergence of the Pharisaic Judaism* (Englewood Cliffs, NJ: Prentice Hall, 1973).

8. E. P. Sanders, *Judaism: Practice and Belief 63BCE–66CE* (London: SCM, 1992), 392–400.

9. A. J. Saldarini, *Pharisees, Scribes, and Sadducees in Palestinian Society* (Grand Rapids, MI: Eerdmans, 2001), 48.

that the Pharisees seemed very active both pre- and post-70 CE and at least two Pharisaic houses were prominent in the early first century. After the Romans destroyed the Second Temple, other Jewish groups appeared to have disappeared while the Pharisees alone survived.[10] The Pharisees, especially the descendants of Hillel, were the guides and teachers who saved the remnant of the Jewish nation from complete ruin and sustained the national identity. This view, though, is a matter of endless debate.[11] Therefore Herford states that the "Judaism which has come down through the centuries is essentially Pharisaism."[12] Perhaps after all, the Pharisees we have seen in the history were not all the "hypocrites and blind guides" described in Matthew 23.

All this fascinated me so much that I wanted to discover the truth about the Pharisees. Who were they? Why does Matthew 23 portray the Pharisees in such a polemical way? Were all the Pharisees at the time opposed to Jesus? What opponents could Jesus have encountered during his ministry? We need to have a clear picture of the Pharisees as they were in history. If there were Pharisees who truly represented the Jewish community and delighted in faithfully observing God's law, we need to examine who was actually the target of Jesus's denouncement. If Jesus's polemic recorded in Matthew only targets some Pharisaic Jewish leaders, who were they? We must investigate whether Matthew portrays the controversy from one side only and generalizes about the Pharisees according to his situation, or examine whether Matthew 23 does reflect the actual roles, character and function of the historical Pharisees in Jesus's time. Therefore, it becomes vital to study the historical Pharisees focusing on first-century CE and to examine how much Matthew 23 reflects the reality of the Pharisees of Jesus in his time.

---

10. R. T. Herford, *The Pharisees* (Boston: Beacon, 1962), 52.
11. Neusner, *From Politics to Piety*, 11.
12. Herford, *Pharisees*, 52.

CHAPTER 1

The Plan of the Study

1.1. Literature Reviews

The following is an examination of the key contributions various scholars have made to the understanding of the Matthean Pharisees in general and in Matthew 23 in particular.

The first group of Matthean scholars maintains that the polemics we see against the Pharisees in Matthew 23 asserted anti-Judaism. Clark claims that throughout Matthew's Gospel, gentile bias is obvious.[1] He believes that a converted gentile Christian from Syria composed this gospel. In his view, Matthew purposefully and repeatedly portrayed a replacement theology of gentile bias through the language he used: "The children of the kingdom will be cast out" (8:12); "In his name will the gentiles trust" (12:21); "The kingdom of God will be taken away from you, and given to a people producing the fruits of the kingdom" (21:43); "Go and make disciples of all the gentile peoples (τα ἔθνη) . . . teaching them to obey all the commands I have laid on you."[2] Some scholars who follow this anti-Judaism position are Hare and Harrington.[3] They argue that Matthew's use of ἔθνος /ἔθνη is to focus on the gentile mission without including the nation of Israel. After a thorough study of ἔθνος /ἔθνη they concluded that "in Matthew's overall view of salvation history the kingdom of God has been taken away from Israel and

---

1. K. W. Clark, "The Gentile Bias in Matthew," *JBL* 66 (1947): 165–172.
2. Clark, "Gentile Bias," 167.
3. D. R. A. Hare and D. J. Harrington, "Make Disciples of All the Gentiles (Mt. 28.19)," *CBQ* 37 (1975): 359–369.

given to nation (ἔθνος) producing fruit of it (Mt 21:43), i.e., the church."[4] Matthew's frequent use of the word ἔθνος /ἔθνη (4:15; 10:5, 18; 12:18; 12:21, 43; 24:14; 25:32; 28:19) indicate an emphasis on non-Jews with Israel excluded. This indicates the gentile bias mission and a replacement theology in Matthew. This motif is also reflected in 23:34–39; 5:10–12; 22:6 for Israel's failure was already foreordained (13:11–15) by Jesus. Since Israel rejected God and his Messiah, they in turn were rejected by God (21:43; 22:7–8; 23:38). Besides, Matthew distinguishes Jewish figures and institutions as other by using the possessive pronouns "their" and "your," rather than the inclusive "we." This reflects the situation of the parting of the ways between Israel and the church.[5] Although Jesus's mission gave first priority to the Jews, with their rejection the time is over and the focus shifts to the gentiles who bear fruits (10:5; 15:24, 26). Therefore, Hare and Harrington consider that in Matthew, Jesus's mission was basically to the gentiles, and the gospel was intended for the whole world. This is because ever since God rejected Israel, Israel was not even on the list of "all the nations" anymore to whom the church was to preach the gospel of Jesus.[6] Although Meier acknowledges the Matthean gentile bias, he hesitates to see God's rejection of the Jews as Hare and Harrington's view.[7] Thus, as for Clark and others who consider the gospel of Matthew as anti-Judaic, the primary concern of Matthew 23 was to contrast the favour shown to the gentiles with God's rejection of the Jews.[8]

The second group of scholars believes Matthew 23 was a product of post-70 conflicts between rabbinic Judaism and the Matthew community. Herford argues that even though Matthew 23 was born out of post-70 CE conflicts between the two different religions, the author of Matthew 23 fatefully misread Pharisaism as religious formalism and attacked the Pharisees as hypocrites.[9] Herford asserts that the group had had centuries of history and

---

4. See further discussion in Hare and Harrington, "Make Disciples," 359.

5. Hare and Harrington, "Make Disciples," 363.

6. Hare and Harrington, 367.

7. J. P. Meier, "Nations or Gentiles in Matthew 28:19?," *CBQ* 39 (1977): 94–102; J. P. Meir, *Vision of Matthew: Christ Church, and morality in the First Gospel* (New York: Paulist Press, 1979), 17–25.

8. Clark, "Gentile Bias," 166.

9. Herford, *The Pharisees*.

they were not "organized hypocrites nor a once living religion."[10] He says that the controversies found in the Gospels, particularly Jesus's declaration of woes to the Pharisees, were written from one side only and that nothing concrete could be learned or known unless we went back to the specific situation.[11] Herford's opinion is that behind the scene of Matthew 23 there was conflict between the two religions – formative-rabbinic Judaism and Christianity. It was a reflection of conflict between the two religions after post-70 CE. As time passed, Pharisaism and Christianity reached a stage when reconciliation was impossible.[12] That was because, while Pharisaism remained a vital current within Judaism, expressing its religion in terms of the Torah, the followers of Jesus progressively changed their faith into a person-centred (Jesus) religion.[13] Never before in all their long history had the Pharisees met such opposition within their own community. The result was an embittered conflict in which the followers of Jesus felt that the Pharisaic leaders had driven them into a situation where they had to turn and fight.[14] For Herford, the author of Matthew composed the woes in order to attack the rival body. Davies also holds such a view and does not think of Matthew 23 as a fictional piece, added by the redactor. He argues that by the time Matthew had composed this writing the rabbis of Yavneh were a leading community amongst the Jews so that the author of Matthew was attacking these so-called rabbi-Pharisees.[15]

However, a third group of scholars disagree. They view Matthew 23 as the work of the redactors rather than a genuine product born out of historical conflict. They consider that Matthew 23 was a redactional and fictional addition written after 70 CE to legitimize the authority of the Matthean community. Garland considers that Matthew 23 was composed for the Matthean community with a certain aim in view.[16] Garland wants to know the intention behind the composition of Matthew 23, and concludes

---

10. Herford, 211.
11. Herford, 214.
12. Herford, 209.
13. Herford, 204.
14. Herford, 210.
15. W. D. Davies, *The Setting of the Sermon on the Mount* (Cambridge: Cambridge University Press, 1964), 106.
16. D. E. Garland, *The Intention of Matthew 23*, NovTSup, 52 (Leiden: Brill, 1979).

that Matthew had composed such an "anti-Judaic" text to warn and teach Christian leaders within his own community. Garland says that the composition of Matthew 23 had two purposes: to clarify the problem of Israel's rejection of Jesus and God's rejection of Israel in the disastrous war with Rome. Matthew exhorts the members of his community not to behave like the generation who had rejected Jesus, urging them to learn a lesson from what had happened in front of their very eyes.[17] As for Garland, Matthew wants Christian leaders to avoid the same judgment and denouncement that the Scribes and Pharisees had fallen under.

Similarly, Saldarini in his book[18] and his essay[19] claims that the context and setting of Matthew 23 was post-70 CE and it cannot therefore be considered as historical.[20] He considers that Matthew 23 was invented in order to challenge and undermine the orthodox leadership of the Jewish community and to build up the legitimacy of Matthew's own group and leadership. The Matthean community was engaged in a critical situation of serious rivalry with the Jewish community at that time, so the author of Matthew attacked the Jewish leaders through Jesus's polemics. Indeed, the final author of Matthew was not attacking the legitimacy of the Jewish community, its structure and its laws but the Jewish leaders of that time, because the author was dissatisfied with their leadership of the Jewish community.[21] It was only a reflection of a fierce rivalry between Jesus's followers and the Jewish leaders.[22] This group of scholars argues that Matthew's presentation of the Pharisees is so fundamentally anachronistic that the passage must be redactional and fictional. Thus, Matthew's picture of the Jewish leaders does not reflect Jesus's time. However, this position has been refuted by the fourth group of scholars who consider Matthew 23 to depict circumstances in Jesus's time.

---

17. Garland, *Intention of Matthew 23*, 215.

18. A. J. Saldarini, *Matthew's Christian-Jewish Community* (Chicago: University of Chicago Press, 1994).

19. A. J. Saldarini, "Deligitimation of Leaders in Matthew 23," *CBQ* 54 (1992), 659–680.

20. Saldarini, *Matthew's Christian-Jewish Community*, 4.

21. Saldarini, *Matthew*, 46.

22. Saldarini, "Delegitimation of Leaders," 665; and Saldarini, *Matthew*, 67.

The Plan of the Study 9

The fourth group of scholars prefers to understand Matthew 23 in the context of Jesus's time rather than regarding the chapter simply as a reflection of the post-70 CE conflict. In his study, Mason raises two distinct but related questions.[23] His first interest is in seeing whether the Pharisees were the dominant party in Palestinian Judaism before the destruction of the Second temple. His second question is to examine whether Jesus of Nazareth had debated with those groups. He concludes that the Pharisees dominated before 70 CE and could have debated with Jesus. For him, the way the Pharisees exercised their religious dominance before 70 CE was the key to understanding Jesus's hypocrisy charge.[24] He does not think a redactor or a final author composed Matthew 23:2–3 since it supported the Pharisees' teachings as a legitimate tradition.[25] Thus for Mason, the best way to understand Matthew 23:2–3 is the context of Jesus's time and not post-70 CE.[26]

Newport goes further in his work *The Sources and Sitz im Leben of Matthew 23* arguing that the various descriptions and aspects of Jewish life depicted in Matthew 23:2–31(for instance, the chair of Moses, phylacteries, tassels and the practices of gnat-straining and cup-washing) fitted into pre-70 CE Judaism.[27] Newport acknowledges that the Gospel according to Matthew was composed after post-70 CE by the author of Matthew for his own purpose. However, the author must have been one very familiar with Jewish laws and regulations since numerous individual references – about the temple and the altar, and the affirmation of Pharisees and Scribes as those who sit on Moses's seat – firmly reflect this very Jewish setting. Thus he suggests that Matthew 23 should be read in the context of pre-70 CE setting and not after. Newport states that the Pharisees of pre-70 CE seem to be a group of scholars who mixed with the common Jews in their daily life and whose concern was to instruct the people in *halakhic* matters.[28] For Newport, Matthew 23 is understandable only when we put it within the

---

23. Mason, "Pharisaic Dominance before 70 CE," 363–381.
24. Mason, 380.
25. See further in Mason, 375.
26. See further in Mason, 378.
27. K. G. C. Newport, *The Sources and Sitz im Leben of Matthew 23* (Sheffield: Sheffield Academic, 1995), 78–79, 116, 156.
28. Newport, *Sources and Sitz*, 114–115.

historical context of Jesus's time. However, he focuses more on pre-70 Jewish customs and practices in Matthew 23 and places little emphasis on how the text reflects the practices of particular Pharisees in Jesus's time.

Neusner allows us to understand more about the pre-70 Pharisees and their tradition.[29] He emphasizes how Pharisaism turned from being a political force to becoming a table-fellowship party. He believes that originally, to be a Pharisee was "not a profession, but an avocation." Pharisaism was one of the philosophical groups within Judaism. However, the members were so expert in both the oral Torah and the written Torah that they claimed the right to rule over all the Jews.[30] They were seen as a political force or party, quite powerful and influential during the Hasmonean period, especially when Salome Alexandra was on her throne. Nevertheless, Hillel (ca. 50 BCE to10 CE), who was nearly a contemporary of Jesus, transformed the Pharisees. Under Hillel's reformation, the Pharisees turned from being a political party to a true piety or table-fellowship sect and with members who also withdrew from normal social and public life. Neusner argues that this fact about the Pharisees is visible in both the gospels and the Talmudic tradition, for the group is portrayed as a religious sect who cares about religious rituals even in their homes.[31] Though Neusner is right in describing the Pharisees' concern for religious ceremonies, he seems to take too narrow a view to make a clear assessment of Pharisaism. As Carson remarks, if the Pharisees were just content to be a table-fellowship party and did not play a leading role within first-century Judaism, why did Jesus curse them?[32] Besides, Neusner mentions the two opposing Pharisaic houses – the House of Hillel and the House of Shammai in the reign of Herod the great. The two houses debated and opposed one another over Mosaic law, its interpretation, traditions and practices. During Jesus's time the followers of the two houses appeared to have had an ongoing debate over their respective rules and regulations. These two houses seemed to have played decisive roles as

---

29. Neusner, *From Politics to Piety*; J. Neuser in his books, *Early Rabbinic Judaism* (1975), 64–69, and also in *History of Religions* 12 (1972/73), 264–269, distinguishes scribes from Pharisees and says that according to Josephus, the scribes were known as rabbis.

30. Neusner, *From Politics to Piety*, 7–11.

31. Neusner, 14.

32. Carson, "Jewish Leaders," 165.

interpreters of the law until 70 CE. After the fall of the temple in 70 CE, the rabbis at Yavneh apparently followed the tradition of the House of Hillel. If this is the case, Jesus could have encountered either the Hillelites or the Shammaites and debated over the Mosaic law, its interpretation and practises during his ministry.[33]

However, as Fornberg in his article *Matthew and the School of Shammai: A Study in the Matthean Antithesis* argues, the author of Matthew never distinguishes between different kinds of Pharisees.[34] Therefore, Fornberg makes a quest to identify a kind of Judaism the final author of Matthew took for granted as his adversary through the analysis of the antithesis in Matthew 5 – the Sermon on the Mount. After carefully analyzing Matthew 5 and comparing it with the legal rules and principles practised by the Hillelite Pharisees and the Shammaite Pharisees, Fornberg states that Jesus's attack seems to have been directed against the Shammaite Pharisees. The polemics do not fit the Hillelites. The Shammaite Pharisees are seen as Jesus's opponents and "the scapegoats for the final redactor of Matthew." It was against the Shammaite-Pharisees that the final redactor of Matthew addressed his polemic. For the Shammaic group fits what is written about laws and oaths in Matthew[35] and thus reflects a pre-Mishnaic level of Pharisaic theology. This then would make it "dubious or rather totally misleading"[36] to see the Pharisaism attacked in Matthew as an invention or the development of a latter rabbinic period. Consequently, the work of Neusner and Fornberg opens the way for further research on the historical Pharisaic group who opposed Jesus since not all the Pharisees seem to have behaved as described in Matthew 23.

1.2. Identifying the Concern of the Study

Throughout Matthean scholarship, the majority of scholars have discussed the Pharisees in Matthew 23, in the situation and context post-70 CE. Although these discussions have taken various forms and have not reached

---

33. Neusner, *From Politics to Piety*, 14.
34. T. Fornberg, "Matthew and the School of Shammai: A Study in the Matthean Antithesis," *Theology of Life* (Hong Kong) 7 (1984): 35–59. *Jewish Dialogue*, 1988, 11–31.
35. Fornberg, "Matthew and the School of Shammai," 31.
36. Fornberg, 11–31.

consensus, scholars generally see the post-70 event as largely explaining the attack on the Pharisees in Matthew 23. They say that the seven woes do not apply to the Judaism of Jesus's time but reflect the situation post-70 CE.

As we have seen above, the first group of scholars interprets Matthew 23 as anti-Judaic in general and anti-Pharisaic in particular. "Replacement theology" is what they see behind Matthew 23. However, the Gospel according to Matthew is also considered the most Jewish gospel, an anti-Jewish stance may not be the focus of Matthew 23.

The second group of scholars believes that Matthew 23 was a product of historical conflict between the Christian community and the leading rabbinic Judaism group in post-70 CE and that it was not written by a redactor or a converted gentile. However, this view has been soundly rebutted by a third group of scholars who consider the text as fictional and unhistorical. For them, Matthew 23 was composed for a certain theological purpose because of post-70 CE events. It was just an invention of the final redactor. Only a few scholars hold that the setting of Matthew 23 is pre-70 CE. For them the traditions of the Jewish leaders described in Matthew 23 are essentially from Jesus's time, and the chapter cannot be understood unless one goes back to the actual situation and setting.

As many scholars hold, there is a possibility that Matthew composed his Gospel after 70 CE. However, it can be misleading if we only place the Pharisees in Matthew 23 within the setting and context of the early Christians' conflict with rabbinic Judaism and only regard the chapter as an invented piece by a redactor or a converted gentile Christian. If Matthew 23, as they think, is just a reflection of post-70 CE circumstances and does not represent the historical Pharisees and their situation in Jesus's time, how can the descriptions and the customs relating to the Pharisees be explained? I am curious to discover more about the roles and traditions of the Pharisees in Jesus's time in order to understand why Jesus attacks them and who he attacked. Although Garland sees Matthew 23 as reflecting the situation and times of Jesus, his study only focuses on the intention behind the chapter, concluding that Matthew wrote it to warn Christian leaders within his own community. He does not examine how far the criticism of Matthew 23 was related to the historical Pharisees of Jesus's time. Likewise, though Mason states that pre-70 Pharisees are the key to understanding Jesus's charge of hypocrisy, he only takes Matthew 23:2–3 into consideration when investigating the actual historical setting of Jesus. He does not examine the rest of the chapter to see whether it fits into the Jesus context. For that, Newport's work on analyzing the traditions and aspects of the first-century Jewish life is astonishingly clear and allows us to understand the Pharisees' customs in the context of the pre-70 setting. However, he does not identify how much the description and criticism of Matthew 23 related to the historical Pharisees in Jesus's time. Thus, this study wants to investigate what Garland, Newport and Mason do not cover in detail.

Furthermore, to understand Jesus's charge of the Pharisees' hypocrisy, it is necessary to do more research on the two Pharisaic houses (Hillel and Shammai) and how they related to Matthew 23. Although Neusner has contributed greatly to the understanding of the pre-70 traditions of the two Pharisaic houses, his focus is on the general sources available, and he makes no connection with how the two houses could relate to Matthew's denunciation. If there were different Pharisaic houses existing in the first century, further investigation on the functions, roles, and practices of the two Pharisaic houses in pre-70 CE are required. That would help us better understand the genuine message of the Pharisees and what role they played during Jesus's ministry. Similarly, though Fornberg in his article specifies the Shammaic house as Jesus's opponents in Matthew 5, this issue still needs to be explored further to see whether the same applies to Matthew 23.

If Matthew is consistent in his presentation of the Pharisees and their relationship with Jesus, he probably must be telling us about the information which contains the historical value. We need to investigate how Matthew 23 fits into the whole Matthean presentation of the Pharisees and how it reflects the historical Pharisees of Jesus's time. Thus, this study proposes to examine whether the Pharisees of Matthew, particularly the Pharisees and their practices in Matthew 23 are traditional materials of pre-70 or post-70 CE. For this reason, special attention and careful research on "the Pharisees in Matthew 23 reconsidered" is essential.

1.3. The Purpose of the Study

Scholars have often suggested that the Pharisees of Matthew 23 were a polemic target in the Matthean community of post-70 CE. They often consider the Pharisees in Matthew 23 as a reflection of the rivalry between rabbinic Judaism and the Matthean community. It may well be that the chapter was composed after 70 CE. However, we still need to be aware that the description and criticism we find there also refer to the Pharisees and their practices in Jesus's time. Matthew 23 may well reflect rivalry between the Christian community and the Jewish community after 70 CE and be interpreted as a warning intended for Christian leaders. That does not necessarily exclude that the chapter is about historical Pharisees and their failures during Jesus's time.

Thus, the purpose of this study is, primarily, to examine whether Jesus's criticism of the Pharisees and their practices in Matthew 23 are traditional or the post-70 CE invention. The hypothesis of this study is that the Pharisees and their materials in Matthew 23 are traditional and yet Matthew uses such material with a purpose for his post-70 community.

1.4. Methodology

1.4.1 Historical Analysis

Historical analysis can be carried our various ways. These include source criticism, form criticism, redaction criticism, textual criticism, and social-scientific analysis of biblical material and so on.[37] Many scholars argue that Matthew 23 bears the hallmarks of a redactional creation and reflect the final redactor's situation.[38] For instance, Garland in his study "The Intention of Matthew 23" uses redaction criticism to place emphasis on the one responsible for the final form of the gospel. It also focuses on the third phase of the gathering of the materials.[39] His redaction criticism emphasizes only two things: Was the final literary composition done by the actual author or by a redactor? And what was the intention of the redactor? Garland's approach neglects the historical context, thus failing to illuminate how the text reflects the authentic issues between the historical Pharisees and Jesus.

---

37. A. Stock, *The Method and Message of Matthew* (Collegeville, MN: Liturgical Press, 1994), 1.

38. Newport also states this fact in his book. See Newport, *Sources and Sitz*, 12.

39. Garland, *Intention of Matthew 23*, 4–5.

Though Saldarini uses a historical-critical and contemporary literary method for the Gospel of Matthew and a sociological approach to Matthew 23, his focus is only on the situation of the Matthean community after 70 CE. Saldarini, therefore, demonstrates how the circumstances of the time in which Matthew wrote and the community he belonged to affected the text. His analysis was more of the situation of the Matthean community and less on that of the Pharisees in Jesus's time. If we want to understand Jesus's words about the Pharisees in Matthew 23, we need to do a historical analysis of Pharisaism – their characters, roles, function, practices and belief. This also means that the extra-canonical Jewish texts and the Greco-Roman literature will be helpful and relevant sources for this study. Thus, this dissertation will first do an historical analysis of Pharisaism to help us understand Jesus's charge of hypocrisy against the Pharisees and to discern how that could relate to the Matthean community.

1.4.2. Literary Analysis

Literary analysis is the second tool I would like to use for this dissertation because a literary analysis will show how a writer tells a story and creates characters and drama. It might also reveal something about the author's intention concerning the Pharisees. By doing this, I hope to discover how Matthew's Pharisees mirror – or not – the historical Pharisees in Jesus's milieu and how the Pharisees in Matthew could be understood. Since the literary world of the gospel could be a reflection of things that happened during Jesus's ministry, we need to examine Matthew's presentation of the plot, characters, setting and the language he uses regarding the Pharisees. Even Schweizer recognized the living voice of Jesus in Matthew 23.[40] Thus, historical analysis seems an appropriate method to apply in order to comprehend and to draw out the whole truth of the historical Pharisees, and the literary analysis will help to understand how Matthew uses the Pharisees in his narrative. We need to go back to the text and its world to have a real idea of the Pharisees in Matthew 23. Otherwise, Matthew 23 will be seen as just a reflection of the Matthean community.

---

40. E. Schweizer, *The Good News according to Matthew*, trans. D. E Green (London: SPCK, 1975), 433. Even Bultmann acknowledges that some of Matt 23 goes back to the ministry of Jesus. See R. Bultmann, *The History of the Synoptic Tradition*, trans. J. Marsh (Oxford: Blackwell, 1963), 147.

1.4.3. The Procedure of the Study

This dissertation has six chapters. The present chapter serves as a general platform for introducing the plan of the whole work. In chapter 2, I will conduct a brief investigation and analysis on the historical Pharisaism from the Second Temple period to the late first century. This chapter will help us to understand the characters, roles, beliefs, traditional law and practices of the historical Pharisees. Particular emphasis will be placed on the Pharisees in Jesus's time. Through the examination of the history of the Pharisees, I hope to see how this can help us to understand Matthew's presentation of the accusations Jesus makes against them.

Once I know as much about the historical Pharisees as possible, I will investigate how Jesus may have interacted with the Pharisees in a literary setting. Thus, in chapter 3, I will study the Pharisees in Matthew to comprehend Matthew's portrayal of the Pharisees and how they interact with Jesus. The chapter will help us to have background material to understand a kind of Pharisees in Matthew 23 more fully.

In chapter 4, I will do literary analysis of Matthew 23. Through exegetical and literal analysis of the text, the study aims to comprehend the tradition, customs, practices, polemical language and messages of Matthew 23 in depth. Through this chapter, I hope to discover whether the Pharisees and materials we find in Matthew 23 are traditional reflection of post-70 Pharisaism or pre-70 Pharisaism of Jesus's time.

Chapter 5 focuses on understanding Matthew 23 in the historical context of the relationship between the Matthean community and Judaism. This chapter will have implications for how we understand the function of Matthew 23, Matthew's way of dealing with his own sources, and his relationship with other Jews in his own time. Chapter 6 is a brief summary of the whole dissertation with some concluding remarks on the study's findings.

CHAPTER 2

The Historical Pharisees from the Second Temple Period to the First Century

Introduction

To understand the polemical charge against the Pharisees, I must begin first to find out what the Pharisees were actually like in the history both during the time of Jesus and then the period when Matthew composed his gospel. Thus, this chapter explores in brief the origin, belief, development, roles, and practices of Pharisaism from the Second Temple period to the first century CE. Basically, there are three sources with information about the Pharisees – the gospels,[1]

---

1. The gospel tradition focuses more on the life, teachings and ministry of Jesus rather than portraying an accurate picture of the Pharisees and Jewish history. This also means that the gospels' portrayal of the historical Pharisees in relation to Jesus is inadequate. However, while the authors portray the life of Jesus, they do not ignore the atmosphere and the world Jesus grew up. The Gospels contain Jewish customs, the Pharisees' practices according to oral tradition. The discussion of Mosaic law in the Gospels reflects Jewish life pre-70 CE. For this reason, even Flusser acknowledges the historical reliability of the three Gospels – Mark, Matthew and Luke, and states that they are far more valuable as historical documents than the Gospel of John. For him the Jesus-portrayal in the Synoptic gospels is, "the historical Jesus, not the Kerygmatic Christ." If the Jesus stories are trustworthy and can be considered as historical documents, the conflict stories he had with the Pharisees are undeniably of historical value. See Flusser's opinion on the Gospels. D. Flusser, *Jesus* (Hebrew University, Jerusalem: The Magnes, 1998), 10, 20.

Josephus,[2] and rabbinic literature,[3] yet all three sources show bias and they were all written after 70 CE.

Besides these sources, some late Second Temple literature gives clues about the movement.[4] Though the information we have about them is very limited, given the nature of the sources, scholars have proposed and constructed various hypotheses about the historical Pharisees and their roles in Judaism. This chapter, too, will draw its basic information from the same primary sources. Although the quest to reconstruct historical Pharisaism is a crucial issue, and, as Neusner states, cannot be moulded into a continuous single narrative, I would like as far as possible to see what I can do based on these available sources. However, the gospel sources will not be discussed in this chapter, but in the next chapter, in order first to obtain a clear understanding of how the other sources portrayed the Pharisees. Thus, this chapter attempts to answer the following questions: What was the origin of the Pharisaic group, and what was the purpose of their existence? How

---

2. Josephus, a Jewish historian, wrote three major pieces: First, a biography of himself between 75 CE and 100 CE; second, biographical sayings about Jesus ca. 50 and ca. 90 CE; third, the laws and sayings attributed to pre-70 CE Pharisees and their successors. However, he presents the pre-70 Pharisees primarily as a political interest party, especially during the time of the Maccabees down to the reign of Herodians. In his *Antiquities* he mentions that the Pharisees numbered roughly 6,000 around the time of the death of Herod the Great. His Pharisees were basically the dominant party with considerable influence over the populace in Palestine from 150 BCE to ca. 50 CE. See M. McNamara, *Palestinian Judaism and the New Testament*, vol. 4 (Wilmington, DE: Glazier, 1983), 168.

3. The traditions in Rabbinic literature (Mishnah, Tosefta and Talmud) assume that the rabbis are the successor of the scribes and of the Pharisaic tradition. In the Mishnah, Rabbinic tradition traces its origin, and the origins of its oral tradition, back to Moses. From Moses it was handed down to Joshua, the elders, the prophets, the men of the post-exilic Great Synagogue, the pairs following on these, then through the last pair Shammai and Hillel (from the two pair – Shammai and Hillel – Hillel had a succession of followers as leaders in Judaism during the formative and consolidating period of the first and second century CE. The Hillelites were seen as, Simon I to ca 25 CE; Gamaliel I (teacher of Paul) 25–55 CE; Simon II 55 to ca 70; Johanan ben Zakkai 70–85 CE; Gamaliel II 85 to ca 135 CE; Simon III 140–175 CE; Judah I Ha-Nasi 175–217). Johanan ben Zakkai was the one who founded Pharisaic-rabbinic academy at Yaveh after the fall of Jerusalem. The nature of rabbinic literature is in part legal and in part non-legal, or haggadic. It comes from two distinct periods – that of the Tannaim (1–200 CE) and of the Amoraim (200–500 CE). Although the dating of rabbinic writing is after 70 CE, the tradition, contained basically in the Mishnah and Tosefta, by large were the traditions and practices of their pre-70 predecessors. See discussion about the matter in McNamara, *Palestinian Judaism*, 162, 166, 177.

4. 1 & 2 Macc, Ben Sirach, 4 Ezra, Baruch, 1 & 2 Enoch, the Book of Jubilees, the Book of Tobit, The Psalms of Solomon, and the Damascus Document. Specific references can be found inside the discussion.

many Pharisaic houses existed in the first century? What practices and roles did they have?

This chapter consists therefore of four parts with the focus on the roles of first-century Pharisaism. First, there will be a brief survey of the origin of the group. Then, there will be an examination of the Pharisees' roles and practice during the Hasmonean period of the Hellenistic era. The third and fourth sections will be on first-century Pharisaism up to the post-70 CE period of the Roman era. In order to comprehend the criticism and description of the Pharisees in Matthew 23, it is essential to study and examine historical Pharisaism.

2.1 The Origin of the Pharisees

The struggle to understand the origin of the Pharisaic development is one of the most crucial and seemingly unending debates for both biblical and Jewish scholars. Based on Josephus's accounts, many Christian scholars and Jewish scholars maintain that the group originated in the Hasmonean period, especially in the time of Jonathan or John Hyrcanus or Alexander Janaeus and it is said that the Pharisees are derived from the *Hasidim*. The idea that the *Hasidim* were the source of Pharisees, Essenes, and Sadducees became a common view of majority biblical scholarship in the nineteenth century,[5] continuing even into the twentieth century.[6] For instance, Gowan states that a kind of Jewish party bearing the name "Pharisees" emerged in the time of

---

5. J. Wellhausen opines that "it was a high degree of probability to see the *Hasidim* as the forerunner for both the Essenes and Pharisees and connect them with the Scribes in 1 Macc 7 as evidence." Cited in J. Kampen, *LXX: The Hasideans and the Origin of Pharisaim* (Atlanta: Scholar Press, 1988), 34.

6. See F. Smith, "A Study of the Zadokite High Priesthood within the Graeco-Roman Age: From Simon the Just to the High Priests appointed by Herod the Great," Dissertation (Harvard, 1961): 6–7; Kampen considers that the Pharisees derived from the Scribal circles of the Hasideans. See Kampen, *Hasideans*, 222. G. Stemberger also sees the Hasidim as the pioneer of both the Pharisees and the Essenes. See G. Stemberger, *Jewish Contemporaries of Jesus* (Minneapolis: Fortress Press, 1995), 97. Saldarini states that religious, intellectual and political life of the Hellenistic and Roman Empires can be the context of the rise of the Pharisees, Sadducees, and other Jewish groups. See Saldarini, *Palestinian Society*, 61–62. H. Koester, *Introduction to the NT, vol I* (Philadelphia: Fortress, 1982), 240. Koester assumes that the Pharisees were descendants of the movement of the Hasidim.

John Hycarnus or Alexander Janaeus.[7] He theorizes that both the Pharisaic party and Sadducees developed from a broader assembly of the *Hasidim* during the Maccabean revolt.[8] Who were the *Hasidim*? Did the Pharisees belong to the *Hasidim* community? According to Stemberger, the term *Asidaioi* is rooted in Aramaic and it corresponds to the Hebrew *Hasidim*. "The name refers to their piety; the Semitic form of the name is perhaps also a conservative, anti-Hellenist usage."[9] Thus, *Asidaioi* is understood as pious Jews who resisted Hellenistic interference in religious affairs.[10] Further explanation about *Asidaioi* is given by Kampen. He says that the word *Asidaioi* is a transliteration of the Hebrew *Hasidim*, and it suggests that the group existed in the second century BCE. He continues with the contention that *Hasidim* in the Hebrew Scripture sometimes refers to the whole of Israel in general, but also sometimes to the righteous ones who remain faithful to God and sometimes to the priests.[11] In all these references, the members of the group must be God's chosen people and faithfulness and loyalty to the cult of Yahweh is essential.[12]

Besides, Kampen assumes that the *Hasidim* in 1 Maccabees have a strong link with the scribes. According to him, the scribes played a pivotal role as leading religious figures after the restoration period, and they committed themselves to the law and the covenant. Kampen further says that the scribes also focused on observing the Sabbath and circumcision, whereas, the Pharisees' concern was on exclusive table fellowship and purity outside the temple.[13] It was the Seleucid King Antiochus IV who had profaned the Jerusalem temple and the Jewish customs, conduct that aroused an angry response from the *scribal-Hasidim* to defend their beliefs for their fellow Jews. For this reason, Kampen believes that the later development of Pharisees

---

7. See D. G. Gowan, *Bridge between the Testaments*, 3rd ed. (Pennsylvania: Pickwick, 1986), 146.

8. Gowan, *Bridge Between the Testaments*, 146; Similarly, Herford thinks that the Pharisees arose during the Maccabean revolt, and they seemed to belong to *Hasidim* community, although the name Pharisees actually appear only in the time of John Hyrcanus' reign. See Herford, *The Pharisees*, 28–29.

9. Stemberger, *Jewish Contemporaries of Jesus*, 98.

10. Stemberger, 98.

11. Kampen, *Hasideans*, 217.

12. Kampen, 218.

13. Kampen, 220–221.

derived from the scribal circles of the *Hasidim*.¹⁴ Kampen seems to believe that he can make the connection from Scribal elements of the *Hasidim* to the development of the Pharisees. This is possible but it cannot be proved definitively due to inconsistent presentation of the two groups and irregular use of pronoun verb forms in the context.¹⁵ For instance, in 1 Maccabees 7:12 the group that approaches Bacchides is a group of scribes. However, in the following verses of 13–14, the *Hasidim* are mentioned as a group who seeks peace from Alcimus and Bacchides. According to Borchardt, the association of the *Hasidim* in these verses is secondary. It appears that they are two separate groups. Besides, 1 Maccabees is inconsistent in dealing with the *Hasidim* as scribes. For, the *Hasidim* in their other appearances are not noted as scribes but simply as mighty warriors of Israel who offer themselves willingly for the law (2:42).¹⁶

Herford elaborated on other functions and beliefs of the *Hasidim,* and how they relate to the Pharisees. He believes that though the name Pharisees actually appeared only in the time of John Hyrcanus's reign, the Pharisees did appear to belong to the *Hasidim* community. Right from the beginning of the Maccabean revolt, there were many defenders of the Torah, and the two groups – the extremist and moderate parties – stood out as prominent figures.¹⁷ The moderate party called the extremists *Hasidim*. These extremists aimed to observe and practice the Torah freely. Though they joined the Maccabean revolt for the sake of religious freedom, once they had religious freedom, they withdrew from all political aspects and seemingly disappeared from public view after the war. After some decades, some disputes appeared between the two groups in the Sanhedrin, and among the people on the law. The moderates considered that only the Written Law was applicable and this group closely mingled with the government (i.e. the priestly family and the nobility).¹⁸ On the other hand, the extremist party associated with the ordinary people and they considered that both the Written and Unwritten Laws

---

14. Kampen, 222.
15. F. Borchardt, *The Torah in 1 Maccabees: A Literary Critical Approach to the Text*, vol. 19 (Berlin: de Gruyter, 2014), 88–89.
16. See further explanation in Borchardt, *Torah in 1 Maccabees*, 88–89.
17. Herford, *Pharisees*, 27.
18. Herford, 28.

were authentic. For them, a true interpretation and teaching was available only when a person held these two traditions.[19] It was in the reign of John Hyrcanus (135–105 BCE) that the group who set such principles for the Torah first made themselves known as Pharisees.[20] Through his depiction, Herford implicitly indicates that the *Hasidim* were the Pharisees and they were the ones who were truly committed to both the Written and "Unwritten Laws and that they were opposed by the Sadducees.

Herford's theory of who the *Hasidim* were and the development of the Pharisaism is interesting. He assumes that certain groups such as the Pharisees and the Sadducees came into being only after the Maccabean revolt, a revolt based on law disputes.[21] However, according to Solomon Zeitlin, the dispute between the two groups about the law had taken place even before the Hasmonean period. More specifically speaking, it was at the end of the fifth century BCE while the Jews were still under Persian rule and during the time of the canonization of the Pentateuch. At that time, according to Zeitlin, the priestly group who came from the sons of Zadok or the Zadokite family acknowledged that only the Written Law was binding and the Unwritten Law was considered heresy.[22] The other group considered that God had given both the Written and Oral[23] Laws and both were binding and authentic. They also practiced the customs and laws according to both traditions and this also became popular among the people as well. Besides, they believed that the God of Israel is not only for Israel but also for all nations. Moreover, they maintained that God did not dwell

---

19. Herford, 28–29.

20. Herford, 29.

21. Herford seems to consider that the disputes between the two groups – the group who favoured both the Written and Unwritten Law, and the group who acknowledged only the existence of the Written law – took place only after the Maccabean revolt.

22. S. Zeitlin, "The Origin of the Pharisees Reaffirmed," in *Origins of Judaism: The Pharisees and Other Sects*, vol. 2: part 2, eds. Jacob Neusner and William Scott Green (New York & London: Garland, 1990), 471–483, 471; According to Rivkin, the controversies between the Sadducees and the Pharisees are recorded in the Mishnah in a dialogue formula. The Tosefta also employs this formula, but it changes the name Sadducees to the Boethusians. See Rivkin, "Defining the Pharisees," 173–217, 210–211.

23. The Oral traditions included laws about ritual purity and other details concerning oaths, Sabbath observance, and marriage. The Oral law is also known as an interpretation of the Written Torah and it is believed to have been originated at the Sinai revelation. See further in K. Hedner Zetterholm, *Jewish Interpretation of the Bible* (Philadelphia: Fortress, 2012), 10, 21.

only in the temple, but his presence could be found everywhere.[24] However, in the eyes of the *Zadukim*, the Sadducees,[25] these people were separating themselves from God and also from their fellow Judeans. For them, whoever held to the Oral Law as binding law, were heretics to be given the name *Perushim*, Pharisees.[26] According to Zeitlin, the Pharisees who held such traditions existed long before the Maccabean revolt so that the theory that the Pharisees derived from the *Hasidim* seems dubious.

Like Zeitlin, there are some scholars (Finkelstein, Beckwith, Gafni, Murphy) who believed the Pharisees' movement originated long before the Maccabean revolt, possibly at the beginning of the fourth century, while the Jews were still under the reign of the Persians.[27] Gafni considers that the Persian period offers precious information on the Pharisees' further development and their teaching extra-biblical traditions.[28] Likewise, Murphy argues that the Persian influence can be seen in some of the Pharisees' beliefs, such as – the "resurrection of the dead, eschatology, hell, angelology, demonology, periodization, and the dualistic concept that there are forces of light and of darkness at odds with each other in the universe."[29] Even though the Persians may have influenced some of their beliefs of the Pharisees, the Persian period seems an unlikely candidate for such a social development as the Pharisees' movement.

---

24. Zeitlin, "Origin of the Pharisees Reaffirmed," 483.

25. S. J. D. Cohen also considers that the name Sadducees derived from the *Zeduqi* and it means "a descendant of Zadok the Priest" see further in S. J. D. Cohen, *From the Maccabees to the Mishnah* (Philadelphia: Westminster, 1987), 159.

26. Zeitlin, "Origin of the Pharisees Reaffirmed," 472, 483.

27. See Zeitlin, "Origin of the Pharisees Reaffirmed," 471; L. Finkelstein, "Origin of the Pharisees Reconsidered," *Conservative Judaism* (Winter, 1969): 25. He says, "The Pharisees existed as a distinct group as early as the beginning of the 4th century BCE."; R. Beckwith also is convinced that the Pharisees movement seems to have arisen before 340 BCE. He states that proto-Pharisaic beliefs before the Maccabees are already seen in some Deutero-canonical books. For instances, the Book of Sirach witnesses belief in the existence of angels and the use of a lunar calendar. Both Judith and Tobit can also be seen as evidence of early Pharisaism since they have descriptions of Pharisaic practices such as tithing (Tob 1:6–8; Jdt 11:13) and purity in eating (Tob 2:5) See further in R. Beckwith, "The Pre-History and Relationship of the Pharisees, Sadducees and Essenes: A Tentative Reconstruction," *RQ* 11 (1982):3–46, 31.

28. I. M. Gafni, "The Historical Background," in *The Literature of the Sages*, eds. S. Safrai and P. J. Tomson (Philadelphia: Fortress, 1987), 8.

29. F. J. Murphy, "Second Temple Judaism," in *The Blackwell Companion to Judaism*, eds. Jacob Neusner & Alan. J. Avery-peck, (Oxford, UK: Blackwell, 2003), 58–77, 63.

Simultaneously, the *Hasidim* was an implausible origin for the Pharisees' development. Though we do not know for sure how the *Hasidim* came into being, it seems quite obvious that the *Hasidim* existed both decades before and during the Maccabean revolt, and the group, too, were the ones who were faithful to the Torah and any political matter was not of interest to them. As we have seen above, many scholars hold that the *Hasidim* were the precursors of the Sadducees, Essenes, Scribes, and more specifically of the Pharisees. However, there seems little chance to know who the *Hasidim* actually were. As Cohen and Tommasoni point out, the source we find in Maccabeans gives an inadequate picture of the actual identity of the *Hasidim*, their beliefs and practices and their roles in Maccabean periods except to tell us that the *Hasidim* had joined the revolt in order to have religious freedom.[30] According to the three references (1 Macc 2:42;[31] 7:13;[32] 2 Macc 14:6[33]) to the *Hasidim*, they appeared to have played an important role in Jewish religious life and were influential in their days.[34] However, that does not mean that they represented a normative religious group at that time. There was no "normative" religious group during the Second Temple period.[35] Furthermore, there is no information about their existence after the revolt. What is more important is that the three sources we have do not agree on the nature of the *Hasidim*. They were defined as (1) mighty warriors for the law with their own identity who had joined Judas' cause; (2) the group who first sought peace from the Hellenizing Alkimus, and associated with scribes; (3) the group which associated with Judas Maccabeus's own movement and his own followers. This indeed shows uncertainty about the *Hasidim*'s origin and nature and can be misleading.[36] Consequently, the community of *Hasidim* can only be said to be one of the Jewish religious groups who

---

30. A. J. Tommasino, *Judaism before Jesus* (Leicester: InterVarsity Press, 2003), 162; Cohen, *From the Maccabees to the Mishnah*, 161.

31. "Then there united with them a company of Hasideans, mighty warriors of Israel, all who offered themselves willingly for the law. (NRS)"

32. "The Hasideans were first among the Israelites to seek peace from them."

33. "Those of the Jews who are called Hasideans, whose leader is Judas Maccabeus, are keeping up war and stirring up sedition, and will not let the kingdom attain tranquillity."

34. Tommasino, *Judaism before Jesus*, 161.

35. J. D. G. Dunn, *The Partings of the Ways*, 2nd ed. (London: SCM, 2006), 16; Tommasino, *Judaism before Jesus*, 162.

36. Borchardt, *Torah in 1 Maccabees*, 88–89.

shared a common heritage of Judaism[37] – such as to be faithful to the Torah, the cult of Yahweh and reverence for Jerusalem.

Though, as Tomasino says,[38] it seems impossible to come to a definite conclusion about the origin of the Pharisees using the available sources, we can still trace the pre-Hasmonean Pharisaic movement and their beliefs. It is highly likely that the Pharisees came into being under the political conditions of the Hellenistic period.[39] After the Seleucids (Syrian Greeks) conquered Jerusalem in 200 BCE, the first consequence for the Palestinian Jews was the impact of Hellenistic cultural influence.[40] Not only did the Palestinian elite collaborate politically, they also fell under the influence of Hellenistic culture. Even the High Priest was not exempt. 2 Maccabees 4:13–15 well reflects the situation of the time:

> There was such an extreme of Hellenization and increase in the adoption of foreign ways because of the surpassing wickedness of Jason, who was ungodly and no high priest, that the priests were no longer intent upon their service at the altar. Despising the sanctuary and neglecting the sacrifices, they hastened to take part in the unlawful proceedings in the wrestling arena after the call to the discus, disdaining the honors prized by their fathers and putting the highest value upon Greek forms of prestige.

It is highly probable that the Pharisees' movement began in the second century BCE, under Seleucid domination before the beginning of the Maccabean wars, as an opposition to the Sadducees. Among the priesthood this opposition grew up when a group of priests, the Pharisaic section, instituted great changes. The Pharisees seemed to have received the title "Pharisees" only in controversies with the Sadducees, who considered them as

---

37. Dunn, *Partings of the Ways*, 25.
38. Tommasino, *Judaism before Jesus*, 167.
39. A. Runesson, *The Origins of the Synagogue: A Socio-Historical Study* (Stockholm: Almqvist & Wiksell International, 2001), 147.
40. G. Vermes, *The Dead Sea Scrolls* (Philadelphia: Fortress, 1981), 139

"*perushim/prusim*-heretics"[41] for accepting the twofold Laws.[42] Consequently, there arose the conflict between the Sadducees and the Pharisees about the rules of purity. Jeremias describes this event as:

> Whereas the Torah laid down rules of purity and rules on food for the officiating priests alone, the Pharisaic group made these rules a general practice in the everyday life of the priests and in the life of the whole people. In this way they mean to build up the holy community of Israel, the true Israel. The Saducean group, on the other hand, was conservative and held that the priestly laws were limited to the priests and the cultus, in conformity with the Scripture. The conflict between Pharisees and Sadducees sprang from this opposition. The Pharisees voluntarily submitted themselves to priestly rules and thus prepared the way for a universal priesthood. The Pharisees' were the people's party because they opposed to the aristocracy on both religious and social matters. They only did they oppose to the Sadducees, but as a true Israel they drew a hard line between themselves and the masses, who did not observe as they did the rules laid down by Pharisaic scribes on tithes and purity.[43]

Another focus of the Pharisaic liturgy was on reading and teaching Torah. They aimed to promote education of the entire people in the law.[44] From this we see that the Pharisees' ambition, was "to address and include the whole Jewish community in their programme, and, therefore, were involved in inner Jewish missionary activities."[45] The Pharisees appeared to be members of a religious association with their own leaders (Ant 15:370), their own

---

41. "In rabbinic Hebrew, the word *Parush* (plur. *Perushim*), whose literary meaning is 'separatist' often is used with a negative valence, e.g. the liturgical condemnation of heretics is described as 'the blessing against separatists' (*perushim*). Occasionally the word appears in passages with the meaning of 'pietist' without the negative overtones. In other passages, the word is used as the name of a group, and that group is the same as that which Josephus and the New Testament call Pharisees." See further in Cohen, *Maccabees to the Mishnah*, 155, 159.

42. Rivkin, *Defining the Pharisees*, 215–216.

43. J. Jeremias, *Jerusalem in the Time of Jesus: An Investigation into Economic and Social Conditions during the New Testament Period*, trans. F. H and C. H. Cave (Philadelphia: Fortress, 1967), 266–267.

44. Runesson, *Origins of the Synagogue*, 134–135.

45. Runesson, 225.

halahkic principles, and the new members of the community were keen to observe the priestly purity and tithes as described by the Pharisees.[46]

It is undeniable that the Pharisees could have died out soon without the impetus of the Maccabean revolt and victory. However, which does not mean that the Pharisaic group came into being only in the Maccabean period.[47] Josephus mentions them at the time of Jonathan:

> Now at this time there were three schools of thought among the Judeans which held different opinions concerning human affair; the first being that of the Pharisees, the second that of Sadducees, and the third that of the Essenes. As for the Pharisees, they say that certain events are the work of Fate, but not all; as to other events, it depends upon ourselves whether they shall take place or not. The sect of Essenes, however, declares that Fate is mistress of all things, and that nothing befalls men unless it be in accordance with her decree. But the Sadducees do away with Fate, holding that there is no such thing and that human actions are not achieved in accordance with her decree, but that all things lie within our own power, so that we ourselves are responsible for our well-being, while we suffer misfortune through our own thoughtlessness.[48]

But he never states that Pharisaism dates from the Maccabean period. Instead, the Pharisees are mentioned as one of three groups (Sadducees and Essenes) in the early period of Jonathan the Maccabee (161–143 BCE), which suggests the Pharisees' existence before the Maccabean revolt.

2.2 The Pharisees in the Hasmonean Period (140–63 BCE)

Although we do not have a full picture of the group's activities from its beginning through the Maccabean revolt, from the Hasmonean period onwards Josephus portrays them as playing an active role. The Hasmonean era is a

---

46. Jeremias, *Jerusalem in the Time*, 251.

47. G. Theissen, *Gospels in Context*, trans. Linda M. Maloney (Minneapolis: Fortress, 1991), 27.

48. Josephus, *Ant.* 13.171–173; Josephus, *War* 2.118.

sub-period within the Hellenistic period. During that time, the Pharisees are depicted as clients dependent on the Hasmonean rulers for their wellbeing and existence; they act with royal approval, and the Hasmonean rulers were understood to be their patrons.[49] They appear to be well known and influential for interpreting the traditional laws not found in the books of Moses. However, Josephus does not clarify what laws and traditions were unique to the Pharisees.[50] The role of Pharisees is noticeably described in relationship with the Hasmonean rulers through three major events.[51]

The Pharisees and John Hyrcanus

The first explicit role of the Pharisees as being a powerful spiritual and religious leading group is seen at the time of John Hyrcanus (134–104 BCE), the fourth successor of the Hasmonean rulers.[52] The Pharisees were described by Josephus as:

> The Pharisees, who are considered the most accurate interpreters of the laws, and hold the position of the leading sect, attribute everything to Fate and to God; they hold that to act rightly or otherwise rests, indeed, for the most part with men, but that in each action Fate co-operates. Every soul, they maintain, is imperishable, but the soul of the good alone passes into another body, while the souls of the wicked suffer eternal

---

49. According to Saldarini, the roles of the Pharisees in this period was better described as "patron-client relationship." He says, "Hyrcanus is the Pharisees' political ruler and patron; the Pharisees are clients dependent on him and act accordingly by not criticizing him. The Pharisees are pictured as part of Hyrcanus's circle of retainers and as a group they have achieved considerable influence, especially over how a proper Jewish ruler ought to carry out the ancestral laws and customs. Though the Pharisees have access to Hyrcanus, any power they have is based on influence with Hyrcanus and not held directly in their hands." See Saldarini, *Palestinian Society*, 87.

50. L. L. Grabbe, *An Introduction to First Century Judaism: History and Religion of the Jews in the Time of Nehemiah, the Maccabees, Hillel and Jesus* (Edinburgh: T&T Clark, 1996), 42–43.

51. Josephus also talks about actions and individuals designated as Pharisees in other passages: *War* 1.5.2–3 (110–114); 1.29.2 (571); 2.17.2–3 (410–411); *Ant*.13.10.5–7 (288–299); 13.15.5–16.6 (398–432); 15.1.1 (3–4); 15.10.4 (370); 17.2.4–3.1 (41–47); *Life* 38 (190–191); Grabbe, *Introduction to First Century Judaism*, 42.

52. Josephus, *Ant.* 13.5.288–292; Saldarini, *Palestinian Society*, 86–87. The Maccabean revolt began in the year 168 BCE by Mattathius and his sons. Mattathius died after a short period and his sons – Judas Maccabee, Jonathan Maccabee and Simon Maccabee continued the revolt.

punishment. . . . The Pharisees are affectionate to each other and cultivate harmonious relations with the community.[53]

And so great is their (the Pharisees) influence with the masses that even when they speak against a king or high priest, they immediately gain credence. Hyrcanus too was a disciple of theirs and greatly loved by them . . . Once he invited them to a feast and entertained them hospitably, and when he saw that they were having a very good time, he began by saying that they knew he wished to be righteous in everything he did try to please God and them – for the Pharisees profess such beliefs; at the same time he begged them, if they observed him doing anything wrong or straying from the right path, to lead him back to it and to correct him.[54]

This passage demonstrates clearly their role and standing both in Jewish society generally and with the monarch in particular. Politically, Hyrcanus is their ruler and the patron, but spiritually and religiously, he is their disciple even though he holds the position of high-priest.[55] Mutual dependence without criticizing one another seemed to be the criteria they followed.

Besides being an influential group in religious matters, the Pharisees appeared to seek power and authority,[56] at the very least so they could directly control religious matters. They appear to have been concerned very much with the right status of the high priest. This is seen when Hyrcanus gave a banquet and invited the Pharisees there. He asked them to correct him and lead him to be a righteous ruler and high priest since the Pharisees were considered as the ones who had knowledge (φιοσοφοῦσιν) because "the Pharisees profess such beliefs." Which means it was believed that the Pharisees knew and so loved God's laws, that whoever pleased them would gain the favour of God.[57]

---

53. Josephus, *War* 2.8.14.162–163, 166.
54. Josephus, *Ant*, 13.5.288–292.
55. Josephus, *Ant.* 13.5.288–292; Saldarini, *Palestinian Society*, 86–87.
56. Saldarini, *Palestinian Society*, 87; Grabbe, *Introduction to First Century Judaism*, 43.
57. Josephus, *Ant.* 13.5.288–292; Saldarini, *Palestinian Society*, 86. Josephus did not specify the customs and regulations of the Pharisees and the Sadducees which John Hyrcanus followed later.

As such, it was not wrong for Hyrcanus to entertain them and to seek their advice regarding what was deemed pleasing to God and also for Hyrcanus's own benefits. However, here, the situation turned out to be different when one of the Pharisees, Eleazar, told Hyrcanus that he should give up the position of the high priesthood and to be just content with being a political ruler. When Hyrcanus asked the reason for this, Eleazar replied, "Because we have heard from our elders that your mother was a captive in the reign of Antiochus Epiphanes."[58] Therefore, Eleazar considered Hyrcanus unworthy to be the high priest.[59] As a result, Hyrcanus became so angry that he transferred his favour to the Sadducees. Therefore, the Pharisees lost royal favour until the end of his reign. Besides, Hyrcanus forbade all their peculiar rules and regulations, which once he had supported and enjoyed so much.[60] Hyrcanus even punished those who observed their regulations. Consequently, Hyrcanus and his sons were bitterly hated by the Pharisees and the populace who supported the Pharisees.[61]

The Jews Executed by Alexander Jannaeus (103–76 BCE)

The Pharisees' leading role in Jewish religious life is seen again when Alexander Jannaeus, one of the sons of John Hyrcanus, came to the throne. He married Salome, the wife of his predecessor Aristobulus I, when she offered him a throne. During his reign, the Pharisees remained out of favour. Though Josephus's sources did not mention the Pharisees' names and their roles directly during the account of the bloody reign of Jannaeus, the Pharisees appeared to show their disapproval of Jannaeus as they had of his father.[62] Consequently, Jannaeus had to face many internal conflicts throughout his reign. Given their influence over the masses, there is no doubt that the Pharisees were probably the ones who aroused the populace against Alexander Jannaeus. They may even have been involved themselves

---

58. Jospehus, *Ant.* 13.292–293.

59. Stemberger, *Jewish Contemporaries of Jesus*, 105; Grabbe, *Introduction to First Century Judaism*, 42; Josephus, *Ant.* 13.5.288–292; Saldarini, *Palestinian Society*, 86–87.

60. Stemberger, *Jewish Contemporaries of Jesus*, 105; Josephus, *Ant.* 13.5.288–292.; Saldarini, *Palestinian Society*, 88.

61. Josephus, *Ant.* 13.5.288–292; Saldarini, *Palestinian Society*, 88.

62. Sanders, *Judaism*, 381.

The Historical Pharisees from the Second Temple Period to the First Century 31

in the uprising against him. We see this event described in both of Josephus's sources as:

> As for Alexander, his own people revolted against him – for the nation was aroused against him – at the celebration of the festival, and as he stood beside the altar and was about to sacrifice, they pelted him with citrons, it being a custom among the Jews that at the festival of Tabernacles everyone holds wands made of palm branches and citrons – these we have described elsewhere ; and they added insult to injury by saying that he was descended from captives and was unfit to hold office and to sacrifice ; and being enraged at this, he killed some six thousand of them, and also placed a wooden barrier about the altar and the temple as far as the coping (of the court) which the priests alone were permitted to enter, and by this means blocked the people's way to him . . . while he feasted with his concubines in a conspicuous place, he ordered some eight hundred of the Jews to be crucified, and slaughtered their children and wives before the eyes of the still living wretches. This was the revenge he took for the injuries he had suffered.[63]

Saldarini considers that the Pharisees continued to seek influence and power and to act as a political interest group.[64] However, as in *Antiquities*, Josephus's account in *War* follows the above version, confirming that the revolt is about the religious objection to the ruler's fitness for the office. Therefore, out of anger and bitterness, Alexander Jannaeus killed 6,000 men and made a way to keep playing his priesthood role unhindered. He again murdered another 800 men after gaining his victory in the civil war. As in the case with John Hyrcanus, Alexander Jannaeus punished those who rose against him for saying he was not qualified to High Priest and not so much on political grounds.

Though Josephus did not mention directly that the Pharisees involved in the uprising, the text makes it clear that the populace moved at the Pharisees' words. Since the Hasmonean rulers did not come from the authorized,

---

63. Josephus, *Ant.* 13.5.372–378; parallel story is described by Josephus in 1.96–98.
64. Saldarini, *Palestinian Society*, 89.

(*Zadokite*) priestly family, both the Pharisees and the populace meant it was important to have a high priest with the right status. Alexander Jannaneus himself conceded that the Pharisees had a great influence over their fellow Jews: on his deathbed, he warned his wife that if she wanted to secure the throne for herself she would have to maintain a good relationship with them.

> Thereupon he (Alexander Jannaeus) advised her to follow his suggestions for keeping the throne secure for herself and her children and to conceal his death from the soldiers until she had captured the fortress. And then, he said, on her return to Jerusalem as from a splendid victory, she should yield a certain amount of power to the Pharisees, for if they praised her in return for this sign of regard, they would dispose the nation favourably toward her. These men, he assured her, had so much influence with their fellow-Jews that they could injure those whom they hated and help those to whom they were friendly; for they had the complete confidence of the masses when they spoke harshly of any person, even when they did so out of envy; and he himself, he added, had come into conflict with the nation because these men had been badly treated by him.[65]
>
> Promise them also that you will not take any action, while you are on the throne, without their consent. If you speak to them in this manner, I shall receive from them a more splendid burial than I should from you; for once they have the power to do so, they will not choose to treat my corpse badly, and at the same time you will reign securely. With this exhortation to his wife he died, after reigning twenty-seven years, at the age of forty-nine.[66]

The Pharisees' were not simply clients for they could help their patron or harm him should they fall out, as Alexander Jannaeus had discovered to his cost.[67] He saw the necessity of restoring the relationship for the benefit of both groups. Though he had punished and even killed many of his ex-clients

---

65. Josephus, *Ant.* 13.400–403.
66. Josephus, *Ant.* 13.404.
67. Saldarini, *Palestinian Society*, 90.

for their rebellion, they exerted so much influence over the nation that they could cause great trouble for the crown. Although they were out of favour throughout his reign, Alexander reached a point where he acknowledged that the Hasmoneans and the Pharisees had to work together. If his wife followed his advice, the Pharisees would be pacified, make their fellow Jews follow them, and she would enjoy a secure and peaceful reign.[68]

Salome Alexandra (76–67 BCE)

According to Josephus, the Pharisees held considerable power and authority during the reign of Salome Alexandra. Once power and authority had been placed in their hands, they seemed however to have become more aggressive. Their interest went beyond the religious affairs to which they had been previously so devoted. As soon as the patronage relationship was restored, the glorious era of the Pharisaic life was inaugurated. They began to act like political rulers and started to get rid of the supporters of the late Alexander Jannaeus. The Pharisees' role during the reign of Salome is depicted by Josephus as:

> Thereupon Alexandra, after capturing the fortress, conferred with the Pharisees as her husband had suggested, and by placing in their hands all that concerned his corpse and the royal power, stilled their anger against Alexander, and made them her well-wishers and friends. And they in turn went to the people and made public speeches in which they recounted the deeds of Alexander, and said that in him they had lost a just king, and by their eulogies they so greatly moved the people to mourn and lament that they gave him a more splendid burial than had been given any of the kings before him.[69]

. . .

> And she permitted the Pharisees to do as they liked in all matters, and also commanded the people to obey them; and whatever regulations, introduced by the Pharisees in accordance with the tradition of their fathers, had been abolished by her

---

68. Josephus, *Ant.* 13.395–403; Saldarini, *Palestinian Society*, 89
69. Josephus, *Ant.* 13.405ff.

father-in-law Hyrcanus, these she again restored. And so, while she had the title of sovereign, the Pharisees had the power. For example, they recalled exiles, and freed prisoners, and in a word, in no way differed from absolute rulers.[70]

According to the sources, Salome followed her husband's instruction and placed all the matters in their hands. Josephus summarized their position during this period: "While she had the title of sovereign, the Pharisees had the power." The Pharisees exercised their power in society. They even took revenge on those who had been involved in the crucifixion of the eight hundred.[71] Thus, as Saldarini rightly puts, "The Pharisees' relationship with Alexandra can best be seen as a religio-political interest group, a corporate, voluntary association, organized for the pursuit of one interest or of several interests in common."[72] At the beginning the Pharisees' interest, commitment and concern was to observe a strict Jewish way of life based on devotion to the covenant and the two-fold traditional laws and to build up the holy community of Israel. As times changed, with the support of those who admired them and the authority they received from their patrons, the Hasmonean rulers, they extended their interest into both religious and political affairs. Indeed, as Sanders states, it was seldom that a group such as the Pharisees exerted governmental power themselves in antiquity. For the Pharisees as a whole were neither of aristocratic nor even prominent lineage although some individuals may have enjoyed social prominence and wealth enough. They were simply a social force group committed to knowledge, interpretation and observance of the ancestral laws of Judaism.[73]

2.3 The Pharisees under the Herodians

2.3.1 The Pharisees and Herod the Great

Josephus's sources do not mention the Pharisees much after the death of Salome Alexandra (47–46 BCE). After her death, the political situation

---

70. Josephus, *Ant.* 13.408f.
71. Josephus, *War* 1.4.6.96-98; Josephus, *Ant.* 13.16.2.410–415; Saldarini, *Palestinian Society*, 91.
72. Saldarini, *Palestinian Society*, 94.
73. Sanders, *Judaism*, 383; Saldarini, *Palestinian Society*, 95.

became increasingly unstable so that the Romans began to interfere in the political affairs of the Hasmoneans.[74] As a result, the Herodian family gained Rome's favour so that the last Hasmonean successor, Antigonus, was dethroned and replaced by Herod the Great with Roman support. Sanders says that during Herod's reign, the Pharisees became a group who lived on their past glory and they were in an ineffective position although they still were a substantial group socially and religiously.[75] Sanders also sees them as a group who were powerless throughout most of the period, although they were still opportunists seeking power to control everything.[76] Sanders, however, is too harsh, as he does not even deign to credit the Pharisees' influence over the general populace at the beginning of Herod's reign. As Sanders states, the Pharisees were powerless at that time; however, they probably were not the only ones looking for opportunities to control everything. One such asset was their *historic* standing and their influence over the populace. This fact was obvious in Herod's early period, during which the Pharisees were still an influential group with the potential to harm or to help the incoming ruler. Though they did not have a chance to exert as much influence as they had done during the time of Salome Alexandra, they still played a major role in helping Herod the Great to besiege Jerusalem in the early period. When Herod the Great managed to become the king of Judea, his initial support came from Samaias who was a prominent member of the Sanhedrin[77] and a disciple of Pollion the Pharisee.[78] Josephus describes this event:

---

74. After Salome's death, her two sons – Aristobulus II and Hyrcanus II – competed for power. When Aristobulus died, his son Antigonus continued to fight his uncle Hyrcanus II with the help of the Parthians. Hyrcanus also sought help from Herod Antipater and his sons, *the Idumeans*, who later began to interfere in the country's political affairs. Later on, Rome backed Herod the Great for the Judean throne, named him a king and deposed Hyrcanus II. Since then, Herod became the official ruler of Judea with the consent and aid of powerful Rome.

75. Sanders, *Judaism*, 395.

76. Sanders, 412.

77. "The Sanhedrin in Jerusalem was the supreme council, which included the most powerful and influential citizens at any given time and thus probably had a shifting membership which reflected the power struggles and social currents of history." See Saldarini, *Palestinian Society*, 97.

78. In Mishnah they are known as Shemaish and Abatalion. m.*Abot* 1:2; "Pollion the Pharisee and his diciples Sameas," (Josephus, *Ant.* 15.1)

But when Herod stood in the Sanhedrin with his troops, he overawed them all, and no one of those who had denounced him before his arrival dared to accuse him thereafter; instead there was silence and doubt about what was to be done. While they were in this state, someone named Samaias,[79] an upright man and for that reason superior to fear, arose and said, " Fellow councillors and King, I do not myself know of, nor do I suppose that you can name, any-one who when summoned before you for trial has ever presented such an appearance. For no matter who it was that came before this Sanhedrin for trial, he has shown himself humble and has assumed the manner of one who is fearful and seeks mercy from you by letting his hair grow long and wearing a black garment. But this fine fellow Herod, who is accused of murder and has been summoned on no less grave a charge than this, stands here clothed in purple, with the hair of his head carefully arranged and with his soldiers round him, in order to kill us if we condemn him as the law prescribes, and to save himself by outraging justice. But it is not Herod whom you should blame for this or for putting his own interests above the law, but you and the king, for giving him such great license. Be assured, however, that God is great, and this man, whom you now wish to release for Hyrcanus' sake, will one day punish you and the king as well.[80]

Samaias states that Herod would one day punish the Hasmonean king and others. He also advised the people to open the gate for Herod and interpreted that God had punished the corruptions and exploitations of the Hasmonean rulers and those who supported them by raising the power of the Herodians.[81] Samaias's prediction came true as Josephus wrote about this event as follows:

---

79. Variant names – Sameas, Samaeus, Samaios. He is mentioned in *Ant.* 15.1 as a disciple of the Pharisee Pollion.

80. Josephus, *Ant.* 14.171–174.

81. Josephus, *Ant.* 14.171–174; Sanders, *Judaism*, 384; Saldarini, *Palestinian Society*, 96.

> When Herod had got the rule of all Judea into his hands, he showed special favour to those of the city's populace who had been on his side while he was still a commoner, but those who chose the side of his opponents he harried and punished without ceasing for a single day. Especially honoured by him were Pollion the Pharisee and his disciple Samaias, for during the siege of Jerusalem these men had advised the citizens to admit Herod, and for this they now received their reward. This same Pollion had once, when Herod was on trial for his life, reproachfully foretold to Hyrcanus and the judges that if Herod's life were spared, he would (one day) persecute them all. And in time this turned out to be so, for God fulfilled his words.[82]

From this we learn that although Herod executed his opponents, he then gave great favours to those who supported him, especially to Pollion and his disciple Samais for advising the people to surrender to him.[83]

However, supporting Herod did not mean the Pharisees' total submission to his rule. Instead, they appeared to defend Herod when necessary and they must have opposed him even though Josephus did not describe clearly in his sources the reason why they offended Herod.[84] This became clear when in the middle of his reign (20 BCE) Herod demanded that they should take a loyalty oath. Pollion, a prominent leader, Samaias and most of their followers did not agree to this. Neither would they swear an oath to Emperor Augustus.[85] Josephus writes:

> As for the rest of the populace, he (Herod) demanded that they submit to taking an oath of loyalty, and he compelled them to make a sworn declaration that they would maintain a friendly attitude to his rule. Now most of the people yielded to his demand out of complaisance or fear, but those who showed some spirit and objected to compulsion he got rid of by every possible means. He also tried to persuade Pollion the Pharisee

---

82. Josephus, *Ant.* 15.1–4.
83. Josephus, *Ant.* 14.175–176; Sanders, *Judaism*, 384; Saldarini, *Palestinian Society*, 96.
84. Josephus, *Ant.* 15.370
85. P. Richardson, *Herod* (Minneapolis: Fortress, 1999), 255.

and Samaias and most of their disciples to take the oath, but they would not agree to this, and yet they were not punished as were the others who refused, for they were shown consideration on Pollion's account.[86]

The reason was that to swear allegiance in the name of God to a mere earthly ruler was to them a blasphemy.[87] Though Herod did not punish Pollion the Pharisee and his disciple Samaias for their refusal because of their earlier assistance to him, he fined over six thousand other Pharisees. However, their fines were paid by a patroness of Herod's court since the Pharisees in general were in charge of the women of the court.[88] Near the end of his life, Herod was probably constantly opposed by the Pharisees and he executed the Pharisees who predicted his fall as well as his younger brother *Pheroras* and his wife who had supported the Pharisees.[89] Josephus tells the story:

> There was also a group of Jews priding itself on its adherence to ancestral custom and claiming to observe the laws of which the deity approves, and by these men, called Pharisees, the women (of the court) were ruled. These men were able to help the king greatly because of their foresight, and yet they were obviously intent upon combating and injuring him. At least when whole Jewish people affirmed by an oath that it would be loyal to Caesar and to the king's government, these men, over six thousand in number, refused to take this oath, and when the king punished them with a fine, Pheroras's wife paid the fine for them. In return for her friendliness they foretold – for they were believed to have foreknowledge of things through God's appearances to them – that by God's decree Herod's throne would be taken from him, both from himself and his descendants, and the royal power would fall to her and Pheroras and to any children that they might have. These things, which did not

---

86. Josephus, *Ant.* 15.369–370. Josephus, *Jewish Antiques: Books 15–17* trans. R. Marcus (London: William Heinemann, 1963).

87. J. Schaper, "The Pharisees" in *The Cambridge History of Judaism*, vol.3 eds. W. Horbury and W. D. Davies (Cambridge: Cambridge University Press, 1999), 402–427; 418.

88. Josephus, *Ant.* 17.41f.

89. Josephus, *Ant.* 17.43f; Josephus, *War* 1.571. Sanders, *Judaism*, 384.

remain unknown to Salome, were reported to the king, as was the news that the Pharisees had corrupted some of the people at court. And the king put to death those of the Pharisees who were most to blame and the eunuch Bagoas and certain karos. . . . He (Herod) also killed all those of his household who approved of what the Pharisees said.[90]

So while Herod would tolerate the situation as long as the Pharisees' opposition was due to religious concerns, if they tried to cause confusion and interfere in politics, he would consider them as dangerous and crush them at all costs.[91] Consequently, "Political quietism"[92] as Joachim Schaper rightly puts it, was the price the Pharisees had to pay for their survival.[93] That does not mean that the Pharisees had no political interest. Even though the majority of Pharisees could not play an open role in political matters in Herod's time, as true Jews, their attitudes on patriotic identity was still based on asocial- religious standpoint.[94]

Nevertheless, not all the Pharisees appeared to have surrendered to this political quietism: the Zealots,[95] the left wing faction of Pharisaism are a good example of that. Josephus's source also mentions the rise of this group in Herod's reign. A revolutionary party, the Zealots were founded by Zadok, a Shammaic-Pharisee (t.*Eduyot* 2:2; b.*Yebamot* 15b),[96] together with Judas

---

90. Josephus, *Ant.* 17.42–45. Josephus, *Jewish Antiques: Books 15–17* trans. R. Marcus (London: William Heinemann, 1963).

91. Schaper, "The Pharisees," 420.

92. In contrast to much of the Hasmonean period, during Herod's time the Pharisees had reached a point where for the sake of their own survival they had to avoid involvement in politics.

93. Schaper, "The Pharisees," 421.

94. I. M. Zeitlin, *Jesus and the Judaism of His Time* (Cambridge: Polity Press, 1988), 14.

95. The origin of this group is a controversial debate. However, the fact that the Zealots appear as the last group to emerge in early first century Judaism is noteworthy. Though the Zealots were not mentioned in the early events, they played a dominant role until the end of the Jewish war. Even Josephus mentioned the Zealots as a party before the winter of 67–68 CE. Thus, this supports the view the Zealots were militant Pharisees. M. Smith, "The Troublemakers" in *The Cambridge History of Judaism*, vol. 3, eds. W. Horbury and W. D. Davies (Cambridge: Cambridge University Press, 1999), 501–568, 545.

96. According to T. *Eduyot* 2:2 and B.*Yebamot* 15b, his full name was known as R. Eleazar b.R. Sadoq and he belonged to the house of Shammai. See also in Marcus Jastrow, and S. Mendelsohn, "Bet Hillel and Bet Shammai," http://www.jewishencyclopedia.com/articles/3190-bet-hillel-and-bet-shammai (accessed 12 October 2015)

the Galilean in 6 CE.[97] Thus, the Zealots were the product of first-century Pharisaism.[98] They acknowledged only the kingship of God and constituted themselves as a distinctive group in Jewish Palestinian society in order to go against all forms of gentile rule.[99] They believed that God needed human help in order to establish his kingdom on earth. Thus, the Zealots were best described as "a Pharisaic-ideology in a more militant manner."[100] Many Jews who had not belonged to any specific group before came to support the Zealots party as they gained some influence in the revolutionary movement in the first century.[101] For the other Pharisees who chose to be contented with the social-religious standpoint, two significant events took place in the history of Pharisaism. The first one was that the Pharisees launched and spread the "conceptualization of oral law" and their traditions in their own association synagogues, as well as in the public synagogues in Palestine. Schaper believes that the synagogues in Palestine became the Pharisees' institution.[102] Schaper seems to indicate the synagogues in general, and argues that the priestly aristocracy in charge of the temple service would have had little interest in competing with the Pharisees at synagogue level. He further argues that there is, in fact, no evidence showing that the priestly aristocrats were even interested in the synagogue service in the pre-Herodian period.[103]

However, Sanders counters such a view and says that the synagogues in Jerusalem were headed and led by aristocratic priests and not by the Pharisees. For Sanders, the Pharisees did not preach nor read the Torah in the synagogue nor governed its functions.[104] Sander was right to some extent, for the Pharisees did not rule all the public synagogues since the synagogue ruler held an administrative office and could be just a wealthy member of

---

97. Josephus, *Ant.* 18.4.

98. A. I. Baumgarten, *The Flourishing of Jewish Sects in the Maccabean Era*, vol 55 (Atlanta: SBL Press, 1997), 19; B. Pixner, "Jesus and His Community: Between Essenes and Pharisees," in *Jesus' Jewishness*, vol. 2, ed. J. H. Charlesworth (New York: Crossroad, 1991), 193–224.

99. Schaper, "The Pharisees," 422; Smith, "The Troublemakers," 545.

100. C. S. Keener, *A Commentary on the Gospel of Matthew* (Grand Rapids, MI: Eerdmans, 1999), 59.

101. Zeitlin, *Jesus and the Judaism of His Time*,15.

102. Schaper, "The Pharisees," 420.

103. Schaper, 421.

104. Sanders, *Judaism*, 398.

the community or from priestly members.[105] There was no specific group that controlled the public synagogues in order to conduct reading the Torah and teaching there.[106] Theodotus's inscription, dating from the first century CE, shows the priests' involvement with the synagogue:

> Theodotos, the son of Vettenos, priest and *archisynagogos*,[107] son of an *archisynagogos*, grandson of an *archisynagogos*, built this synagogue for the reading of the law (i.e. the Torah) and the study of the commandments, and a guesthouse and rooms and water installations for hosting those in need from abroad, it (i.e. the synagogue), having been founded by his fathers, the presbyters, and Simonides.[108]

According to Levine, by the first century CE, the Torah reading and study, alongside the temple, had become the most important and holiest thing in Judaism. Therefore, Torah reading became part of the Jewish worship in the pre-70 synagogue.[109]

While the Pharisees did not run or control the public synagogues, they did run their own association synagogues or the assembly house for Torah education. According to Runesson, there were two kinds of synagogues existed in Palestine: (a) public synagogue or town assembly, originated in Persian period ca. 450 BCE and everyone could use it freely. (b) Parallel to the public synagogue, the other type of synagogue was voluntary association and it originated ca. 200 BCE. This type of synagogue belonged to a specific group or was dominated by a certain group for Torah studies.[110] Subsequently, the Pharisees who were devoted to the study of Torah and its interpretation focused more on their association synagogue. In that sense, the Pharisees and

---

105. L. I. Levine, *The Ancient Synagogue: The First Thousand Years* (New Haven: Yale University Press, 2000), 126.

106. Runesson, *Origins of the Synagogues*, 222.

107. "The *archisynagogue* was not only a communal leader, but also a wealthy member of the community who participated in the ritual, administrative, and financial aspects of the institution" see further in Levine, *Ancient Synagogue*, 126.

108. Levine, *Ancient Synagogue*, 55.

109. Levine, 136.

110. A. Runesson, "The Origins of the Synagogue in Past and Present Research," *Studia Theologica* 57 (2003): 60–76; and "Rethinking of Early Jewish-Christian Relations: Matthean Community History as Pharisaic Intragroup Conflict," *JBL* 127, no. 1 (2008), 95–132.

the association type of Synagogue were inseparable. Nevertheless, there is no doubt that the Pharisees associated with a local synagogue ruler to align practice there with Pharisaic *halakhah*, and to debate with other groups regarding the interpretation of Torah.[111] Thus, it was highly likely that the Pharisees conceptualized the tradition of the twofold Torah in their own association synagogues, as well as in the public synagogues.

The second event in the Pharisaic community was the separation of the Pharisaic Houses. The split was between the Houses of Hillel and Shammai, with the latter dominating until the revolt.[112] Schaper states that with the rise of the pair of Pharisaic leaders, Hillel and Shammai, a period of intense interest in purity-related *halakha*[113] started.[114] The Pharisees began to focus more on their commitment to the tradition of the twofold laws, their interpretation and purity concerns. Since the temple was deemed by the Pharisees as already polluted by illegitimate priests and by their services, the right to conduct purity laws became a matter for the Pharisees. According to Neusner, Hillel was the one who shifted the focus of the Pharisees from politics to piety.[115] Although, as Neusner states, all the Pharisees may not have turned to a life of piety the majority of Pharisees did appear to desire ritual purity by applying the Levitical purity rules even at home. While eating ordinary meals like any of their fellow Jews, they cared for ritual purity as if they were temple priests.[116] R. Deines states that archaeological findings, dating from around the last third of first-century BCE, provide evidence of the Pharisees' practices in the stone vessels they used in many areas of

---

111. Runesson, *Origins of the Synagogues*, 222; "Origins of the Synagogue," 60–76; and "Rethinking of Early Jewish-Christian Relations," 95–132.

112. Fornberg, "Matthew and the School of Shammai," 35–59; McNamara, *Palestinian Judaism and the New Testament*, 163; H. Falk, *Jesus the Pharisee: A New Look at the Jewishness of Jesus* (New York: Paulist, 1985). cited in D. J. Harrington, "The Jewishness of Jesus: Facing Some Problems," J. H. Charlesworth, ed., *Jesus' Jewishness*, vol. 2 (New York: Crossroad, 1991), 123–152, 126.

113. "Jewish religious law. It is also used to refer to the legal portions of rabbinic literature. Halakhah deals with details of how and when commandments are to be observed." See in Zetterholm, *Jewish Interpretation of the Bible* (Philadelphia, PA: Fortress, 2012), 189.

114. Schaper, *The Pharisees*, 420. We will discuss more about the two Pharisaic houses in the next section.

115. Neusner, *From Politics to Piety*,

116. Neusner, 83.

their daily life.[117] Although all may not agree with R. Deines that the stone vessels connect with the Pharisaic practices, the latter's emphasis on purity concerns is quite clear. At this point, Pharisaism as a whole was being torn apart by internal clashes such as the rise of Zealots, and the constant rivalry between the houses of the Pharisaic leaders – Hillel and Shammai.[118]

2.3.2. The Two Pharisaic Leaders[119] – Hillel and Shammai

As we have seen above, Hillel and Shammai emerged as the two most important Pharisaic leaders during Herod the Great's reign in the early first century CE.[120] They were Jesus's older contemporaries and the rivalry between the followers of the two houses continued after Jesus's death.[121] The House of Hillel and the House of Shammai were the titles of the two parties that clashed on the interpretation of the laws. Hillel was moderate[122] and Shammai conservative.[123] Despite their disagreements, both houses stood

---

117. Cited in Schaper, *The Pharisees*, 420.

118. Schaper, *The Pharisees*, 423.

119. The sources we are about the two leaders and their stories are historically controversial. Therefore, Neusner states that the historical Hillel hardly existed. Neusner was right to some degree. For we know about them was only through rabbinic literature in which Hillel and his teachings were presented in a positive manner. The rabbis' main attention was solely on how they handed down the oral traditions from their predecessors. Although a Jewish historian, like Josephus did not inform us the historical person Hillel the Pharisee, there are good reasons for believing Hillel was a prominent Pharisaic leader who lived sometime before the destruction of the temple. The Acts of Apostles mentions Hillel's grandson, Gamaliel I as, ". . . a Pharisee in the Sanhedrin named Gamaliel I, a teacher of the law held honour by all the people (Acts 5:34–39). The rabbi's information about Hillel's former teachers – Semaias and Abatalion and his later successors – Gamaliel I and his son, Simon – is consistent with Josephus's information about the Pharisaic leaders in the Herodians' reign. See Josephus, *Ant.* 14.171–173). This at least confirms the existence of Hillel. We have little information about his rival, Shammai, except the parallel presentation of both rivals' opinions by the Hillelites. So, even if we only have one side's view of the dispute, surely the Hillelites provide testimony to Shammai's existence?

120. L. H. Schiffman, "Beit Hillel and Beith Shammai," in *The Oxford Dictionary of the Jewish Religion*, eds. R.J. Zwi Werblowsky and Geoffrey Wigoder, 108 (Oxford: Oxford University Press, 1997); Gowan, *Bridge between the Testaments*, 147; Gafni, "Historical Background," 10.

121. Gafni, "Historical Background," 11; Sanders, *Judaism*, 422.

122. By this I mean that Hillel was flexible and willing to teach the Torah to anyone. Besides, he was patient and the purpose of his teaching was to make it applicable in daily life.

123. By this I mean to say that Shammai was strict in interpretation of the laws and its practices. He did not aim to adopt the Torah to the needs of the situation but stuck to his own way. Besides, he only wanted pupils from noble families and refused to teach the Torah to commoners.

together for the nation when the Roman procurator Coponius attempted to tax the Jews and ordered a strict census to be taken after the Romans had dethroned Herod the Great's successor Archelaus (6 CE) in Judea. At that time, according to Neusner, both houses strongly opposed the Romans.[124]

Hillel's contribution to historical Pharisaism was to adapt the law to everyday life. Moreover, his successors have adopted his teachings about the law and moderate interpretation so they have continued to be relevant. This may explain why his name is predominant and highly honoured in rabbinical tradition after 70 CE. Another reason may be that Hillel's followers won the Pharisaic leadership from the followers of Shammai after 70 CE,[125] thus promoting Hillel to the most important figure. For these reasons Neusner views him as the founder of Pharisaic pious life.[126] Most scholars believe that he lived ca. 50 BCE to ca. 10 CE[127] or 20 CE.[128] There are two conflicting stories concerning Hillel's life. One story describes Hillel as already well-trained in the Torah when he came from Babylonia to Palestine to interpret the law (y.*Pesahim* 6:1). Another version portrays Hillel's lifespan as being quite similar to Moses's. In that version, he was not a learned man before he came to Palestine at the age of forty. After his arrival in Palestine, he studied the Torah for forty years, then served forty years and eventually died at the age of 120 years.[129] Though we do not know anything for sure about Hillel's early life, according to the available sources, Hillel was portrayed as a pious

---

124. J. Neusner, ed., *Dictionary of Ancient Rabbis: Selections from the Jewish Encyclopaedia* (Peabody, MA: Hendrickson, 2003), 106. Although Josephus did not mention the opposition from both houses specifically, he did mention Judas (the founder of Zealot), who organized a revolt not to pay tribute to the Romans at the time. See Josephus, *War* 2.118 (*Ant.* 17.349). "The territory of Archelaus was now reduced to a province, and Coponius, a Roman of the equestrian order, was sent out as procurator, trusted by Augustus with full powers, including the infliction of capital punishment Under his administration, a Galilean, named Judas, incited his countrymen to revolt, upbraiding them as cowards for consenting to pay tribute to the Romans and tolerating mortal masters, after having God for their lord. This man was a sophist who founded a sect of his own, having nothing in common with the others."

125. We will discuss more about this in the last section of this chapter.

126. Neusner, *From Politics to Piety*, 13–14.

127. S. E. Karesh and Mitchell M. Hurvitz, *Encyclopaedia of Judaism* (New York: Facts on File, 2006), 211; Neusner, *From Politics to Piety*, 13.

128. H. Koester, *History, Culture, and Religion of the Hellenistic Age*, vol. I (Philadelphia: Fortress, 1982), 406.

129. J. Neusner, ed., *Dictionary of Judaism in the Biblical Period: 450 B.C.E to 600 C.E* (Peabody, MA: Hendrickson, 1999), 294.

person, a man of gentle heart, peace-loving and accommodating himself to bringing both Jews and gentiles alike nearer to God.[130] Scholars believe that Hillel was from a wealthy family. However, he chose to study the Torah as a poor and simple man and did not receive any financial aid from his family while studying in Jerusalem.[131] As a poor man, he learned the Torah faithfully in his daily life and he was wise enough to approach the interpretation of the law, the nature of God and how they related to humanity.[132] The sources also depict that all of Hillel's deeds and teachings were "for the sake of heaven" and he only had the singleness of mind to serve God and do his will. In a rabbinic text, there is a story about how Hillel brings others to the Torah:

> He stood in the gate of Jerusalem and met people going to work. He asked, "How much will you earn to-day?" One said, "A denarius," the other said, "Two denarii." He asked them, "What will you do with the money?" They gave answer, "We will pay for the necessities of life." Then he said to them, "Why don't you rather come with me and gain knowledge of the Torah, that you may gain life in this world and life in the world to come?" Thus Hillel was wont to do all his days and has brought many under the wings of heaven.[133]

Hillel also probably criticized the luxurious lifestyle of the powerful and rich people in his days.[134] *Avot* 2:7 also provides his teaching, which says, "The more flesh the more worms; the more possessions the more care; the more women the more witchcrafts; the more bondwomen the more lewdness; the more bondmen the more thieving; the more study of the law the more life." During his time in Jerusalem, the House of Shammai preferred to have pupils from wealthy families and well-educated disciples. Shammai maintained that only such worthy persons could study the Torah. Such discrimination was unacceptable to Hillel. In his understanding, the law

---

130. Neusner, ed., *Dictionary of Ancient Rabbis*, 105.
131. Karesh and Hurvitz, *Encyclopaedia of Judaism*, 211.
132. Neusner, ed., *Dictionary of Judaism*, 108.
133. ARN A 27. Cited in D. Flusser, "Hillel and Jesus: Two Ways of Self-Awareness," in *Hillel and Jesus* eds. J. H. Charleswort and L. L. Johns, (Minneapolis, MN: Fortress, 1997), 75.
134. G. Wigoder, ed., *New Encyclopaedia of Judaism* (1989): 364–365.

was for everyone to learn, and a person must study the Torah in order to become a worthy person. With this in mind, he taught the law even to common labourers on their way to work and he welcomed everyone to discuss and clarify the matters of the law in his house. Hillel was described as the one who was convinced the law should be studied unselfishly, and thus he was called the teacher of the Torah (b.*Sukkah*.20a;[135] m. *Avot* 1:12–13[136]).[137] As such, he was also known for his humility and pious life. The Shammai may have dominated before 70 CE,[138] but most ordinary Jews favoured Hillel. There were good reasons for this. He had experienced poverty, which enabled him to put himself in the position of the common people and to pass judgement in a way that they could apply in their lives.[139] The House of Hillel was said to be founded, shaped and driven according to Hillel's personality and his disciples followed their master's way.[140] Their intention was to make the law possible and applicable for people to follow in their daily lives. Consequently, the House of Hillel represented the poor and ordinary people and was merciful whereas, the House of Shammai favoured the elite. For the House of Shammai say, "A *Zab*(the name of a Hebrew boy) who is a Pharisee should not eat with a *Zab* who is a common person." But the House of Hillel permits it.[141] Comparing the rulings and the disputes between the two houses, the House of Hillel's ways were more considerate than the House of Shammai's. Furthermore, Hillel taught that "A person should always show sympathy to other people" (b.*Ketubot* 17a) and he always accommodated himself to others.[142] He teaches,

---

135. R. Simeon b. Laqish said, "Lo, I am atonement for R. Hiyya and his sons, for in the beginning, when the Torah was forgotten in Israel, Ezra came up from Babylonia and placed it on solid foundations. When it was once more forgotten, Hillel the Babylonian came up and placed it on solid foundations (b.*Sukkah*, 20a).

136. Hillel said: "Be of the disciples of Aaron, loving peace and pursuing peace, loving mankind and bringing them nigh to the law".

137. Wigoder, ed., *New Encyclopaedia of Judaism*, 346.

138. Neusner, ed., *Dictionary of Judaism*, 294; Schiffman, "Beit Hillel and Beith Shammai," 108.

139. Karesh and Mitchell M. Hurvitz, *Encyclopaedia of Judaism*, 211.

140. Neusner, ed., *Dictionary of Judaism*, 293.

141. t. *Shabbat* 1:15 in J. Neusner, trans., *The Tosefta*, vol. 1 (Peabody, MA: Hendrickson, 2002).

142. Neusner, *Babylonian Talmud*, 2009.

Do his will as if it was thy will that he may do thy will as if it was his will. Make thy will of none effect before his will that he may make the will of others of none effect before thy will . . . judge not thy fellow until thou art come to his place, and say not of a thing which cannot be understood that it will be understood in the end (m.*Avot* 1.4–5).[143]

In contrast, Shammai was considered to have originated from a wealthier and aristocratic Sadducee background,[144] and he was depicted as arrogant, impatient and patriotic. Neusner believes that Shammai had two interests – basically playing a prominent role in religious matters and also in political affairs.[145] Probably, his followers mostly came from aristocratic families. His religious views and interpretation were strict in the extreme. These would have been difficult for the common people to understand and to apply in their daily lives.[146] Although Shammai had good sayings such as, "Make your Torah study a regular practice," "Say little and do much," and "Greet everyone with a cheerful face," in reality he was portrayed as a person would not tolerate any poor man who loved to study the Torah, let alone any gentile who wished to be a proselyte. His reaction towards them was "rigorous, conservative, impatient and irascible in nature."[147] Thus he was disliked by common people because of his perceived lack of human qualities – sympathy, gentleness, patience and hospitality towards others.[148]

In addition, as a true Palestinian Jew, Shammai did not submit to any aspects of heathen rule. Hence, he participated in his land's politics as much as possible. This is obvious in the later period,[149] for his disciples followed the same pattern, held the same principles as their master and ran the House of Shammai accordingly. According to the Mishnah and Talmudic writings, Hillelites gained the more dominant leadership position in the late

---

143. m. *Avot* 2.4–5 in Danby, *The Mishnah*.
144. Koester, *History, Culture, and Religion*, 403; Schiffman, "Beit Hillel and Beith Shammai," 108.
145. Neusner, ed., *Dictionary of Ancient Rabbis*, 384.
146. Neusner, 384; Fornberg, "Matthew and the School of Shammai," 35–59.
147. Wigoder, ed., *The New Encyclopaedia of Judaism*, 705. How Hillel and Shammai responded to gentile proselytes will be discussed later.
148. Neusner, *Dictionary of Ancient Rabbis*, 384.
149. Detailed discussion will be in section 2.3.4.

first-century CE, whereas before that the Shammaites dominated. In the rabbinic literature, the disputes of both leaders comprised a large corpus and the House of Shammai was the one that appeared first and always had the last word as authoritative.[150] Accordingly, the House of Shammai probably triumphed over the House of Hillel in pre-70 CE, but after the fall of Jerusalem in 70 CE, the Hillelites were probably seen as the dominant leaders, as they had gathered at Yavneh for the continuation and survival of Pharisaic Judaism.[151]

2.3.3 The Teachings and Practices of Hillel and Shammai

The teachings and practices of Hillel and Shammai are seen largely and in an expanded manner in rabbinic sources.[152] Some examples of the two masters' controversies, seen in Talmud and Mishnah, are noted below. These are quoted directly in order to give a clear picture of the two masters' attitudes toward the law, their personalities, characters and the way they dealt with proselytes and others.[153]

Narrative Depiction of Shammai and Hillel

1. Admission to Torah Study

An ancient teaching of the Men of the Great Assembly urges, "Raise up many disciples."[154] Shammai and Hillel held different opinions on the standard to be an eligible disciple:

Shammai says, "One should not teach [the Torah] except to one who is wise, meek, and a member of distinguished family and wealthy;" but the House of Hillel say, "One should teach anyone."[155] According to Sotah, the House of Shammai

---

150. Neusner, *Dictionary of Judaism*, 293.

151. Schiffman, "Beit Hillel and Beith Shammai," 108.

152. Neusner, *Dictionary of Ancient Rabbis*, 105.

153. The Talmud and Mishnah sections quoted below are taken from Jacob Neusner, *Introduction to Rabbinic Literature* (New Haven, CT: Yale University Press, 1988). Reproduced with permission of the Licensor through PLSclear.

154. m.*Abot* 1:1

155. Abot &Rabbi Nathan Version A (ARN-A), ch. 3. Y. Buxbaum, *The Life and Teaching of Hillel* (New York: Rowman & Littlefield, 1994); L. Finkelstein, "The Pharisaic Leadership after the Great Synagogue (170 B.C.E.-135 C.E.)," in *The Cambridge History of*

preferred and believed that only worthy students should be allowed to study Torah whereas the House of Hillel believed that Torah study is available to everyone, hoping that they will repent and become worthy.[156]

Shammai only wanted to train disciples from the wealthy, the noble and the religious parents whereas Hillel was very eager to teach all people, whether rich or poor, Jew or gentile, and even to sinners.[157]

2. Concerning Proselytes[158]

A) A gentile once came before Shammai and asked him: "How many Torahs do you have?" He replied: "Two, a Written Torah and an Oral Torah." The gentile said to him, "I believe you with reference the Written Torah, but with reference to the Oral, I do not believe you. Make me a proselyte by teaching me the Written Torah." Angrily he scolded him and told him to leave. He then came before Hillel, who made him a proselyte. The first day he taught him *aleph*, *beth*, *gimmel*; the second day he reversed the names of the letters. He protested to him: "But yesterday you did not teach them to me thus!" Hillel replied to him: "Did you not depend on me [with reference to the names of the letters of the alphabet?]. Then depend on me also with reference to the Oral Torah." (b.*Shabbath* 30b–31a)

B) In another occasion it happened that a certain gentile came before Shammai and said to him, "Make me a proselyte, on condition that you teach me the whole Torah while I stand on one foot." There upon he repulsed him with the builder's cubit which was in his hand. [When] he went before Hillel, he converted to him. Hillel said to him, "What is hateful to you, do not do to your neighbour. That is the whole Torah, while the rest is commentary thereof; go and learn [it]."

Judaism, vol. 2, eds. W. D. Davies and L. Finkelstein (Cambridge: Cambridge University Press, 1989), 250.
    156. ARN-B, ch.4, "Jewish Encyclopaedia: School of Shammai and Hillel, b.*Sotah*," 47b.
    157. ARN-A, ch. 3 in Buxbaum, *The Life and Teaching of Hillel*, 128.
    158. b.*Shabbath* 30b–31a in Neusner, *Babylonian Talmud*, 2009.

C) On another occasion it happened that a certain heathen was passing behind a school and heard the voice of a scribe reciting, "And these are the garments which they shall make: a breastplate, and an ephod." Said he, "For who are these?" "For the High Priest," they said. Then said that heathen to himself, "I will go and become a proselyte, that I may be appointed a High Priest." So he went before Shammai and said to him, "Make me a proselyte on condition that you appoint me a High Priest." But he repulsed him with the builder's cubit which was in his hand. He then went before Hillel and. He made him a proselyte. Said he to him, "Can any man be made a king but he who knows the arts of government? Go and study the arts of government!" He went and read. When he came to *And the stranger (a non-Levite) who comes to attend the work (of tabernacle) shall die*, he asked him, "To whom does this verse apply?" "Even to David, king of Israel," was the answer. There upon that proselyte reasoned within himself a fortiori: "If Israel, who are called sons of the Omnipresent, and whom in His love for them He designed Israel is my son, my first born (Exod 4:22), yet it is written of them, *And the stranger (a non-Levite) who comes to attend the work (of tabernacle) shall die* – how much more so a mere proselyte, who comes with his staff and wallet!" Then he went before Shammai and said to him, "Am I then eligible to be a High Priest? Is it not written in the Torah, *And the stranger that cometh nigh shall be put to death*?" He went before Hillel and said to him, "O gentile Hillel: blessings rest on your head for bringing me under the wings of the *Shekhinah* (divine presence)!" Sometime later the three met in one place. Said they, "Shammai's impatience sought to drive us from the world, but Hillel's gentleness brought us under the wings of the *Shekhinah (divine presence)*.[159]

---

159. b.*Shabbath*. 30b–31a, cited in Neusner, *From Politics to Piety*, 38–39.

3. Their Teachings over Practicing the Law

The time to recite the Shema

The House of Shammai say, "In the evening everyone should recline in order to recite (the Shema) and in the morning they should stand," as it says (in the passage of Shema), when you lie down and when you rise (Deut 6:7). But the House of Hillel says, "Everyone may recite according to his own manner (either reclining or standing)," as it says, And as you walk by the way. (m.*Berahkot* 1:3)[160]

Benedictions[161]

The House of Shammai say, "One recites the blessing over the day then one recites the blessing over the wine." The House of Hillel say, "One recites the blessing over the wine then one recites the blessing over the day." (m.*Berahkot* 8:1)

As regards a field which was improved during the Sabbatical year

The House of Shammai say, "They do not eat its produce (which grows) during the Sabbatical year." The House of Hillel says, "They do eat its produce which grows during the Sabbatical year." The House of Shammai says, "They do not eat produce of the Sabbatical year which was given by the owner of a field as a favour." The House of Hillel say, "They eat produce of the Sabbatical year it was given by the owner of a field as a favour or not." The House of Shammai says, "During the Sabbatical year a person may not sell to another a heifer used for ploughing." But the House of Hillel permits one to sell such a heifer because he (the buyer) may slaughter it. The House of Shammai say, "Also one may not sell vegetables in bunches." The House

---

160. m.*Berahkot*. 1:3 in J. Neusner, trans., *The Mishnah: A New Translation* (Yale University, 1988), 3.

161. m.*Berahkot*. 8:1 in Neusner, *The Mishnah*, 12. The term is used for blessing, thanksgiving, prayer and intercessions. See further in H. Danby, *The Mishnah* (London: Oxford University Press, 1933), 2.

of Hillel says, "Vegetables which one is accustomed to bind into bunches in the home."[162]

Heave-offerings[163]

A seah of unclean heave offering which fell into a hundred (seahs) of clean heave offering. The House of Shammai declares (the mixture) to be [forbidden for consumption by a priest]. But the House of Hillel permits.[164]

Tithes[165]

Children who hid [untithed] figs away [intending to eat them on] the Sabbath. The House of Shammai declare it exempt [from the removal of tithes; one who snacks on the produce prior to the Sabbath need not tithe]. But the House of Hillel declares it [liable to the removal of tithes; one who snacks on the produce prior to the Sabbath must tithe].

The Sabbath[166]

The House of Shammai say, "They do not [on Friday afternoon] soak ink, dyestuffs, or vetches, unless there is sufficient time for them to be [fully] soaked while it is still day." And the House of Hillel permits.

The House of Shammai say, "They do not sell [anything] to a gentile or bear a burden with him, "and they do not lift up a burden onto his back, "unless there is sufficient time for him to reach a nearby place [while it is still day]." And the House of Hillel permits.

---

162. m.*Shebit.* 4:2; 5:8; 8:3, in Neusner, *The Mishnah*, 76, 81, 86.

163. According to Num 18:18–20 and Deut 18:4, a portion of the produce of the harvest had to be given to the priests and the produce was forbidden to be used by non-priests until this portion was set aside. McNamara, *Palestinian Judaism*, 203.

164. m.*Terumot.* 5:4 in Neusner, *The Mishnah*, 104.

165. m.*Maaserot.* 4:2 in Neusner, 128.

166. m.*Shabbat.* 1:5; 1:7 in Neusner, 180.

Feast of Passover[167]

The House of Shammai says, "They do not move a ladder from one dovecot to another. But one may lean it from one window to another." And the House of Hillel permits (moving it).

The House of Shammai say, "One may not take [pigeons for slaughtering on the festival day] unless he [physically touched and] stirred them up while it was still day." And the House of Hillel say, "One may stand [at a distance] and say, 'This one and that one I shall take.'"

The House of Shammai says, "They do not remove cupboard doors on the festival." And the House of Hillel permit, even putting them back [if the festival] coincided with the day after the Sabbath [Sunday]. The House of Shammai says, "They immersed everything before the Sabbath." And the House of Hillel says, "Utensils [are to be immersed] before the Sabbath. But man [immerse] on the Sabbath [itself]."

The House of Shammai says, "[On a festival] they bring peace offerings, but they do not lay hands on them. But [they do] not [bring] whole offerings [at all]." And the House of Hillel says, "They bring peace offerings and whole offerings, and they lay hands on them."

Women[168]

The House of Shammai says, "Only girls who are (merely) betrothed exercise the right to refusal." And the House of Hillel says, "Those who are betrothed and those who are married."

The House of Shammai says, "A man divorced his wife only because he has found grounds for it in unchastity, since it is said, *because he has found in her indecency in anything* (Deut 24:1)." And the House of Hillel say, "Even if she spoiled his dish, since it is said, *because he has found in her indecency in anything.*"

---

167. m. *Besta.* 1:3; 1:5; 2:2; 2:4 in Neusner, 291, 293–294.
168. m. *Yebamot.* 13:1; 9:10 in Neusner, *The Mishnah*, 366, 487.

Since the Shammaic Pharisees are the dominant group until the fall of Jerusalem, there are occasions that the House of Hillel reverted and accepted the teaching of the House of Shammai. Here we take example from *Eduyyut*-the testimonies,

Testimonies[169]

The House of Shammai say, "she may remarry and collect her marriage settlement." And the House of Hillel say, "She may remarry, but she may not collect her marriage settlement."

Said to them the House of Shammai, "You have permitted the matter involving sexual relations, which is subject to a severe rule. Will you not now permit the matter involving property, which is subject to a much more lenient rule?" Said to them the House of Hillel, "But we find that the brothers do not take over the estate [of deceased] on the basis of her testimony." Said to them the House of Shammai, "But do we not learn the following from the contract covering her marriage settlement: 'If you marry another person, you will collect what is written over to you [in this document].'" The house of Hillel reverted and accepted the teaching of the House of Shammai.

Purities[170]

Nails known to have been made from other utensils – The House of Shammai declare unclean. And the House of Hillel declares clean.

A chair of the bride of which the seat boards [or coverings] have been removed. The House Shammai declare unclean. And the House of Hillel clean. Shammai says, "Also the frame of the chair is unclean."

A chair which one affixed onto a trough – The House of Shammai declare [the chair] unclean. And the House of Hillel

---

169. m.*Eduyyot*. 1:12 in Neusner, , 642.
170. m. *Kelim*. 11:3; 22:3 in Neusner, *The Mishnah*, 913, 934.

declare [it] clean. Shammai says, "Even that which is made inside it."

The above-mentioned disputes between the House of Shammai and the House of Hillel are just a few examples basically from the Mishnah. From this, we see that Shammai focuses more on the formal act of strictness while Hillel stresses more the intention of the heart and the requirements of the situation.[171]

The House of Shammai is concerned about what is proper and what is improper activity in the synagogue on the Sabbath while Hillel's interpretation is based on the requirements of the situation.[172] As we have seen, the disputes of the two houses are basically over the laws of purity, Sabbath, festivals and table fellowship. Besides these, agricultural tithes, offerings and other taboos, also legal matters are the Pharisees' concern. In every case, whatever the House of Shammai forbids, it seems the House of Hillel permits.[173] Flusser states that Hillel's moderate interpretation of the law is based on his understanding of humanity and how one relates to the image of the creator. For Hillel, human beings were created in the image and form of God. Thus, he makes God's law applicable to every individual so as to help them draw closer to God.[174] Consequently, Hillel's humanity and his principle of interpretation became decisive for his followers. In contrast, Shammai's principle of interpretation was difficult for common people to follow, according to Koster, as his exegetical principle basically was linked to the Jerusalem temple.[175]

2.3.4 The Hillelites and the Shammaites

During Jesus's ministry, when Tiberius was the Roman Emperor, Herod Antipas was the tetrarch of Galilee and Pontius Pilate was a prefect[176] in

---

171. M. Weinfeld, "Hillel and the Misunderstanding of Judaism in Modern Scholarship," in *Hillel and Jesus*, eds. J. H. Charlesworth and L. L. John (Minneapolis: Fortress, 1997), 67.

172. t. *Shabbat.* 16:22, Levine, *Ancient Synagogue*, 57.

173. Cohen, *From the Maccabean to Mishnah*, 157.

174. D. Flusser, *Judaism of the Second Temple Period*, trans. Azzan Tadin, vol. 2 (Jerusalem: Hebrew University Press, 2002), 215.

175. Koester, *History, Culture, and Religion*, 406.

176. According to the Caesarea Maritima inscription discovered in 1961, Pilate was prefect of the Roman province of Judea from 26–36 CE. J. D. Kingsbury, "The Developing

Judea, the followers of the two houses appeared to be the most antagonistic Pharisaic houses in Palestine.[177] The debates between the two houses were not conclusively resolved until after the fall of Jerusalem. The process is reflected in the Mishnah.[178] Saldarini says that after the death of the two masters, their disciples probably institutionalized what was a faction into formal organisation which constituted part of first-century social structure.[179] The successor of Hillel was Gamaliel I,[180] who was believed to be the son of Hillel.[181] Others believe that Gamaliel I was the son of Simeon ben Hillel and the grandson of Hillel.[182] In any case, he was a direct descendant of Hillel. The Hillelites followed their master's principles and values and maintained the teachings and practices of their founder. Their intention was to study the law, to bring all men nearer to God and to his neighbour. Therefore they kept themselves quiet, and were peace-loving men, accommodating themselves to circumstances and times.[183] As a result, the Hillelites were described as, "the pious and gentle followers of Ezra."[184]

The Shammaites also faithfully followed the same pattern as their master in characteristics, such as being intensely nationalistic, intemperate, and severe.[185] According to the Mishnah, Hananiah b.Hezekiah b.Gorion was the head of the House of Shammai in the generation before the destruction of Jerusalem.[186] Besides, they had a more conservative tendency and

---

Conflicts between Jesus and the Jewish Leaders in Matthew's Gospel: A Literary-Critical Study," *CBQ* 49 (1987): 59.

177. Neusner, *Dictionary of Ancient Rabbis*, 104.

178. Gafni, "Historical Background," 11.

179. Saldarini, *Palestinian Society*, 210.

180. He became the successor of the Pharisees during 20–50 CE. He was described as a man of great respect who spoke in favour of the arrested apostles of Jesus in Act 5:34 and also mentioned as the master of the apostle Paul in Acts 22:1–3. According to Gafni, Gamaliel I (the Elder) was merely a Pharisaic member of the Sanhedrin. See Gafni, "Historical Background," 12.

181. Koester, *History, Culture, and Religion*, 406.

182. L. M. Abrami, "Were All the Pharisees 'Hypocrites'?" *Journal of Ecumenical Studies* 47, no. 3 (Summer 2013): 427–435.

183. b.*Berakoth*. 60a; b.*Shabbath*. 31a. Neusner, *Dictionary of Ancient Rabbis*, 105.

184. b.*Sanhedrin*. 11a. Neusner, 105.

185. b.*Berakhot*. 60a; b.*Shabbat*.31a.

186. See Danby, *The Mishnah*, 100.

preferred literal readings when interpreting the laws, just like their master.[187] Moreover, the Shammaites' religious standpoint was combined with hatred of the gentiles, and this principle directed their zeal and attitude towards dethroning the power of the gentile ruler. At the time their beliefs were similar to the Zealots. Consequently, the Shammaites received much support from them.[188] Since the Shammaites dominated before 70 CE, they seemed to decree whatever rules they like. This fact is recorded in the Mishnah as:

> When they (the House of Shammai and the House of Hillel) went up to visit him (Hananiah b.Hezekiah b.Gorion) they voted, and they of the House of Shammai outnumbered them of the House of Hillel; and eighteen things did they decree on that day.[189]

It was in the leader of the House of Shammai (Hananiah b.Hezekiah b.Gorian) while the Pharisees from both Houses were gathering, the House of Shammai decreed various legal regulations, including the rigorous observance of the Sabbath in accord with their teachings.[190] The 18 decrees, they formulated probably were also rules for the Jews to further distance themselves further from the gentiles.[191] Subsequently, their attitudes towards the gentiles later led them to participate in the Jewish revolt. As the conflict grew and continued with the Romans in the time of Nero, the Shammaites became more in line with the revolutionary Zealots who openly opposed the Romans. Due to their political cooperation with Zealots at the time, the Shammaites also received support from the majority of the Jews, and even from the Sanhedrin council to fight against their oppressors. In contrast, most of the Hillelites who loved a peaceful life and sought to foster their attention only on the law became powerless, as they could not stem public indignation against the Romans at this point.[192] The House of Hillel was

---

187. G. Stemberger, *Introduction to the Talmud and Midrash*, trans. and ed. M. Bockmuehl, 2nd ed (Edinburgh: T&T Clark, 1996), 66; Neusner, *Dictionary of Ancient Rabbis*, 105.
188. Schaper, *Pharisees*, 423.
189. m.*Shabbat* 1:4.
190. C. Roth, "The Pharisees in the Jewish Revolution of 66–73," in *Origins of Judaism*, vol. 2 , ed. J. Neusner (London: Garland, 1990), 270.
191. Gafni, "Historical Background," 11.
192. Schaper, *Pharisees*, 426.

not only opposed to "a priestly oligarchic leadership based on hereditary authority, it also appeared to be diametrically opposed to the elitist attitudes expressed by the followers of the Shammai."[193] As a result, the two houses could not be together under one roof, not even in public worship, and the conflict intensified.[194]

Besides, it was the Shammaites who brought up the idea that all the Jews must detach themselves completely from being involved in commerce and communication with their gentile neighbours. The House of Shammai say, "They do not sell (anything) to a gentile or bear a burden with him, and they do not lift up a burden onto his back."[195] When the Hillelites disagreed with such exclusivity, the Sanhedrin called together the matter to discuss. There, the Zealots, the militant-Pharisees, took the side of the Shammaites, so that finally the council had to agree with the Shammaites' proposal in relation to foreign policy. Subsequently, misfortune and calamity for the Hillelites was waiting when the leader of the Zealot militants, Eleazar ben Ananias called the Pharisees from both houses to meet at his house. The Hillelites were told they should adopt all the rules and principles the Zealots had set up against the Romans. This the remaining Shammaites were able to do so.[196] When the Hillelites disagreed on the matter and started to leave they were killed by the armed men placed by Eliezer at his door.[197] When the war actually broke out in 68 CE, the House of Shammai joined the Pharisaic war party. Nevertheless the armies of the powerful Romans triumphed; the temple in Jerusalem fell in 70 CE and all the nationalists and the Zealots, including the Pharisaic war party composed largely of the Shammaites, perished.[198]

---

193. Gafni, "Historical Background," 11.

194. t.*Shabbath*.1:16; Koester, *History, Culture, and Religion*, 406; Neusner, *Dictionary of Ancient Rabbis*, 105–106.

195. t.*Shabbat*. 1:22 in trans. J. Neusner, *The Tosefta*, vol. 1.

196. H. Graetz, *History of the Jews*, vol. 2, *From the Reign of Hyrcanus (135 B.C.E) to the Completion of the Babylonian Talmud 500 C.E*, (New York: Cosimoclassic, 2009), 270; M. Jastrow and S. Mendelsohn, "Bet Hillel and Bet Shammai" (accessed 15 December 2014).

197. m.*Shabbat*. 1:4; t.*Shabbath*.1:16; b.*Shabbath*.13a; y.*Shabbath*.1:3c.

198. Koester, *History, Culture, and Religion*, 406; Neusner, *Dictionary of Ancient Rabbis*, 106.

2.4 The Pharisees in Post-70 CE

What happened to the existence of the Pharisaic community after the fall of Jerusalem in 70 CE? Davies believes that the so-called rabbis – Pharisees at Yavneh were a leading community of the Jews – were against the Christians, especially in that they had clashed with the Matthean community.[199] Similarly, Maccoby states that the Pharisees dominated throughout the whole period from 175 BCE to 135 CE and they had many followers.[200] Likewise, Herford says that after the Romans destroyed the Second Temple in 70 CE, those groups that had supported the Jewish revolt disappeared; one major group of Pharisees alone survived and they took the lead for the continuation of Judaism.[201]

According to the sources we have, this surviving group of Pharisees did not dominate the Jewish community as a whole right after post-70 CE. Yet the Jewish war with the Romans inaugurated a new beginning and direction for Pharisaic Judaism, and it was this new direction that became mainstream Judaism in the third or the fourth century. The founder of this new movement was Yohanan ben Zakkai. Sanders accepts the view that Yohanan ben Zakkai was a disciple of both Hillel and Shammai based on the description in *Avot* 2:8 as "Rabban Johanan ben Zakkai received the law from Hillel and from Shammai."[202]

However, other sources like b.*Suk.28a* write, "Our rabbis have taught: Hillel the elder had eighty disciples, thirty of whom were worthy of the divine spirit resting upon them, as it did upon Moses our Master . . . the greatest 9 of them was Jonathan b.Uzziel, the smallest of them was Johanan b.Zakkai." In this source, ben Zakkai was described only as the disciple of

---

199. W. D. Davies, *The Setting of the Sermon on the Mount* (Cambridge: Cambridge University Press, 1964), 106.

200. H. Maccoby, *Revolution in Judea*, 164–167, cited in Sanders, *Judaism*, 400.

201. With the destruction of the Qumran community by the Romans in 68 CE, the Essene group disappeared. The Jewish nationalists such as Zealots and Sicarii also perished. Many priestly, Sadducees and lay aristocrats who controlled Jerusalem were killed or taken as prisoner to Rome after the fall of Jerusalem. Still, many appeared to survive the disaster. The only significant number who survived the disaster were the Pharisees, which many survivors from different groups joined later. See J. P. Meier, *A Marginal Jew*, vol. 3 (New York: Doubleday, 2001), 298–299; Herford, *The Pharisees*, 52.

202. m.*Abot* 2:8 see H. Danby, *The Mishnah*, 448.

Hillel.²⁰³ Thus, the majority of scholars see him as the disciple of Hillel rather than Shammai. While he was still the youngest disciple of Hillel, his future leadership had been already predicted as "the father of wisdom" and "the father of younger generations" by Hillel before his death.²⁰⁴ With ben Zakkai's wisdom and wise leadership, Pharisaic rabbinic Judaism came into existence as a reality and the only academic centre was in Jamnia or Yavneh (modern Yebna) where all the remnant of the Pharisees had come together to foster Torah after the war. Yohanan ben Zakkai had opposed the Pharisaic war party and he had disengaged himself from the war even before the end of the revolt. During the war he and some of his disciples managed to get out of Jerusalem to meet Vespasian, the Roman commander of Nero. Yohanan ben Zakkai had put himself in a coffin that was carried out of the city by his disciples. When they were stopped and questioned, they said that they were on their way to bury their master.²⁰⁵ That was the story of how he and his disciples managed to escape from the war and came to the place where Vespasian had settled. Yohannan requested Vespasian to grant him permission to found a school in Yavneh (Jamnia), on the coast of Palestine. He also prophesied imperial glory for the general.²⁰⁶ Since Vespasian himself had been interested in encouraging moderate Jewish leadership in Palestine, after seeing the true passion of Yohannan in wishing to set up a school there, permission was granted.²⁰⁷ Under this disciple of Hillel and his leadership, Jewish identity survived. Consequently, it is likely that the "Judaism which has come down through the centuries is essentially Pharisaism," as Herford states.²⁰⁸

However, Sigal denies any link between the Pharisees and the rabbis of the Yavneh period and beyond. Sigal argues that there is little evidence of

---

203. Ben Zion Bokser, trans., *The Talmud: The Selected Writings* (New York: Paulist, 1989), 223; I. B. Gottlieb, "Yohanan Ben Zakkai" in *The Oxford Dictionary of the Jewish Religion*, eds. R. J. Zwi Werblowsky and Geoffrey Wigoder (Oxford: Oxford University Press, 1997), 748; Neusner, *Dictionary of Ancient Rabbis*, 239.

204. Neusner, *Dictionary of Ancient Rabbis*, 239.

205. Neusner, 240.

206. Neusner, *Dictionary of Ancient Rabbis*, 240; Koester, *History*, 407.

207. Neusner, 240; Koester, 407.

208. Herford, *The Pharisees* 52.

the connection between pre-70 Pharisees and the rabbis of the Mishnah.[209] Likewise, Cohen says that, after the revolt, there was no particular sect that had control over the others. Post-70 CE was not marked by sectarianism since the war made the people realize that sectarianism was dangerous. He argues that the Yavneans never called themselves Pharisees. Therefore, he states that the view that there was a Pharisaic triumph at Yavneh is misinformed. He further argues that the rabbis in the early Tainnaitic period[210] did not describe the members of the Yavnean community as Pharisees but as the "sages of Israel."[211] None of the rabbis' works carried any connotation of a Pharisaic self-consciousness nor had spoken of Pharisees as their predecessors or presented their opponents as Sadducees (and Boethusians, a group mentioned only in rabbinic literature).[212] According to Cohen, at Yavneh there is an early prayer against all heretics who try to cause sectarian division.[213]

The observations of Sigal and Cohen are right to some extent. As they understand, the earliest Yavneans, around Yohanan ben Zakkai, did not have a direct connection and relationship with the Pharisees. Although Yohanan ben Zakkai was a disciple of Hillel and Shammai or just Hillel, he never explicitly identified himself as a pupil of either. The early Yavneans appeared to realize that the disputes of sectarianism and exclusivity meant division which in turn had brought about the disaster not only upon the respective group or sect but also to the entire nation. Consequently, the Yavneans avoided identifying themselves as Pharisees since the early rabbinic movement was likely composed of a variety of people.[214] It may well be as Cohen says, to avoid sectarian division that the early Yavneans simply avoid using the name "Pharisees" in the most historically critical period.

On the other hand, we see in Talmudic literature that the term "Pharisees" was used to address the rabbis/Sages. For instances, whenever the Sadducees

---

209. Sigal rejects the link between the Pharisees of Josephus and the New Testament and the rabbis of post-70 CE. See P. Sigal, *The Halakhah of Jesus of Nazareth According to the Gospel of Matthew* (Boston: Brill, 2008), 59–60.
210. Tannaitic period is from ca. 70–225 CE.
211. S. J. Cohen, "The Significance of Yavneh: Pharisees, Rabbis, and the End of Jewish Sectarianism," *Hebrew Union College Annual* 55 (1984): 39.
212. Cohen, *From the Maccabean to Mishnah*, 226.
213. Cohen, 227.
214. Zetterholm, *Jewish Interpretation of the Bible*, 12.

disputed with rabbis/Sages, they addressed the Sages as the Pharisees. Another point is that the rabbis/Sages addressed themselves as the Pharisees when they themselves speak of their own negative traits (y.*Berakhot* 9, 14b).[215] Besides, the Yavnean literature, especially Mishnah provides a detailed picture of the legal disputes of the two Pharisaic Houses (Shammai and Hillel). This suggests that the surviving disciples of disciples of those houses joined Yohanan ben Zakkai in the work of Yavneh and began to record and preserve the traditions they had learned before 70 CE.[216] Most of the rabbis who joined Yohanan ben Zakkai shortly before or after the end of the war were possibly from the House of Hillel.[217] The rabbis at Yavneh followed Pharisaic traditions such as the careful observation of the Written and Oral Laws. For the Mishnah's central focus was "ritual purity, eating, festivals, agricultural regulations, and laws relating to the exchange of women (betrothal, marriage, divorce)."[218] As Cohen himself acknowledges, (whereas Sigal denies) most of the characteristics of the Mishnah account have to do with the disputes between the House of Hillel and the House of Shammai of pre-70 CE although the disputes after post-70 CE had shifted from the two houses' to individual rabbinic masters.[219] The fact that the Mishnah account favoured the Pharisees indicated that the rabbis at Yavneh had implicitly adopted the Pharisees as their ancestors.[220] For instance, whenever the rabbis presented the disputes between the Sadducees and the Pharisees, they always supported the Pharisees. Whenever they provided the disputes between the House of Hillel and Shammai, Hillel would receive the more honour.[221] Thus, as Saldarini rightly puts, the Mishanic editors' purpose was not simply to report the disagreements between the Pharisees and the Sadducees but to recount and preserve stories and the traditions of their legal precedents.[222]

---

215. D. Flusser, *Jewish Sources in Early Christianity* (Tel-Aviv, Israel: MOD, 1993), 28.
216. Neusner, *From Politics to Piety*, 100.
217. Koester, *History, Culture, and Religion*, 407.
218. L. L. Grabbe, *Introduction to Second Temple Judaism, History and Religion of the Jews in the Time of Nehemiah, the Maccabees, Hillel and Jesus* (London: T&T Clark, 2010), 53.
219. Cohen, *From the Maccabean to Mishnah*, 228.
220. Saldarini, *Pharisees*, 231.
221. Zetterholm, *Jewish Interpretation of the Bible*, 12.
222. Saldarini, *Pharisees*, 231.

Moreover, the Yavneans were most likely headed and led by the Hillelites after 70 CE since Yohanan ben Zakkai was mostly accepted as Hillel's disciple and he was later replaced by rabbi Gamaliel II (the grandson of Hillel and the son of Gamaliel I) possibly around 90 CE or 100 CE. This does not mean that the remaining Shamaites were excluded from a new form of Pharisaic-rabbinic community. This also suggests that there is a tie between the Pharisees and the rabbis at Yavneh.[223] Therefore, considering all these factors, although the rabbis/Sages at Yavneh, as Cohen states, avoided any sectarian division, the evidence above supports that the Pharisees, particularly the Hillelites, still appeared to play leading roles by the exegetical principles, traditions and practices they followed at Yavneh.

Since the temple was the heart of their cult, the effect of the loss of the temple was profound for every Jew. They also realized that the temple could not be rebuilt as long as the Flavians (Vespasian, Titus and their descendants) were on the throne.[224] Therefore, individual and communal prayer and the study of Torah took the place of temple sacrifice.[225] Even before 70, the Pharisees comprised a variety of subgroups with somewhat differing interpretations of the Torah. Moreover, the emphasis has already shifted from the temple rites to everyday purity. This seems to have made it possible for them to adjust well to the crisis.[226] Consequently, the first priority of the practice of the Yavnean community appeared to be studying the Torah (both the Oral and Written Law), the practice of Torah and the performance of good deeds.[227] This is reflected in Yohannan ben Zakkai's words of comfort to his student:

> When rabbi Joshua looked at the Temple ruins one day, he burst to tears. Alas for us! The place which atoned for the sins of the people of Israel lies in ruins! Then Yohannan ben Zakkai spoke to him these words, "Be not grieved my son.

---

223. B. Pixner, "Jesus and His Community," 211; Zetterholm, *Jewish Interpretation of the Bible*, 12; Neusner, *From Politics to Piety*, 101.

224. In late 70 CE Titus proclaimed the Jerusalem cult illegitimate by the fact that his actions had caused its destruction. See M. Goodman, *Mission and Conversion* (Oxford: Clarendon, 2001), 44.

225. Goodman, *Mission and Conversion*, 44.

226. A. Runesson, "Rethinking of Early Jewish-Christian Relations," 109.

227. Neusner, *From Politics to Piety*, 91.

There is another way of gaining ritual atonement, even though the Temple is destroyed. We must now gain ritual atonement through deeds of loving-kindness."[228]

This altered emphasis led to a shift in Judaism which has no longer centred on the temple. According to Zetterholm, the early rabbis did not take leading roles in the synagogues. Each synagogue was led by prominent or affluent members of the local community and frequented by ordinary people, whereas the rabbis rather preferred to study the Torah at their respective houses.[229] Another major concern for them was to preserve the houses' traditions and their legal disputes.[230] The laws of tithing and ritual purity of pre-70 Pharisaic traditions were highly developed and set as discussion matter.

This supports the view that the majority of the early masters of Yavneh carried forward and preserved old Pharisaic traditions. It is especially true of Yohanan ben Zakkai, an important Jerusalemite Hillelite teacher was the founder of Yavneh.[231] Although the Yavneans preserved the traditions of the pre-70 Pharisaic laws and their legal disputes, the community at this point, as Cohen states, learnt to accept the rabbis' individual differences of the rabbis. In spite of their legal disputes, the community appeared to maintain social stability and seemed prepared to tolerate and foster legal diversity within the community.[232] In short, the Yavnean community at this point maintained legal inclusiveness but avoided exclusiveness. On the other hand, this community in the history of Pharisaic Judaism is important for this was the place where we see the link between the rabbinical traditions of pre-70 Pharisaism and their legal disputes. The Yavnean community survived from 70 CE to ca. 125 CE.[233]

---

228. Abot D' rabbi Nathan 94:5.
229. Zetterholm, *Jewish Interpretation of the Bible*, 15.
230. Neusner, *From Politics to Piety*, 121.
231. Neusner, 122.
232. Cohen, *From the Maccabean to Mishnah*, 228.
233. Neusner, *From Politics to Piety*, 99.

Chapter Findings

According to our findings, the Pharisees existed long before the Maccabean revolt, more likely in the time of Hellenistic period in opposition to the Sadducees. While the Sadducees only accepted the Written Law as authentic, the Pharisees accepted both oral and written laws and practised accordingly. Besides, they were keen to build the holy Jewish community by encouraging the people to observe priestly rules, and thus prepared the way for a universal priesthood and Torah-focused education for the entire people. Therefore, they were called *perushim* (separatists) by their opponents, the *zadoqims*.

Though we do not know the role of the Pharisees in the early Maccabean revolt in the Hellenistic era, it became clear that they were already there as a solid group by the time they were mentioned along with Jonathan, the Maccabee. During the Hasmonean period, they appeared to play significant roles as religious as well as and also political advisers for the Hasmonean rulers who were both kings and priests. Patron-client best describes the relationship between the Hasmonean rulers and the Pharisees. By the time Salome Alexandra was on the throne, the Pharisees had become the most powerful group, since authority was placed in their hands. Then they began to misuse their authority and exercised their power excessively. That was the time when they lost their purpose as Pharisees and became political opportunists.

By the time the Herodians became powerful, the Pharisaic community had begun to focus more on the study of the twofold Laws, their interpretation and the practice of ritual purity. That was also the time Pharisaism split into a left-wing party, the House of Shammai and the House of Hillel. The left-wing party or Zealots were the Pharisees who chose not to bend to any foreign rulers and to fight at any cost. The House of Shammai stood for both religious-political interests while the House of Hillel did not encourage so much political involvement, rather they were whole-heartedly devoted to fostering the Torah and committed to drawing humanity nearer to their God. In short, the two Pharisaic houses existed in the first century and the Hillelites were moderate while the House of Shammai were conservative and strict in interpretations. Besides, the Shammaic Pharisees dominated until the fall of the temple.

After 70 CE, the Pharisees and other remaining groups gathered at Yavneh under the leadership of one of the Hillelites, Yohannan ben Zakkai.

Though the Yavneans explicitly did not speak of the Pharisees as their predecessors, the work and the practice of the community revealed that the Yavneh community was indeed led by the Hillelite Pharisees. At this point, they inaugurated a new form of inclusive religious society for the continuation of Judaism. Thus, they maintained a peaceful social order by performing loving-kindness and good-deeds for the benefit and survival of Pharisaic-rabbinic-Judaism.

CHAPTER 3

The Pharisees in Matthew

Introduction

The preceding chapter discussed the historical Pharisees. The present chapter deals with how the Pharisees interact with Jesus and Matthew's intention in portraying the Pharisees in his Gospel. To get a better understanding of Matthew's purpose here, I will begin first by studying the Pharisees in Matthew from a literary perspective. After that I will observe Matthew's redaction of the Pharisaic matter on Mark and the Q-source he shares with Luke. Which means I follow the consensus of the two-document theory – the Markan priority and the existence of Q.[1] Apart from providing background

---

1. It is not my focus to give further discussions and solutions to the synoptic problem in this chapter. The two-document hypothesis, despite having complexities and problems, is one of the most widely accepted conclusions of the twentieth century. This hypothesis accepted that Mark was the earliest written gospel, that Matthew and Luke use Mark and a second source, designated as "Q." Scholars who support the two document hypothesis are: O. E. Evans, "Synoptic Criticism Since Streeter," *ET* 72 (1961): 295–299; W. G. Kummel, *Introduction to the New Testament* (London: SCM, 1975), 44–52; W. R. Farmer, *The Synoptic Problem: A Critical Analysis* (Dillsboro, NC: Western North Carolina Press, 1976); A. J. Bellinzoni, ed., *The Two-Source Hypothesis: A Critical Appraisal* (Macon, GA: Mercer University Press, 1985); W. G. Kummel, "In Support of Markan Priority," in *The Two-Source Hypothesis: A Critical Appraisal*, ed. A. J. Bellinzoni (Macon, GA: Mercer University Press, 1985), 53–84; J. A. Fitzmyer, " The Priority," in *The Two-Source Hypothesis: A Critical Appraisal*, ed. A. J. Bellinzoni (US: Mercer University Press, 1985), 37–52; B. H. Streeter, "The Priority of Mark," in *The Two-Source Hypothesis: A Critical Appraisal*, ed. A. J. Bellinzoni (Macon, GA: Mercer University Press, 1985), 23–36; C. M. Tuckett, *Q and the History of Early Christianity* (Edinburgh, T&T Clark, 1996); C. M. Tuckett, "Synoptic Problem," in *The Anchor Bible Dictionary*, ed. D. N. Freedman (New York: Doubleday, 1992), 6:263–270; J. S. Kloppenborg, ed., *The Shape of Q* (Minneapolis, MN: Fortress, 1994); J. S. Kloppenborg, *Q and the Earliest Gospel* (London: John Knox, 2008).

for the next chapter, this chapter will focus on what type of Pharisee Matthew portrays and what is Matthew's purpose in portraying them in this way.

3.1. The Pharisees in Matthew

I need to examine the part played by the Pharisees in Matthew's narrative. How do they interact with Jesus in this Gospel? How are they portrayed, and what role do they play? However, the focus of this section is not to do exegetical analysis, rather it is to examine the narrative account of the Pharisees in order to figure out how they were portrayed and given a role in the gospel of Matthew.

The Pharisees and John the Baptist (3:1, 5–9)

Matthew introduces the Pharisees in the wilderness of Judea, where John the Baptist is baptizing those who repent in the River Jordan (Matt 3:5–12). The Judean wilderness is located to the west of the Jordan, between the mountain ridge and the Dead Sea.[2] Although the text does not make the nature of John's baptism clear,[3] it appears to be more a sign of repentance and preparation for the way of the Lord than a ritual purification. John's reaction to the presence of the Pharisees is unpleasant. As soon as John sees them coming, he calls them γεννήματα[4] ἐχιδνῶν[5] – brood of vipers. Although the Pharisees pride themselves on being "Abraham's off-spring," John pronounced that they are like vipers, they should be exterminated. They are like trees that cannot bear fruit and should be axed. John shames them in the presence of the crowd. Since we have no prior information about the Pharisees, this is quite an introduction – extremely hostile.

The Pharisees in Galilee

The name of the Pharisees was mentioned next in Jesus's speech, which comes after the Sermon on the Mount, and forms a contrast to this opening,

---

2. G. Theissen, *Gospels in Context*, 40.

3. John's baptism is seen as "Jewish proselyte baptism, and with the washings of Qumran; wider Baptist movement in the first century Judaism, the baptism based primarily upon certain OT texts (Ps 51:6–9; Isa 4:4; Ezek 36:25; Zech 13:1). See W. D. Davies and D. C. Allison, *Matthew* (London: T&T Clark, 2004), 40.

4. Creatures, children or offspring.

5. Vipers or snakes.

because Jesus seemingly acknowledges their reputation for righteousness (Matt 5:17–20). However, soon this impression is corrected, for if listeners are first told they need to surpass the righteousness of the Pharisees, in Matthew 6:1–5 and 16 they are told not to do their acts of righteousness so as to be seen, nor to boast about it as hypocrites do. As Jesus continues his speech, the Pharisees became negative example for the crowd because of their failures as religious leaders. The Pharisees, who love to practice piety and prayer in the synagogues and at the corner of the street, and who conduct fasting in order to be seen by others, were sharply criticized as 'οἱ ὑποκριταί[6] – the hypocrites. For Jesus, although the Pharisees are authorities on Mosaic law, they are more interested in receiving praises and rewards than in pleasing God.

In Matthew 9:9–13 the Pharisees are astonished at Jesus being friends with tax-collectors and sinners, even dining with them. Tax collectors collaborated with the Roman occupiers, sinners did not observe the law; therefore, anyone who associated with them, let alone shared the table with them, became tainted by their impurity.[7] How could one who mingled with the like be a pious teacher? Maybe Jesus even reclined while eating like the Romans.[8] Jesus overhears their questioning and silences them by saying what God desires most is mercy and not sacrifice. Here Jesus cites Hosea 6:6 to argue that traditional practice of cultic purity is subordinate to the demands of God's mercy and compassion. Then he makes it clear that his association with sinners and tax-collectors does not contradict the law, but is in line with it.[9] In the following verses (vv. 14–17), John the Baptist's disciples come and ask Jesus why they and the Pharisees fast while Jesus's disciples do not. This seems to be a genuine question, rather than an accusation. The Pharisees themselves are not mentioned as being present on this occasion.

However, they are present when Jesus performs a series of healings. After he has healed a demon-possessed man (Matt 9:32–34), the crowd bursts out

---

6. Pretenders, dissemblers, or play-actors.

7. Davies and Allison, *Matthew*, 135.

8. Keener refers to Jeremias (1966a:20–21) and says that ἀνακειμένου indicates that this is special meal, a banquet which is set in honour of the teacher. Palestinian Jews normally sat on chairs for ordinary meals. See Keener, *Gospel of Matthew* (Grand Rapids, MI: Eerdmans, 2009), 296.

9. D. Senior, *Matthew* (Nashville: Abingdon Press, 1998), 106

in amazement: "Nothing like this has been seen in Israel." This provokes the jealousy of the Pharisees, therefore they claim that he has used the power of demons to do this. The Pharisees' concern here is to convince the crowd that Jesus worked with the demoniac power and not of God.

Jesus and the Pharisees clash twice over the Sabbath, first in 12:1–8, then, more seriously in 12:9–14. The first clash occurs when the Pharisees accuse the disciples of breaking the law by picking and eating some heads of grain as they were passing through a field on the Sabbath. There might be two possible objections to this: (1) that they were travelling on the Sabbath, and (2) that plucking grain might be considered work. The Pharisees interpreted the Sabbath restrictions very strictly. What Exodus says about holding the Sabbath holy is general and not detailed: oral tradition supplements the written law by filling in the gaps.[10] The Pharisees spell it out in detail.[11] Although most Jews limit their travel on the Sabbath, at least in first-century Galilee they were not very strict. So we see that Jesus, his disciples and the Pharisees were legitimately in the field.[12] Jesus urges the Pharisees to apply the Sabbath principle in the light of Hosea 6:6. He also recalls the story of King David in which David gave the bread to his men out of compassion.[13] Jesus does not say disregard the law; he says apply it with compassion.[14] This is the second time Jesus quotes Hosea 6:6, urging them to consider God's mercy. Seemingly, the dispute ends there, because the Pharisees do not reply.

However, the second Sabbath story (12:9–14) shows that the dispute did not end there. The next time Jesus is in a synagogue on a Sabbath, there is a man with a withered hand. The Pharisees have reached a point where they could no longer tolerate another defeat. They are looking for a reason to accuse Jesus. Provocatively, they ask whether it is allowed to heal

---

10. There are 39 categories of forbidden work the Jews have to follow on the Sabbath. Some of them are: No work shall be done by persons or animal on the Sabbath (Exod 20:10; Deut 5:14); people are to observe the Sabbath rest because it is a sign of the covenant, the day is holy and must be sanctified, and commemorates God's completion of creation (Exod 31:13–17; Gen 2:2–3); no food is to be prepared (Exod 16:22–30); fire may not be kindled and penalty can be stoned to death (Exod 35:2–3; Num 15:32–36); no transportation (Jer 17:21–22; Neh13:15–22).

11. Keener, *Commentary on the Gospel of Matthew*, 350.

12. Saldarini, *Matthew*, 128.

13. 1 Sam 21:1–6

14. Senior, *Matthew*, 136.

on the holy day. They are the ones who initiate a quarrel. They know that Jewish tradition does not allow healing on the Sabbath unless a person is in a life-threatening situation. This man's condition is chronic and not life-threatening.[15] They are just waiting to see if Jesus will violate the Sabbath by healing a man. Jesus argues that if a mere animal that fell into a pit could be rescued on the Sabbath, human life is more important. In that sense, Jesus underscores that his action is not violation of the law but valid and authoritative. As the Pharisees have expected, Jesus performs a miracle. Now they begin to conspire to destroy him.

The conflict between the Pharisees and Jesus intensifies when Jesus heals a demoniac man who is both blind and mute (12:22–37). This is a similar case to that in 9:32–34. Here too the crowd is astounded, only this time they wonder, "Could this be the Son of David?" The Pharisees though accuse him of using the help of the ruler of demons – *Beelzebub*. Jesus knows what they are thinking and roundly refutes their accusation: "If Satan drives out Satan, he is divided against himself . . . every sin and blasphemy will be forgiven men, but the blasphemy against the Spirit will not be forgiven." Matthew's Jesus explains at length the difference between the power of God and the power of demons and warns them against sinning against the Holy Spirit. For Matthew, Jesus's ministry also involves expelling unclean spirits (12:43–45; cf Zech 13:2), demons (8:16; 9:32–33; 10:6–8; 17:18), and unclean animals (8:30–32) from the holy land where God's presence dwells.[16] Matthew's Jesus lets the Pharisees know that "the kingdom of God has not merely drawn near but has reached (φθάνω) the Pharisees."[17] For Jesus casts out demons in the Spirit of God, but they have not realized its manifestation in Jesus's exorcisms.[18] Therefore he harshly criticizes them for being extraordinarily blind and calls them a "brood of vipers" (12:34), the term we are already familiar with from John the Baptist.

---

15. Senior, *Matthew*, 138.

16. A. Runesson, "Purity, Holiness, and the Kingdom of Heaven in Matthew's Narrative World," in, *Purity, Holiness, and Identity in Judaism and Christianity: Essays in Memory of Susan Baber*, eds. C. S. Ehrlich, A. Runesson and E. Schuller, (Tubingen: Mohr Siebeck, 2013), 144–180, 155.

17. M. Marshall, *The Portrayals of the Pharisees in the Gospels and Acts*, vol. 254 (Gottingen: Vandenhoeck & Ruprecht, 2015), 102.

18. Marshall, *Portrayals of the Pharisees*, 102.

Later in the narrative (12:38–42), teachers of the law join the Pharisees, and ask Jesus for some miraculous sign, as if the miracles he had already performed were not enough. By addressing Jesus as "a teacher," they asked not for another exorcism or healing but for a reliable sign, probably for a sign such as Moses's shining face, so they can accept him as an agent of God. However, Jesus knows that their requests are not genuine but intended to entrap him and test him.[19] Therefore, he refuses them to show any other sign except for the sign of Jonah who was three days and three nights in the belly of the whale and so with the Son of Man who will be three days and three nights in the heart of the earth.

The next occasion (Matt 15:1–20) is when a group of Pharisees and teachers of the law come from Jerusalem to seek Jesus at Gennesaret[20] in Galilee. They criticize Jesus's disciples for not observing the traditional laws by washing their hands before eating. The Pharisees considered the washing of hands as a sign of purity and righteousness. Jesus accuses them of only offering lip service. He gives the example of the commandment to honour your father and mother. According to the Pharisees, a son was excused from using his property to support his parents if he vowed to make a gift to the temple. Maybe tradition allowed this, but in fact it was a serious transgression of God's commandment.[21] Jesus uses his expertise in biblical law to show that washing your hands before eating is a tradition, not a biblical law, but that what the Pharisees themselves teach others contradicts the law. This is why Jesus calls them "hypocrites and blind guides of the blind." Once more, the Pharisees demand a sign from heaven (16:1–4), and once more Jesus refuses. Afterwards he departed from them but warned his disciples to be aware of the yeast of the Pharisees.

The Pharisees in Jerusalem

Jesus now enters Judea on his way to Jerusalem. Yet again the Pharisees come to test him (19:1–9). This time they ask him if it is lawful for a man to divorce his wife "for any and every reason." The debate refers to Deuteronomy

---

19. Marshall, 87.
20. According to 14:34.
21. H. Clarke, *The Gospel of Matthew and Its Readers* (Bloomington, IN: Indiana University Press, 2003), 136; Saldarilni, *Matthew*, 137.

24:1, which permits this. However, Jesus refers back to Genesis where it is written that God made them "one flesh" and that "what God has joined together, let man not separate." When the Pharisees ask why, if this is the case, Moses allowed men to divorce their wives, Jesus replies that it was because of men's hard hearts. The only rightful ground is unfaithfulness.

From Matthew 21:23ff, the setting is Jerusalem and the temple becomes the focal point. Jesus enters the temple, cleanses the temple, teaches people there and his teachings become provocative to the authorities. As the chief priests control the temple, they become the principal opponents of Jesus, but the Pharisees are mentioned later (21:45) alongside the priests. The chief priests and elders ask by what authority he is teaching and healing. Jesus answers with a question about whether John's baptism came from heaven or man. If they answer from man, they risk the anger of the public; if they answer from heaven, they risk being asked why they did not believe John. So they keep silent. Jesus then tells the great parables (21–22) – the two sons, the parable of the wicked tenants, and the wedding banquet. He sums up by telling the priests and the Pharisees, "The kingdom of God will be taken from you and given to a people that produces the fruits of the kingdom." Jesus is so provocative that the religious leaders in Jerusalem want him out of the way.

The Pharisees plan to trap Jesus and collect evidence against him (Matt 22). So they send their own disciples and Herodians as witnesses when they ask him whether it was right to pay taxes to the Romans. If he says no, that will make Jesus a rebel against Roman authority; if he says yes, that will make him unpopular with the people. However, Jesus knows their intention and calls them hypocrites. He avoids the trap by telling them to give to Caesar what is Caesar's and to God what is God's. Their second question is about the greatest commandment (vv. 34–40). Jesus refers back to Deuteronomy 6:1–7 and Leviticus 19:18, combining them in a double commandment, saying that all the commandments hang on these two. For Matthew, unlike that of the Pharisees, Jesus's opinion on the Torah is "authoritative and definitive."[22] It is now Jesus's turn to ask them a question. Unlike previous

---

22. Marshall, *Portrayals of the Pharisees*, 89.

conflicts, Jesus initiates the discussion here.²³ He quotes a verse (22:44), and then asks if David calls the Messiah Lord, how can the Messiah be David's son. This shuts them up. After that no one dared ask him any more questions. After Jesus silences them, he denounces the Pharisees along with the Scribes (Matt 23) calling them "hypocrites," "blind guides," and "blind fools" for their misconduct in religious roles. These are Jesus's final words to the Pharisees. After this the Pharisees disappear from the narrative with the exception of a brief mention in 27:62–64. What follows next is the plot to kill Jesus arranged by the priests and the elders (Matt 26–27).

Admittedly, the Pharisees accompany the chief priests to ask Pilate to place guards at the tomb of Jesus (27:62–66), but they are otherwise altogether absent from the passion narrative. For Matthew, as Runesson states, "the blame for the death of Jesus is related primarily to the temple authorities" and not so much on the Pharisees.²⁴

From the above analysis, we see that Matthew keeps the Pharisees in focus. Matthew's Pharisees were keen on observing oral traditions in addition to the written Torah. They are presented as Jesus's most prominent dialogue partners concerning the Mosaic law and its application in daily life. At the same time, Matthew presents them as the villains of the piece who seek Jesus's doom in cooperation with the chief priests, the Herodians and the elders in Jerusalem. Their character will be discussed in more detail in section 3.3 of this chapter.

3.2. Matthew's Redaction

In this section, I will examine Mathew's redaction on Mark and Q. This will support what my analysis has already shown – that Matthew focuses on the Pharisees as a bad example. I will compare the material in Matthew and Mark on the Pharisees. In addition, I will compare some passages Matthew shares with Luke. Most scholars think that Matthew and Luke use the material in Mark. In fact, Matthew shares 90 percent of the subject matter with Mark. But in addition to this matter, Matthew and Luke share material which is not in Mark. The Q hypothesis claims that Matthew and Luke were using a

---

23. Marshall, 90.
24. Runesson, "Purity, Holiness, and the Kingdom," 150.

common source, Q. The Q-hypothesis assumption depends on Mark being written first. Regardless of the correctness of the consensus, a comparison of the non-Markan matter on the Pharisees in the two other synoptic gospels could shed light on the way Matthew redacted the material to suit his ends. General consensus of the scholars is that Luke maintains the Q source in his gospel more than Matthew does, since Matthew seems to redact the Q source material to reach his purpose.[25]

3.2.1. Matthew's Redaction on Mark

Matthew places greater emphasis on the Pharisees, contrasting them even more negatively with Jesus. Matthew contains more material on the Pharisees and the conflicts between the Pharisees and Jesus than does Mark (3:7; 5:20; 9:11–13; 9:32–34; 12:1–7; 12:9–14; 12:24; 12:38–42; 15:1–12; 16:1; 19:1–9; 21:45; 22:15–22; 22:34–36; 22:41–42; 23; 27:62–64). This becomes clear if we compare the two gospels and note the changes Matthew makes to Mark as related to the Pharisees. We can do this graphically as follows:

Table 1. The Portrayal of the Pharisees in Mark and Matthew

Mark	Matthew
1.	3:7 But when he saw many of the **Pharisees** and Sadducees coming for baptism, he said to them, "You brood of vipers! Who warned you to flee from the wrath to come?"
2.	5:20 For I tell you, unless your righteousness exceeds that of the **scribes and Pharisees**, you will never enter the kingdom of heaven.

---

25. A. J. Bellinzoni, *The Two-Source Hypothesis*, 14–18; see further discussion in W. G. Kummel, "In Support of Markan Priority," 53–84; J. A. Fitzmyer, "The Priority," 37–52; B. H. Streeter, "The Priority of Mark," 23–36; C. M. Tuckett, *Q and the History of Early Christianity*; C. M. Tuckett, "Synoptic Problem," 6:263–270; J. S. Kloppenborg, *The Shape of Q*; J. S. Kloppenborg, *Q and the Earliest Gospel*

	Mark	Matthew
3.	2:16–17 And **the scribes of the Pharisees**, when they saw that he was eating with sinners and tax collectors, said to his disciples, "Why does he eat with tax collectors and sinners?"	9:11–13 And when **the Pharisees** saw this, they said to his disciples, "Why does your teacher eat with tax collectors and sinners?" Go and learn what this means, "**I desire mercy, and not sacrifice.**"
4.		9:32–34 Behold, a dumb demoniac was brought to him. And when the demon had been cast out, the dumb man spoke; and the crowds marvelled, saying, "Never was anything like this seen in Israel." But **the Pharisees** said, "He casts out demons by the prince of demons."
5.	2:23–28 One Sabbath he was going through the grainfields; and as they made their way his disciples began to pluck heads of grain. And **the Pharisees** said to him, "Look, why are they doing what is not lawful on the Sabbath?"	12:1–7 At that time Jesus . . . his disciples were hungry, and they began to pluck heads of grain and to eat. But when **the Pharisees** saw it, they said . . . "Or have you not read in the law . . . **I tell you, something greater than the temple** is here." And if you had known what this means, "**I desire mercy, and not sacrifice,**" you would not have condemned the guiltless.'

	Mark	Matthew
6.	3:1–6 Again he entered the synagogue, and a man was there who had a withered hand. And they watched him, to see whether he would heal him on the Sabbath, so that they might accuse him. And he said to the man who had the withered hand, "Come here." And he said to them, "Is it lawful on the Sabbath to do good or to do harm, to save life or to kill?" But they were silent. And he looked around at them with anger, grieved at their hardness of heart, and said to the man, "Stretch out your hand." He stretched it out, and his hand was restored. **The Pharisees** went out, and immediately held counsel with the Herodians against him, how to destroy him.	12:9–14 And he went on from there, and entered their synagogue. And behold, there was a man with a withered hand. And they asked him, "Is it lawful to heal on the Sabbath?" so that they might accuse him. He said to them, **"What man of you, if he has one sheep and it falls into a pit on the Sabbath, will not lay hold of it and lift it out? Of how much more value is a man than a sheep!** So it is lawful to do good on the Sabbath." Then he said to the man, "Stretch out your hand." And the man stretched it out, and it was restored, whole like the other. But **the Pharisees** went out and took counsel against him, how to destroy him.
7.	3:22 And **the scribes** who came down from Jerusalem said, "He is possessed by Beelzebul, and by the prince of demons he casts out the demons."	12:24 But when **the Pharisees** heard it they said, "It is only by Beelzebul, the prince of demons that this man casts out demons."
8.		12:38–42 Then **some of the scribes and Pharisees** said to him, "Teacher, we wish to see a sign from you."

	Mark	Matthew
9.	7:1, 5 Now when **the Pharisees** gathered together to him, with some of **the scribes**, who had come from Jerusalem (v. 1). And **the Pharisees and the scribes** asked him, "Why do your disciples not live according to the tradition of the elders, but eat with hands defiled?" (v. 5)	15:1–12 Then **Pharisees and scribes** came to Jesus from Jerusalem and said, "Why do your disciples transgress the tradition of the elders? . . . then the disciples came and said to him, "Do you know that **the Pharisees** were offended when they heard this saying?"
10.	8:11–13 **The Pharisees** came and began to argue with him, seeking from him a sign from heaven, to test him.	16:1 And **the Pharisees** and Sadducees came, and to test him they asked him to show them a sign from heaven.
11.	10:2–10 And **Pharisees** came up and in order to test him asked, "Is it lawful for a man to divorce his wife?"	19:1–9 And **Pharisees** came up to him and tested him by asking, "Is it lawful to divorce one's wife for any cause?"
12.	11:27 And they came again to Jerusalem. And as he was walking in the temple, **the chief priests** and **the scribes** and the elders came to him.	21:45 When **the chief priests and the Pharisees** heard his parables, they perceived that he was speaking about them.
13.	12:13–14 And they sent to him some of **the Pharisees** and some of the Herodians, to entrap him in his talk. And they came and said to him, "Teacher . . . is it lawful to pay taxes to Caesar, or not?"	22:15–22 Then **the Pharisees** went and took counsel how to entangle him in his talk. And they sent their disciples to him, along with the Herodians, saying, "Teacher . . . is it lawful to pay taxes to Caesar, or not?"

Mark	Matthew
14. 12:28 And one of **the scribes** came up and heard them disputing with one another, and seeing that he answered them well, asked him, "Which commandment is the first of all?"	22:34–36 But when **the Pharisees heard** that he had silenced the Sadducees, they came together. And one of them, a lawyer, asked him a question, to test him. "Teacher, which is the great commandment in the law?"
15. 12:35 The presence of scribes is seen in the temple for Jesus said, "How can **the scribes** say that the Christ is the son of David?"	22:41–42 Now while **the Pharisees** were gathered together, Jesus asked them a question, saying, "What do you think of the Christ? Whose son is he?"
16. 12:38–39 And in his teaching he said, "Beware of **the scribes**, who like to go about in long robes, and to have salutations in the market places and the best seats in the synagogues and the places of honor at feasts."	23:1–2, 6–7a **The scribes and the Pharisees** sit on Moses's seat . . . and they love the place of honor at feasts and the best seats in the synagogues, and salutations in the market places.
17.	23:3–5, 7b–39 The Woes against the scribes and the Pharisees.
18.	27:62–64 Next day, that is, after the day of Preparation, **the chief priests** and **the Pharisees** gathered before Pilate and said, "Sir, we remember how that impostor said while he was still alive, 'After three days I will rise again'."

The parallel table shows that although Matthew follows all Markan uses of pericopes in relation to the Pharisees and arranges them in the same order, in most cases, Matthew makes the Pharisees the main players in his controversial stories. Matthew changes Markan scribes into Pharisees several times in his gospel. For instance, the "scribes of the Pharisees" in Mark 2:16 are simply "Pharisees" in Matthew 9:11. The scribes who come from Jerusalem in Mark 3:22 are designated as Pharisees in Matthew 12:24. Although Mark's scribes (7:1, 5) are mentioned together with the Pharisees in Matthew 15:1, at the end Matthew makes it clear that the criticism is aimed at the Pharisees (15:12). "The chief priests, the scribes, and the elders" in Mark 11:27, 12:1–12 are identified in Matthew 21:45 as "the chief priests and the Pharisees." A scribe who asks about the greatest commandments in Mark 12:28–34 becomes a Pharisee in Matthew 22:34–40. In Mark 12:35–37, the presence of scribes is seen when Jesus gives the riddle about Messianic sonship, but Matthew changes it to the Pharisees (22:41–46). Finally, Jesus's criticism of the scribes' love of honour, banquets and places in Mark 12:38–40 becomes the most detailed and sharpest criticisms directed against "the scribes and the Pharisees" in Matthew 23.[26] Matthew seems to consider Mark's scribes as Pharisees. Matthew makes clear this point in 22:34–36. After Jesus silences the Sadducees, the Pharisees come together and one of them, **a lawyer or a scribe**, asks him a question to test him: "Teacher, which is the great commandment in the law?" Matthew sticks to Mark's version by writing that it is a scribe who asks Jesus the question, but he makes it clear that the scribe is a Pharisee. Although Matthew does not present all the scribes as identical with the Pharisees, for Matthew, there is an "unholy alliance" between individuals from different groups against Jesus.[27] Matthew 23 is the evidence that Matthew puts them all into one bag regardless of their differences.[28] In all these references, Matthew keeps the Pharisees in focus.

Not only does Matthew focus on the Pharisees and make them Jesus's main opponents, he makes the point that the Pharisees do not understand the implications of their own *Halakah*. The uniqueness of Matthew against

---

26. M. Pickup, "Matthew's and Mark's Pharisees," in *In Quest of the Historical Pharisees*, eds. J. Neusner and B. D. Chilton (Waco, TX: Baylor University Press, 2007), 93–94.

27. Runesson, "Purity, Holiness, and the Kingdom," 150; Kingsbury, "Developing Conflicts between Jesus," 60–61.

28. Saldarini, *Palestinian Society*, 165.

the Pharisees is the use of the quotation from Hosea 6:6.[29] In Mark 2:15–17, the scribes of the Pharisees ask the disciples why Jesus mixes with sinners and tax collectors. Jesus only answers that he has come to call sinners without giving any further comments, whereas in Matthew 9:11–13, Jesus tells them to go and learn until they get a better understanding of what God wants in Hosea 6:6, "I desire mercy, and not sacrifice." Again in Mark 2:23–28 when Jesus's disciples pluck grain on the Sabbath, the scribes want to know why they are breaking the Sabbath (2:23–24). Jesus defends their actions by referring to the precedence of David and his men, who ate the showbread when they were hungry.[30] Jesus says, "The Sabbath was made for humankind, and not humankind for the Sabbath; so the Son of Man is Lord even of the Sabbath." Jesus does not provoke the anger of the Pharisees in the first Sabbath conflict in Mark,[31] but he does in Matthew. Although Matthew (12:1–7) follows Mark's pericope, he adds more material: (1) the temple priest breaks the Sabbath yet remains guiltless, (2) arguing Jesus is greater than the temple, and (3) pointing out the Pharisees misread Scripture and the will of God in Hosea 6:6. Through these additions and by using the words of Hosea 6:6 twice in 9:1–13 and 12:1–7, Matthew points out that the Pharisees have failed to understand the core biblical demands of God in order to preserve their human traditions.[32] Matthew emphasizes that the Pharisees' failure to recognize Jesus as greater than the temple is their failure to recognize the new demands of the kingdom of God.[33]

Matthew highlights and develops the ideas that are hidden in Mark in relation to the Pharisees and includes more materials that are not found in Mark. For instance, Mark's parable of the wicked tenants, which indicts the Jewish leaders for the rejection of God's emissaries, is taken over by Matthew and applied to the Pharisees. Matthew has John the Baptist's polemic against the Pharisees (3:7f) right from the beginning; in the Sermon on the Mount (5:20) Jesus accuses them of falling short in their pursuit of righteousness. The conflict escalates. Later (9:32–34) the Pharisees claim Jesus is using the

---

29. Marshall, *Portrayals of the Pharisees*, 91.
30. Pickup, "Matthew's and Mark's Pharisees," 69.
31. Cook, "Gospel Portrait of the Pharisees," 222.
32. Marshall, *Portrayals of the Pharisees*, 90.
33. Marshall, 123.

power of demons to heal the demon-possessed dumb man. The Pharisees demand that Jesus show them a sign as proof (12:38–42). Jesus's criticism of the Pharisees' misconduct reaches a peak in chapter 23 (vv. 1–5, 7b–39). The Pharisees are afraid Jesus's grave will be robbed, so they go with the chief priests to Pilate to ask for guards to be posted there (27:62–64). All this shows that Matthew presents the Pharisees as the main opponents of Jesus.

3.2.2. Matthew's Redaction on Q

We can also see Matthew's purpose in the Pharisaic material in his redaction on the Q source he shared with Luke. Matthew's redaction on the Q source helps us to understand that his primary focus was on the Pharisees and how they were a bad example. The first passage comes when John preaches repentance in the wilderness. The parallel passages are Matthew 3:7–9 and Luke 3:7–8:

Table 2. The Baptism of John the Baptist in Matthew 3:7–9 and Luke 3:7–8

Matthew 3:7–9	Luke 3:7–8
ἰδὼν (Ἰωάννης) δὲ πολλοὺς τῶν Φαρισαίων καὶ Σαδδουκαίων ἐρχομένους ἐπὶ τὸ βάπτισμα αὐτοῦ εἶπεν αὐτοῖς· γεννήματα ἐχιδνῶν, τίς ὑπέδειξεν ὑμῖν φυγεῖν ἀπὸ τῆς μελλούσης ὀργῆς; ποιήσατε οὖν καρπὸν ἄξιον τῆς μετανοίας καὶ μὴ δόξητε λέγειν ἐν ἑαυτοῖς· πατέρα ἔχομεν τὸν Ἀβραάμ. λέγω γὰρ ὑμῖν ὅτι δύναται ὁ θεὸς ἐκ τῶν λίθων τούτων ἐγεῖραι τέκνα τῷ Ἀβραάμ.	Ἔλεγεν (Ἰωάννης) οὖν τοῖς ἐκπορευομένοις ὄχλοις βαπτισθῆναι ὑπ' αὐτοῦ γεννήματα ἐχιδνῶν, τίς ὑπέδειξεν ὑμῖν φυγεῖν ἀπὸ τῆς μελλούσης ὀργῆς; ποιήσατε οὖν καρποὺς ἀξίους τῆς μετανοίας καὶ μὴ ἄρξησθε λέγειν ἐν ἑαυτοῖς· πατέρα ἔχομεν τὸν Ἀβραάμ. λέγω γὰρ ὑμῖν ὅτι δύναται ὁ θεὸς ἐκ τῶν λίθων τούτων ἐγεῖραι τέκνα τῷ Ἀβραάμ.

Within the parallel narrative of John's preaching, two things need to be highlighted. First, Luke has John addressing "the crowds – τοῖ ὄχλοι" while in Matthew John addresses "the Pharisees and the Sadducees – τῶν Φαρισαίων καὶ Σαδδουκαίων."[34] We do not have the presumed Q source, so we do not know whom John might have addressed there. Nonetheless, the difference

---

34. D. Zeller, "Redactional Process and Changing Setting," in *The Shape of Q*, ed. J. S. Kloppenborg (Minneapolis: Fortress, 1994), 120.

between Matthew and Luke is quite clear: Matthew has John attack the Pharisees.[35] The second thing to be noticed is that "the crowds – τοῖς ὄχλοις" in Luke came "to be baptized by John – βαπτισθῆναι ὑπ' αὐτοῦ" whereas in Matthew, the Pharisees come ἐπὶ τὸ βάπτισμα (on his baptism or to his baptism) is ambiguous. The Greek word "ἐπὶ" does not really imply the Pharisees and Sadducees came there to accept John's baptism. Rather, as Tuckett points out, Matthew appears to inform us that the Pharisees came "only to look at John, without being baptized themselves."[36]

Another Q source Matthew shares with Luke is the saying of the sign of Jonah (Matt 12:38–42; Luke 11:29–32):

Table 3. The Sign of Jonah in Matthew 12:38–39 and Luke 11:29–30

Matthew 12:38–39	Luke 11:29–30
Then **some of the scribes and Pharisees** said to him, "**Teacher, we wish to see a sign from you.**" But he answered them, "An evil and adulterous generation seeks for a sign; but no sign shall be given to it except the sign of the prophet Jonah."	When **the crowds** were increasing, he began to say, "This generation is an evil generation; it seeks a sign, but no sign shall be given to it except the sign of Jonah. For as Jonah became a sign to the men of Nineveh, so will the Son of man be to this generation."

In Luke's narrative, Jesus delivers his speech about the sign of Jonah as the crowd increases, whereas in Matthew it is the Pharisees/Scribal-Pharisees who demand that Jesus gives them a sign of his authority. Once again we cannot know which version is closest to Q, but the comparison of Luke and Matthew shows that Matthew insists on making the Pharisees Jesus's main opponents. We can go on to compare Matthew 21:1–45 with Luke 20:1–19, where the chief priests and teachers of the law in Luke (20:1) and the chief priests and the elders in Matthew (21:23) question the authority of Jesus. In Matthew verse 45 the questioners become the chief priests and Pharisees, whereas Luke maintains in verse 19 that it is the teachers of the law and the chief priests. Teachers of the law might mean the same as Pharisees, but not necessarily so. Clearly, Matthew is intent on making the

---

35. C. M. Tuckett, *Q and the History of Early Christianity*, 110.
36. Tuckett, 113.

Pharisees the culprits. Furthermore, unlike Luke, Matthew concentrates the passages where Jesus condemns the Pharisees. The following table shows shared material and Matthew's additions:[37]

Table 4. The Portrayal of the Pharisees in Matthew 23:1–39 and Luke

Matthew 23:1–39	Luke
Then said Jesus to the crowds and to his disciples,	And in the hearing of all the people he said to his disciples, (20:45)
²"**The scribes and the Pharisees** sit on Moses's seat; ³so practice and observe whatever they tell you, but not what they do; for they preach, but do not practice.	
⁴They bind heavy burdens, hard to bear, and lay them on men's shoulders; but they themselves will not move them with their finger. ⁵They do all their deeds to be seen by men; for they make their phylacteries broad and their fringes long, ⁶and they love the place of honor at feasts and the best seats in the synagogues, ⁷and salutations in the market places, and being called rabbi by men.	Woe to you **lawyers** also! for you load men with burdens hard to bear, and you yourselves do not touch the burdens with one of your fingers. (11:46) Woe to you **Pharisees!** for you love the best seat in the synagogues and salutations in the market places. (11:43)

---

37. B. H. Throckmorton, ed., *Gospel Parallels: A Synopsis of the First Three Gospels* (Nashville, TN: Nelson, 1967), 148–152.

⁸But you are not to be called rabbi, for you have one teacher, and you are all brethren. ⁹And call no man your father on earth, for you have one Father, who is in heaven. ¹⁰Neither be called masters, for you have one master, the Christ. ¹¹He who is greatest among you shall be your servant; ¹²whoever exalts himself will be humbled, and whoever humbles himself will be exalted.

¹³But woe to you, **scribes and Pharisees,** hypocrites! because you shut the kingdom of heaven against men; for you neither enter yourselves, nor allow those who would enter to go in.

¹⁵Woe to you, **scribes and Pharisees,** hypocrites! for you traverse sea and land to make a single proselyte, and when he becomes a proselyte, you make him twice as much a child of hell as yourselves.

Woe to you **lawyers!** for you have taken away the key of knowledge; you did not enter yourselves, and you hindered those who were entering. (11:52)

¹⁶Woe to you, blind guides, who say, "If any one swears by the temple, it is nothing; but if any one swears by the gold of the temple, he is bound by his oath." ¹⁷You blind fools! For which is greater, the gold or the temple that has made the gold sacred? ¹⁸And you say, "If any one swears by the altar, it is nothing; but if any one swears by the gift that is on the altar, he is bound by his oath." ¹⁹You blind men! For which is greater, the gift or the altar that makes the gift sacred? ²⁰So he who swears by the altar, swears by it and by everything on it; ²¹and he who swears by the temple, swears by it and by him who dwells in it; ²²and he who swears by heaven, swears by the throne of God and by him who sits upon it.

²³Woe to you, **scribes and Pharisees**, hypocrites! for you tithe mint and dill and cumin, and have neglected the weightier matters of the law, justice and mercy and faith; these you ought to have done, without neglecting the others. ²⁴You blind guides, straining out a gnat and swallowing a camel!

But woe to you **Pharisees**! for you tithe mint and rue and every herb, and neglect justice and the love of God; these you ought to have done, without neglecting the others. (Luke 11:42)

²⁵Woe to you, **scribes and Pharisees**, hypocrites! for you cleanse the outside of the cup and of the plate, but inside they are full of extortion and rapacity. ²⁶You blind **Pharisee**! first cleanse the inside of the cup and of the plate, that the outside also may be clean.	Now you **Pharisees** cleanse the outside of the cup and of the dish, but inside you are full of extortion and wickedness. ⁴⁰You fools! Did not he who made the outside make the inside also? ⁴¹But give for alms those things which are within; and behold, everything is clean for you. (11:39–41)
²⁷Woe to you, **scribes and Pharisees**, hypocrites! for you are like whitewashed tombs, which outwardly appear beautiful, but within they are full of dead men's bones and all uncleanness. ²⁸So you also outwardly appear righteous to men, but within you are full of hypocrisy and iniquity.	Woe to you! for you are like graves which are not seen, and men walk over them without knowing it." (11:44)
²⁹Woe to you, **scribes and Pharisees**, hypocrites! for you build the tombs of the prophets and adorn the monuments of the righteous, ³⁰saying, "If we had lived in the days of our fathers, we would not have taken part with them in shedding the blood of the prophets." ³¹Thus you witness against yourselves, that you are sons of those who murdered the prophets. ³²Fill up, then, the measure of your fathers. ³³You serpents, you brood of vipers, how are you to escape being sentenced to hell?	Woe to you! for you build the tombs of the prophets whom your fathers killed. (11:47)

So you are witnesses and consent to the deeds of your fathers; for they killed them, and you build their tombs. (11:48) |

³⁴Therefore I send you prophets and wise men and scribes, some of whom you will kill and crucify, and some you will scourge in your synagogues and persecute from town to town, ³⁵that upon you may come all the righteous blood shed on earth, from the blood of innocent Abel to the blood of Zechariah the son of Barachiah, whom you murdered between the sanctuary and the altar. ³⁶Truly, I say to you, all this will come upon this generation.	Therefore also the Wisdom of God said, "I will send them prophets and apostles, some of whom they will kill and persecute," ⁵⁰that the blood of all the prophets, shed from the foundation of the world, may be required of this generation, ⁵¹from the blood of Abel to the blood of Zechariah, who perished between the altar and the sanctuary. Yes, I tell you, it shall be required of this generation. (11:49–51)
³⁷O Jerusalem, Jerusalem, killing the prophets and stoning those who are sent to you! How often would I have gathered your children together as a hen gathers her brood under her wings, and you would not! ³⁸Behold, your house is forsaken and desolate. ³⁹For I tell you, you will not see me again, until you say, "Blessed is he who comes in the name of the Lord."	O Jerusalem, Jerusalem, killing the prophets and stoning those who are sent to you! How often would I have gathered your children together as a hen gathers her brood under her wings, and you would not! ³⁵Behold, your house is forsaken. And I tell you, you will not see me until you say, "Blessed is he who comes in the name of the Lord!" (13:34–35)

Although Luke has scattered passages condemning the Scribes and the Pharisees in his gospel, Matthew has put it all in one place and added extra materials related to the Pharisaic *halakhic* traditions. Q might well be the origin of Jesus's condemnation of the Pharisees because both gospels share some material doing so. Matthew provides us more and makes sure that the Pharisees are the main target of Jesus's criticisms.

One important thing to be noted is that Luke gives his woes against the scribes and the Pharisees in the house of an anonymous Pharisees outside Judea (11:37–54) whereas Matthew sets Jesus's denunciation in the temple.[38]

---

38. J. S. Kloppenborg, *Q the Earliest Gospel*, 30.

Thus, from Matthew's redaction of Q source, we see that Matthew chooses to present more about the Pharisees and their frauds than Luke does. Matthew's addition of the materials is to make the Pharisees the main target of Jesus's criticisms and to point out their evil intention toward Jesus.

3.3. The Characteristic of the Matthean Pharisees

It is clear from the above examination of Matthew, his redaction on Mark and Q that Matthew has intend to give more space for the Pharisees and gives them a major role as the opponents of Jesus. They are the experts in Mosaic law, practice and interpretation. They regard themselves as the guardians of Jewish oral traditional law that lays out how Mosaic law should be practised. They are determined to maintain their reputation and status among the Jewish people and use their strict observance as a means of doing so. They seem to work well with the authorities holding religious and political offices, and they appear to be quite popular with the crowd over whom they have some influence. When the crowd praises Jesus, they are jealous of his popularity.

As in Mark, the Pharisees test Jesus to bring about his fall. It is noteworthy that the Pharisees almost disappear from the narrative after the woes in chapter 23. For that reason, Simmonds considers that they do not take part in the plot to bring Jesus to trial and execution.[39] Although the narrative does not explicitly mention their involvement, their desire for Jesus's downfall is clear enough.[40] For Matthew writes that the Pharisees' wanted to get rid of Jesus. After the crucifixion, they went with the chief priests and elders to Pilate to ask for guards at the tomb (27:62–64). For the Pharisees remembered Jesus said that he would rise from the dead on the third day. Thus, we may conclude that although Matthew avoids directly involving the Pharisees in Jesus's arrest and crucifixion, by their attitude, behaviour and support for Jesus's downfall, they are, as Marshall states, implicated.[41]

---

39. A. R. Simmonds, "Woe to You . . . Hypocrites! Re-Reading Matthew 23:13–36," *Bibliotheca Sacra* 166 (July–Sept 2009): 349.

40. Runesson, "Rethinking Early Jewish-Christian Relations," 129.

41. Marshall, *Portrayals of the Pharisees*, 122.

Matthew provides the Pharisees' present in every region watching over every deed and teaching of Jesus. Matthew gradually builds up the Pharisees as the main opponents of Jesus in Galilee; they appear twice in the Judean desert, as well as in the final destination in Jerusalem. In Capernaum they are the only opponents. Afterwards, they are joined by the Scribes, the Herodians, the elders and the chief priests. Jesus's disputes with the Pharisees take various forms. One is in the form of questions to Jesus and his responses, which include scriptural quotations and his questions to them. After a series of tests by the Pharisees, the plot has reached a point where they no longer dare to dialogue with Jesus. His indictments of the Pharisees follow in Matthew 23.[42] It is then quite clear that in Matthew the Pharisees have a double role: first, as Jesus's main opponent in the debate on the practice of the Mosaic law; second, as protagonists in the plot that leads up to the Passion narrative.[43]

Furthermore, Matthew places the Pharisees' rejection of Jesus within a broader history of opposition to those sent by God. The Pharisees' rejection of Jesus and his disciples has become one of Matthew's Pharisaic themes. They bear responsibility for the rejection of Israel's prophets. Matthew makes it clear in his gospel that the Pharisees rejected John the Baptist, who was sent ahead of Jesus, and have continued by rejecting Jesus and whomever Jesus will send in the future. They criticize the nature of Jesus's ministry, misattribute his power to Beelzebul and refuse to recognize the power of the Spirit of God that has been placed before them. For that reason, Matthew's Jesus utters the parable of the wicked tenants, which indicts the Pharisees for the rejection of God's emissaries.[44]

Moreover, Matthew characterizes the Pharisees under the main theme of impurity. Under the headings "brood of vipers," "hypocrites," and "blind guides/fools," Matthew stresses that the Pharisees are ritually unclean as brood of vipers (Lev 11:42).[45] This polemical language appears at the very

---

42. D. L. Turner, "Jesus' Denunciation of the Jewish Leaders in Matthew 23, and Witness to Religious Jews Today," in *To the Jew First*, eds. Darrell L. Bock and Mitch Glaser (Grand Rapids, MI: Kregel, 2008), 68.

43. A third major role of the Pharisees as causing the fall of the temple will be discussed in section 5:3 of chapter 5.

44. Marshall, *Portrayals of the Pharisees*, 122–123.

45. Runesson, "Purity, Holiness, and the Kingdom," 161.

beginning with John the Baptist, continues throughout the gospel, and reaches a peak in the denouncement in Matthew 23. Matthew gives us a hint that the Pharisees' impurity would defile the land and the people in the near future. We can summarize Matthew's stress on this progression graphically as follows:

Table 5. The Depiction of the Pharisees in Matthew

No.	Text	Title
1.	3:7	γεννήματα ἐχιδνῶν (Brood of vipers)
2.	6:5	οἱ ὑποκριταί (the Hypocrites)
3.	12:34	γεννήματα ἐχιδνῶν (Brood of vipers)
4.	15:7	ὑποκριταί (Hypocrites)
5.	15:14	τυφλοί εἰσιν ὁδηγοί (Blind guides)
6.	22:18	ὑποκριται (Hypocrites)
7.	23:13	ὑποκριται (Hypocrites)
8.	23:15	ὑποκριται (Hypocrites)
9.	23:16	ὁδηγοὶ τυφλοί (Blind guides)
10.	23:17	μωροὶ καὶ τυφλοί (Blind fools)
11.	23:19	τυφλοί (Blind men)
12.	23:23	ὑποκριται (Hypocrites)
13.	23:24	ὁδηγοὶ τυφλοί (Blind guides)
14.	23:25	ὑποκριτα (Hypocrites)
15.	23:26	Φαρισαῖε τυφλέ (Blind Pharisees)
16.	23:27	ὑποκριται (Hypocrites)
17.	23:29	ὑποκριται (Hypocrites)
18.	23:33	γεννήματα ἐχιδνῶν (Brood of vipers)

Matthew highlights their hypocritical way of life and their misconducts in the religious sphere. Up to Matthew 23, Matthew points out that the Pharisees are blind guides, hypocrites and offspring of a brood of vipers. John's attack is reinforced by Jesus throughout the narration.[46] "Matthew

---

46. J. C. Anderson, *Matthew's Narrative Web* (Sheffield: JSOT Press, 1994), 103; Marshall, *Portrayals of the Pharisees*, 75.

views them as evil and hypocritical blind guides who have misled the crowds."[47]

Chapter Findings

We have seen that Matthew has more material on the Pharisees and places more emphasis on the negative. Though Matthew closely follows Mark's account, he spends more time on the Pharisees. Matthew makes it clear in his narrative that Mark's scribes or teachers/experts in the law are the Pharisees. He makes them play a bigger role in Jerusalem and the temple itself, the very centre of Judaic cult. The Pharisees' frauds are exposed plainly in the temple. Moreover, he gives them a bigger role in conspiring with others to bring about Jesus's downfall, thus strengthening the case against them. Likewise, Matthew's redaction of Q helps us to see that Matthew's Pharisees are depraved. Consequently, Jesus's denunciation of them is given greater emphasis. They are a "brood of vipers," "hypocrites," and "blind." The Pharisees are in a state of ritual impurity.

Second, Matthew presents more conflicts between Jesus and the Pharisees. The conflicts are about Sabbath observance, table fellowship, observing the tradition of the fathers regarding hand washing, the issue of divorce, paying taxes, and the interpretation of Mosaic law. Matthew appears to present the Pharisees as the most legitimate dialogue partners of Jesus on Mosaic law at the time. Since the *halakhic* debates on Sabbath observance, ritual purity, the issue of divorce, and paying taxes or tithing were the focus of the Pharisees' attention until the fall of the temple, therefore, Matthew's accounts of the conflict stories between Jesus and the Pharisees are of historical value. The next chapter will make it clearer that the Pharisees and their materials in Matthew 23 are of a traditional nature.

---

47. A. J. Saldarini, "Reading Matthew without Anti-Semitism," in *The Gospel of Matthew in Current Study*, ed. David E. Aune (Cambridge: Eerdmans, 2001), 168.

CHAPTER 4

The Literary Analyses of Matthew 23

Introduction

The previous chapter already gives us initial background to understand the type of the Pharisees we see in Matthew. This chapter explores literary analyses of Matthew 23. However, the chapter does not intend to do exhaustive exegetical commentary on each sentence. Rather, the literary analysis in this chapter focuses mainly on whether the description and criticism of the Pharisees' practices and customs in the text fit the historical practice and customs of the Pharisees at Jesus's time or not. The chapter claims that the Pharisaic-materials we see in Matthew 23 are traditional and they are not invented by Matthew after 70 CE.

To better understand Jesus's confrontations with the Pharisees and their practices I shall use primarily rabbinic sources, more specifically the Mishnah and Tosefta, but also Tannaic authority in Talmudic sources when necessary. Although the rabbinic literature – the Mishnah, Tosefta, and Talmud – are written mostly by the disciples of Hillel before 200 and 600 CE respectively, however, the discussion and information there are still useful, and it is still possible to date the *halakhic* debates among the Pharisees back to Jesus's time for the following reasons: First, they claim to contain the discussions and conflicts between the House of Hillel and the House of Shammai regarding *halahkic* matters in the first century, if not earlier. Therefore the Mishnah and Tosefta are considered to have historical value. One can also argue that the Mishnah, Tosefta, and Talmud depict Hillel as a hero, and Shammai often plays the role of "the bad guy." Yet the nature of rabbinic literature reflects the discussion and conflicts of both houses. The Hillelites' position can be seen and appreciated only when viewed alongside the Shammai's position.[1]

Second, the Hillelites at Yavneh are not supporters of Matthew – they do not have anything to do with Matthew nor do they bother about what the Christians say. Thus, when what is stated in the Mishnah, Tosefta, and the Talmud about the practice of the Pharisees parallels what is stated in Matthew, it may very well reflect the practice of the Pharisees before 70 CE.

Third, the information and practices of the Pharisees we find in the rabbinic literature are the traditions they received from their predecessors. It is not that the rabbis at Yavneh sit there and invent something which was not practiced before the fall of the temple, rather it was a tradition they practiced throughout the generations alongside the written Torah. As long as the temple is there, the practices of oral traditions are there, but once the temple is gone, they need to write down oral traditions. It is the disappearance of the temple that obliges the rabbis to collect oral tradition handed down to them. For this reason, the rabbinic literature can be used to understand more fully the Pharisees' practices, traditions and Jesus's charges of hypocrisy against them.

4.1. The Setting, Literary Context and Structure of Matthew 23

The narrative analysis of the Pharisees in Matthew in the previous chapter already shows that the setting of the text is in the temple, and it reaches a decisive moment, a turning point in the narration of Jesus's mission in Jerusalem. Matthew's temple-centred motif is reinforced from Matthew 21 with Jesus's entry into Jerusalem. Since Matthew portrays the temple as holy place, Jesus purifies the uncleanness of the temple by driving out all who were doing business in the temple and overturning the tables of the money-changers and the seats of those who sold pigeons. According to Matthew's Jesus, the temple is defiled and it is like a den of robbers because of their corruption (21:12–13). This section reaches a climax with Jesus's denunciation of the Pharisees in chapter 23. After his denunciation, he predicts the fall of the temple. Afterwards on the Mount of Olives, his disciples ask him about

---

1. M. Weinfeld, "Hillel and the Misunderstanding of Judaism," 69.

this; he reaffirms this prophesy and talks of the end of the age and signs of his coming (24:1–2). Within this literary setting, Matthew presents Jesus as the Messiah who is rejected by the Pharisees, scribes and other temple authorities.[2] There is a dramatic contrast between the reception Jesus gets on arrival and the reception he gets once he has entered the temple. Outside the temple, a tumultuous crowd proclaims Jesus as the son of David; inside the temple, Jesus cleanses the temple and clashes fiercely with the Pharisees and other Jewish leaders. He has pointed out their inadequacy as religious leaders in three great parables (the parable of the two sons, the parable of the wicked tenants, and the parable of the wedding banquet).[3] Now at this point Jesus debates with the Pharisees and lashes out at the Pharisees, revealing at length their failure before God.

The text is also a long and unique discourse, placed in a "narrative-critical" literary context and it has the function to move the narrative to the next level.[4] Within the gospel narrative, the text is quite distinctive and cannot be compared with anything else in Matthew since it has no ending formula.[5] It is formed as a series of lengthy and sharp denunciations. It is negative and condemnatory and appears to target a specific group.[6]

Although the discourse of Matthew 23 is not included in the five discourses formula, it plays a decisive role in the narrative.[7] According to Luz

---

2. D. L. Turner, *Israel's Last Prophet: Jesus and the Jewish Leaders in Matthew 23* (Minneapolis: Fortress, 2015), 311–330; D. R. Bauer, *The Structure of Matthew's Gospel* (Sheffield: Almond Press, 1988), 137–138.

3. G. R. Osborne, *Exegetical Commentary on the New Testament* (Grand Rapids, MI: Zondervan, 2009), 832; Luz, *The Theology of the Gospel of Matthew* (Cambridge: Cambridge University Press, 1995), 117.

4. "In narrative terms this discourse has the function of bringing to an end Jesus' conflict with his opponents, of pronouncing judgment on them, and of preparing for the final departure from the temple (21.1–2)." See Ulrich Luz, *Matthew 1–7* (Minneapolis: Fortress, 2007), 12.

5. D. A. Hagner, *WBC: Matthew 14–28*, 33b (Dallas, TX: Word Books, 1995), 653.

6. Hagner, *WBC: Matthew 14–28*, 653.

7. Specified discourses or the five-discourse formula begin with, "when he had finished speaking" and are seen in 7:28; 11:1; 13:53; 19:1; 26:1. It gives us a clue to understand that Matthew structured his gospel within the five-discourse formula. Base on that, Bacon understands the five discourses of Matthew against the Five Books of Moses. See B. W. Bacon, "'The Five Books' of Matthew against the Jews," *Expositor* 15 (1918): 56–66; B. W. Bacon, "Jesus and the Law: A Study of the First Five 'Books' of Matthew (Mt. 3–7)" *JBL* 47 (1928): 203–231.

and Staton, this chapter is seen as a single unit or part of a larger unit with chapters 24–25. They argue that Matthew joins the three chapters to create a bigger narrative frame.[8] Though I do not see Matthew 23 to 25 as a single unit, mainly because of the change of audience in chapter 24, the temple-centred motif is noticeably emphasized from 21:12 to 24:1–2 – Jesus enters the temple, cleanses the temple, teaches in the temple, condemns the Pharisees in the temple, and foretells the doom of the temple. Thus, Matthew 23 should be read within the frame of this temple-centred motif.

Matthew 23 also stands as a bridge between the concluding narratives of chapters 19–22 and the new emphasis in chapter 24–25.[9] It serves as a transition between the various conflicts Jesus had with the Pharisees and the story of Christ's passion and resurrection. The structure of Matthew 23 falls into three sections.[10]

The first section, verses 1–12, is a discourse where Jesus recognizes the authority and rightfulness of the Pharisees as religious leaders but makes known their failure before God. The second segment, verses 13–36, is the "Seven Woes" denunciation of the Pharisees, and the third is the future destruction of Jerusalem's temple and Jesus's second coming (vv. 37–39).

4.2 General Exegesis of Matthew 23

The beginning of the first verse provides a clue that this long discourse was intended for the crowd and the disciples. It is understandable why they were the audience of this discourse, for from verse 2 onwards Jesus is going to criticize the Pharisees for the role they play in the religious community. Though the Pharisees are not directly mentioned in verse 1, the adverb

---

8. Luz, *Theology of the Gospel of Matthew*, 121; G. Stanton, *A Gospel for a New People* (Edinburgh: T&T Clark, 1992), 165.

9. Osborne, *Exegetical Commentary on the New Testament*, 832.

10. The three-part structure of Matt 23 is proposed by many Matthean scholars. For instance, Luz, *Theology of the Gospel of Matthew*, 121; Ulrich Luz, *Matthew 21–28: A Commentary* (Minneapolis: Fortress, 2005), 92; D. Senior, *The Gospel of Matthew* (Nashville: Abingdon, 1997), 158; M. Pickup, "Matthew and Mark's Pharisees," 102; and Osborne, *Exegetical Commentary on the New Testament*, 832. Although Senior and Osborne have three parts of structure, they have taken the second part from verses 13 up to 36. As for me, I follow more specific structure of Luz and Pickup.

"Τότε" suggests a connection with the previous chapter where they are definitely present.[11]

Matthew 23:2–3a

The Pharisees' position is declared in verses 2–3a, "They sit on Moses' seat." The authority of the Pharisees is recognized and it is related to the actual meaning of τῆς Μωϋσέως καθέδρας. Roth states that the Pharisees sat on the seat of Moses as a means to indicate the Pharisees' intellectual arrogance.[12] However, scholars understand "the seat of Moses" either literally or metaphorically. Newport,[13] Hagner,[14] Albright and Mann,[15] and Rabbinowitz[16] consider that Moses's seat has to be understood literally. "The seat of Moses" was a real chair used by the authorized interpreter of the Torah in the synagogue. Rahmni's understanding is slightly different from theirs. He supposes that "the seat of Moses" was a chair on which the Torah scroll was placed. No one sat in this chair during the synagogue service.[17] In contrast, Keener,[18]

---

11. Hagner, *WBC*, 658.

12. C. Roth, "The 'Chair of Moses' and Its Survivals," *Palestine Exploration Quarterly* 81 (1949): 110.

13. Newport gives this view by using Hill's work of E. L. Sukenik, who gives several examples of "chairs of Moses" found by archaeologists. The first was seat was that of Hammath-by-Tiberius and it was made of a single block of white limestone and measures 94cm by 60 cm. The seat faced the congregation and back towards Jerusalem. Another one was found in Chorazim. This seat too was made of a single block of stone and it is 56cm high and 76 cm wide. All these discoveries proved the dating back to pre-70 CE. See further in Newport, *The Source and Sitz im Leben, 23*, 81–85; G .C. Newport, "A Note on the 'Seat of Moses,'" *AUSS* (1990) 53–58.

14. Hagner states that the term has to do more with an actual chair in the synagogue in which an authorized person expounded the Torah to the congregation. See Hagner, *Matthew 14–28*, 659.

15. "'Moses' seat which is the literal translation and is the name given to the seat in the Synagogue." See W. F. Albright and C. S. Mann, *Matthew: The Anchor Bible*, vol. 26 (London: Doubleday, 1971), 278.

16. N. S. Rabbinowitz, "Matthew 23:2–4: Does Jesus Recognize the Authority of the Pharisees and Does He Endorse Their Halakah?" *JETS* 46, no. 3 (September 2003): 423–447.

17. L. Y. Rahmni, "Stone Synagogue Chairs: Their Identification, Use and Significance," *International Endodontic Journal* 40 (1990): 192–214.

18. C. S. Keener, *A Commentary on the Gospel of Matthew* (Grand Rapids, MI: Eerdmans, 1999), 541.

Powell,[19] Davies and Allison,[20] and Senior[21] think that the term is to be understood metaphorically to indicate the Pharisees' role as the interpreters of Mosaic law.[22]

In fact, archaeologists have discovered a stone chair in a synagogue setting before 70 CE on the Greek island of Delos and which may have been sat on by the preacher.[23] It is unlikely that the Torah Scroll was placed on such stone chair as Rahmni considers. However, whether they were called the seat of Moses is doubtful. Although we are uncertain as to whether Moses's seat refers to the actual seat or authority, indeed Moses's seat and authority are inseparable, because only a person who has authority can use Moses's seat and preach the Mosaic law. The seat of Moses may refer to public function to convey the Mosaic law by the ones devoted to study the law of Moses,[24] or by the ones who control it. Powell does not consider that the term refers to the Pharisees' role as authoritative teachers, rather it was Jesus's simple acknowledgement of the Pharisees' control of the Torah scroll in the synagogues and their powerful social and religious position in an illiterate world.[25] Powell's observation fits the Greek word Matthew's Jesus uses in 23:3. It solves the problem of the apparent contradiction between Jesus's warning against the Pharisees as blind leaders (Matt 15:14)[26] and his telling them to do everything the Pharisees say in Matthew 23:3. How can the same Jesus speak such a contradictory words? In the first place, Jesus seems to use the term metaphorically to indicate the Pharisees' authority in interpreting Mosaic law. However, it seems that the Greek word λέγω does not refer to

---

19. M. Powell, "Do and Keep What Moses Says (Matthew 23:2–7)," *JBL* 114 (1995): 419–435.

20. Davies and Allison states that "the name Moses connotes authority; and the image of Moses sitting on Sinai was well known in ancient Judaism." See W. D. Davies and D. C. Allison, *Matthew*, vol. 3.19–28 (Edinburgh: T&T Clark, 1997), 268.

21. Senior assumes that "the seat of Moses referred to the authority of the teacher whose interpretation of the tradition provided a link to Moses, the lawgiver and teacher par excellence." See Senior, *Matthew*, 257.

22. Keener, *Commentary on the Gospel of Matthew*, 541.

23. I thank Anders Runesson for the information of this knowledge.

24. Marshall, *Portrayal of the Pharisees*, 85.

25. Powell, "Do and Keep What Moses Says," 419–435.

26. Jesus said that the Pharisees are blind leaders for the blind, and that both these leaders and their followers will fall into the pit.

teaching here,[27] rather to what they say in relation to Torah, that is, you obey and follow them when they read or say a word from the Torah. Thus, the disciples and Jesus's audience should do and keep what Moses says, even when the words coming from the mouths of Pharisees. However, they do not keep the commandments of Moses, even if they read them correctly to everyone. Their sayings and their *halakhic* practices do not match, but they simply control the Torah – the seat of Moses. Therefore, Jesus's disciples and the crowd must not follow the example of the Pharisees, for they do not practice what they preach. Their practice is not that of the law, but the result of their *halakhic* understanding of the Mosaic law. In other words, for Matthew the Pharisees simply do not follow Torah when they create their *halakhic* rules and regulations. However, when they are the readers of Torah, one must listen, since it is Mosaic law that is being read.[28] Thus, the notion of "the seat of Moses" is best understood as Jesus's acknowledgement on the Pharisees' position as the ones who control access to the Torah in an illiterate community.[29]

The reason for such controlling of the seat of Moses or Mosaic law may be because of their commitment to studying Mosaic law. Many references in the NT, Josephus, and also in rabbinic literature (m.*Abot* 1:1), show this. Josephus informs us about the Pharisees' domination of religious and social norms in the Jewish community before 70 CE. He mentions Samaias and Pollion, the Pharisees, as influential Pharisaic leaders in Herod the Great's early days.[30] So too in his account of his life he writes,

> At about the edge of sixteen (53 CE), I determined to gain personal experience of the several sects into which our nation is divided. These, as I have frequently mentioned, are three in number—the first that of the Pharisees, the second that of the Sadducees, and the third that of the Essenes. I thought that, after a thorough investigation, I should be in a position to select the best. So I submitted myself to hard training and laborious

---

27. In Matt 15:9, διδάσκω is used about Pharisaic teaching and their teaching is condemned.
28. Powell, "Do and Keep What Moses Says," 435
29. Powell, 419–35.
30. Josephus, *Ants*. 14.171–174.

exercises and passed through these the three courses . . . Being now in my nineteenth year (56–57 CE) I began to govern my life by the rules of the Pharisees, a sect having points of resemblance to that which the Greeks called the Stoic school.[31]

He describes how he was also inspired by Pharisees' way of life and behaved accordingly when he began his public life. He also acknowledged that the Pharisees were "considered the most accurate interpreters of the laws, and hold the position of the leading sect, attribute[ing] everything to fate and to God."[32] Josephus consistently presents the Pharisees as the dominant school with the mass following their lead in all religious aspects of life.[33] He tells that even Sadducees needed to submit to the Pharisees in order to assume their power.[34]

Although the Pharisees play such a role in social and religious sphere, Jesus's word, "πάντα οὖν ὅσα ἐὰν εἴπωσιν ὑμῖν" as Powell correctly points out, is merely an acknowledgement of the reality of the situation in which the Pharisees control the Torah and their authority to access to the preaching of Mosaic law.[35]

Matthew 23:3b–12

Jesus charges the Pharisees with hypocrisy after he has acknowledged the Pharisees' role as the ones who control Mosaic law. The issue now is the Pharisees' failure to practice what they preach, and their pretence of piety.[36] Although the Pharisees are commended for preaching Mosaic law, they are now denounced for not doing their preaching – τὰ ἔργα αὐτῶν μὴ ποιεῖτε.[37] Both Second Temple Jewish literature (e.g *Enoch*) and later rabbinic literature (e.g. Lev; Rab. 35:7),[38] emphasize the need to match word

---

31. Josephus, *The Life against Apion: Loeb Classical Library*, trans. H. S. T. J. Thackeray (London: William Heinemann, 1926), 10–12.
32. Josephus, *War* 2.162–163; Josephus, *Life*, 38.
33. Josephus, *Ant.* 18.15.
34. Josephus, *Ant.* 18.17; S. Mason, *Josephus and The New Testament* (Peabody, MA: Hendrickson, 1992), 143.
35. Powell, "Do and Keep What Moses Says," 435.
36. Mason, *Josephus and The New Testament*, 145.
37. Powell, "Do and Keep What Moses Says," 423.
38. D. J. Harrington, *The Gospel of Matthew: Sacra Pagina Series*, vol. 1 (Minnesota: Liturgical Press, 1991), 320.

and deed, so there is no doubt that this can also be applied in Jesus's time. Even b. *Yebamot* 14a provides the deeds of the Shammaic Pharisees for not matching their teachings.

> "Do you think that the House of Shammai actually acted in accord with their position? The House of Shammai never really acted in accord with their position." R. Yohanan said, "they most certainly acted in accord with their position." Rab says, "The House of Shammai never really acted in accord with their position." Afterwards, Samuel gave a lengthy [defence of the] Shammai' position (b. *Yebamot*.14a).[39]

First, Jesus charged them with hypocrisy for binding heavy burdens – "δεσμεύουσιν δὲ φορτία βαρέα [καὶ δυσβάστακτα]" – on others but not themselves. This refers to the Pharisaic emphasis on the traditions of the fathers (oral traditions) as a complement to and enhancement of the Torah. However, Gundry states that the heavy burdens do not refer to the Pharisees' traditions and interpretation of the law, but rather to the Pharisees' attempt to win public respect and honour everywhere and to be called "my Great One."[40] This seems dubious, for within verses 4–7 we are told that the Pharisees put heavy burdens on others and loved the best seats. The most plausible explanation seems to be "the practice of the Pharisees in placing upon the people numerous *halakhic* formulations."[41] In other words, "lay the burden" to mean "lay the burden of the commandments on other people's shoulders."[42] Through their oral traditions they tried to fill in the details that Moses's written law had left out. For instance, the law said to keep the Sabbath and not to work on God's holy day. Yet, what was work and what was not? How far could a person walk on the Sabbath without it being work? Even Josephus mentions that the Pharisees observed "regulations handed down by former generations and not recorded in the laws of Moses."[43] Josephus further specifies that the Pharisees' focus on such

---

39. Neusner, *Babylonian Talmud*, 2009.
40. R. Gundry, *Matthew*, 2nd ed. (Grand Rapids, MI: Eerdmans, 1994), 455–456.
41. Newport, *Source and Sitz im Leben*, 127.
42. Flusser, *Jewish Sources in Early Christianity*, 29.
43. Josephus, *Ant.* 13.297–298.

traditions and practices flourished more popularly in Palestine from the time of Salome Alexandra. For during her reign, she restored the Pharisees' traditions and practices which her father-in-law, Hyrcanus, had once abolished. Although Josephus did not mention the practice and tradition of the Pharisaic houses in detail, the rabbinic literatures had recorded rules and regulations of the Pharisaic houses prior to 70 CE. Some laws attributed to the Hillelite Pharisees were purity rules, temple rites, and agricultural taboos.[44] Similarly, the Shammai's rulings also related to Sabbath observance, phylacteries, heave-offering,[45] second tithe, purity, ploughing in the seventh year, uncleanness from a bone in a tent, the obligation for children to observe on particular occasions.[46]

The two houses common traditions before 70 CE included, (1) an attitude of ritual purity in all aspects of daily life which involved food; (2) absolute obedience in regard to biblical laws of tithing and the offering and raising of agricultural crops; (3) unusual emphasis on the observance of the Sabbath and religious festivals; and (4) introducing the laws of cultic purity usually observed by the priests into the lives of ordinary Jews in order to renew Jewish piety and to provide a stronger sense of Jewish identity in the face of incursions.[47] Thus, it is possible that their traditions and practices could have been well established during Jesus's time, and that it was even the case that the Houses of Shammai and Hillel disputed how far one should go to fulfil such traditions. As often, the House of Shammites was portrayed as extremely strict over the observance of the traditions of the law, but the House of Hillel adapted to the needs of the situation. Jesus may mean that the Pharisees' excessive emphasis on tradition and practice of the law has laid heavy burdens on others.

The second charge of hypocrisy against the Pharisees was their love of honour, position and showing off (vv. 5–6) – "they make their phylacteries broad and their fringes long; love the place of honour at feasts and the best

---

44. J. Neusner, "Pharisaic Law in New Testament Times," *Union Seminary Quarterly Review* 24, no. 4 (Summer, 1971): 333.

45. A kind of offering which associated with great offering and which has to be consumed by Cohen the priest.

46. Neusner, "Pharisaic Law in New Testament Times," 334.

47. Neusner, 331; Culbertson, "Changing Christian Images of the Pharisees," *ATR* 64, no. 4 (1982): 542; Harrington, *Gospel of Matthew*, 323; Senior, *Matthew*, 258.

seats in the synagogues; salutations in the market places, and being called rabbi by men." Jesus accuses them not because they follow the law but because they are boastful and full of pride in how they do so. They are charged with vanity. What they do is interpret Moses in ways that are burdensome for others (23:4) and in ways that bring glory to themselves (23:5–7).[48]

In fact, wearing the phylactery (Exod 13:9, 16; Deut 6:4–9) and tassels on the corner of the garment (Num 15:38–39; Deut 22:12) are direct commandments from God for all Jewish men. Consequently, in order to be seen as God's chosen people, they keep the fringes or tassels on the corner of each garment as a unique nation before God, and they wear the phylactery, a small leather box which contains the text of Deuteronomy 6:4–9 and other passages. They are bound by leather straps to the forehead during prayer as a reminder of God's commandment.[49] Numerous facts indicate that the phylacteries can be equated with *tefillin*.[50] For *tefillin* are phylacteries, small leather cases holding biblical passages that are worn on the head and arm of Jews during prayers. Josephus also mentioned the practice of wearing phylacteries on arms and he called them *tefillin*.[51] Archaeologists have discovered Essene leather phylacteries in caves 1, 4, 5 and 8 at Qumran.[52] This shows that Jesus's speaking of the Pharisees' enlarging their phylacteries may refer to *tefillin* of the forehead, the wearing of which may have been commonly practised at his time. The Greek word, "φυλακτήρια – *pylakteria*," means a safeguard and is not to be misunderstood φυλακτήρια as amulet or charm.

---

48. Powell, "Do and Keep What Moses Says," 432.

49. Senior, *Matthew*, 258.

50. J. Magness, *Stone and Dung, Oil and Spit: Jewish Daily Life in the Time of Jesus* (Grand Rapids, MI: Eerdmans, 2011), 112; J. Bowman, however, did not consider the practice of equating phylacteries with *tefillin*. He said that the phylacteries in Matt 23:5 were "amulets." He pointed out that there was no evidence in early Jewish literature of *tefillin* being called phylacteries. Nevertheless, Newport responded to Bowman by retorting that Bowman's examples of "amulet" being identified with phylactery were in fact of a late date. Although there was no early Jewish source that called the phylacteries *telfillin*, the Peshitta version of the New Testament (c.450 CE) translates τὰ φυλακτήρια αὐτῶν in Matthew *tephlaihom*. See Newport, *Source and Sitz im Leban*, 88.

51. Josephus, *Ant.* 4.213.

52. Harrington, *Gospel of Matthew*, 321; Newport, *Source and Sitz im Leban*, 86.

For φυλακτήρια is also something which worn between the two eyes and it serves "as a *bona fide* connection to God."[53]

Similarly, the literal practice of wearing tassels was based upon the commandment of Numbers 15:37–41, making it compulsory for the Jews to place tassels on the four corners of their robe in order to remember God's commandments (Num 15:38–39; Deut 22:12).[54] Thus, it is quite clear that the Pharisees' practice of wearing tassels that Jesus mentions originated in biblical times. Although we do not know for sure whether the Jews wore tassels or not in OT times, at least we know they did in NT times. That Jesus wore tassels is made clear in Matthew 9:20, and the woman who suffered from haemorrhaging touched the fringe or tassel of Jesus – τοῦ κρασπέδου τοῦ ἱματίου αὐτοῦ. The Qumran community appeared to wear the tassels attached to their garments and carefully followed the clothing instruction of God. As contemporary religious leaders known for their piety, there can be no doubt that the Pharisees wore tassels. However, Jesus claims that true piety has nothing to do with showing off or seeking marks of honour. Jesus also accuses the Pharisees of being too fond of their own honour, getting the best seats, and being called rabbi. The New Testament, Josephus, and rabbinic literature inform us that these privileges were reserved for the leaders of the religious community. Honourable places and titles were reserved for the powerful and the rich. This was true both for secular (places at the dinner table, the market place) and religious life (Luke 14:7–11).[55] While Jesus is dining at the house of a prominent Pharisee, he advises his listeners not to take the most honourable places (18:1–5; 19:27; 20:9–16, 20–28).[56] The general tenor of them is not to seek honour in this world, and that the humble on earth will be rewarded with honour in heaven. There is no doubt that Jesus was sick of the Pharisees' desire to be better than others.[57] However, according to rabbinic source, not all the Pharisees desired honour

---

53. Rabbi Shraga Simmons, http://www.aish.com/jl/m/pb/48969816.html (accessed 5 October 2015).

54. F. D. Bruner, *The Church Book Matthew 13–28*, vol. 2 (Grand Rapids, MI: Eerdmans, 1990), 435.

55. R. T. France, *NICNT: The Gospel of Matthew* (Grand Rapids, MI: Eerdmans, 2007), 862.

56. Bruner, *Church Book Matthew*, 435.

57. Bruner, 435.

and position. Hillel was portrayed as a meek man who humbled himself even before an arrogant Shammai, the opponent. b.*Shabbat* 17a says,

> They (the Shammaites) plunged a sword into the schoolhouse saying, "Let anyone come in who wants, but no one is going to get out of here," and on that day, Hillel sat humble before Shammai just like another disciple."

Shammai, on the other hand, was depicted as arrogant, basking in his own power and influence.

Jesus also condemns the love of being called "rabbi." The title "rabbi" means "my great one or master," and was used to address the teacher of Mosaic law.[58] In Matthew, both *rabbi* and *rabboni* are translated into Greek with teacher (*didaskale*). Thus, it indicates that *rabbi* and *teacher* are synonyms.[59] For instance, Gamaliel the Elder, who died before 70 CE, was called "rabban," the teacher. Although the term "rabbi" was identical with *teacher* in Jesus's time, it was not used as an official title as it was in the later period.[60] The gospel evidence suggests that the term was used as an unofficial title for the teachers of Mosaic law and honorific teachers in Jesus's days.[61] Flusser also affirms that the term rabbi was popular and used as a common title for scholars and teachers of the law. Since the term was not restricted and confined only to certain expert teachers in the academic sense, every teacher of the law can expect to be called *rabbi*.[62] From what we know of the two Pharisaic houses, the Shammaites were composed of students from wealthy noble families and associated only with people of status. Consequently, Shammai's followers were described as the ones who considered themselves superior to the followers of Hillel (b.*Erubin* 13b).[63] For Jesus, such pretentious piety is

---

58. France, *NICNT*, 862–863.
59. France, 927.
60. Hagner, *WBC*, 660.
61. Newport, *Source and Sitz im Leban*, 90–95.
62. Flusser, *Jesus*, 32.
63. Said Rabbi, "The only reason I am sharper than my colleagues is that I saw R. Meir from the back, and if I had seen him from the front, I would have been still sharper, as it is written: 'But your eyes shall see your teacher' (Isa 30:20)." Said R. Abbahu and R. Yohannan, "R. Meir had one disciple, named Sumekhos, who could give forty-eight reasons to confirm the uncleanness of something that was unclean, and who could give forty-eight reasons to confirm the cleanness of what was clean." b.*Erubin* 13b. R. Meir was considered to be the disciple of Shammai.

unacceptable: loving the best seats and seeking one's own honour is like abusing and mistreating God's honour and glory. For that reason, Jesus taught his disciples not to be like the Pharisaic-status-seekers, but recommended humility. Matthew here contrasts the humbleness of Jesus, who is the only instructor and Messiah, with the pride of the Pharisees, who desire to be called "rabbi" in God's appointed ministry.

Matthew 23:13–36

Jesus makes his seven woes pronouncements between verses 13 to 36 before he prophesies that the temple will be destroyed as a result (37–39). He accuses them of various practices – such as shutting the door to heaven, putting heavy burdens on proselytes, taking oaths, tithing, neglecting justice, mercy and faith, gnat-straining, and insisting on ritual purity while ignoring inward purity, justice, mercy and faithfulness.

The first woe (v. 13) – Once more Jesus acknowledges the Pharisees' influential role in religion. The first woe charges them with abusing this role to prevent others from entering the kingdom of heaven. Garland states that "these masters of the Torah, who sat on Moses' seat, obstructed God's will and side-tracked his law with their contravening traditions, precedents and pettifogging rules"; and "their teaching fogged the simple and central truths of the law with casuistry."[64] Nevertheless, Newport considers that shutting the door to heaven has nothing to do with the Pharisees' interpretation of the law. Rather, it has to do with their failure to recognize who Jesus was. Their failure to recognize Jesus as the key to heaven has caused others to turn away from Jesus.[65] Although Garland and Newport differ on the matter, they both acknowledge the authoritative role of the Pharisees in the Jewish social-religious domain. What the Pharisees said and taught affected the spiritual life of the Jews who followed the Pharisees' teaching where Mosaic law was concerned. Nolland's view is that the words, "for you neither enter yourselves, nor allow those who would enter to go in" is much more a reflection of the opposition of Jewish leaders at the time of the Matthean

---

64. Garland, *Intention of Matthew 23*, 127.
65. Newport, *Sources and Sitz im Leban*, 134.

community (that is after 70 CE).⁶⁶ However, the latter word, "nor allow those who would enter to go in," may imply the Pharisees' public influence and their critical stance against Jesus's mission during his ministry. Newport asserts that this verse is to be understood in the Jewish context, for the Jews considered themselves the custodians of the kingdom. If Newport is right, although the Pharisees were not the key to heaven, they were considered the guardians of the Mosaic law, and their teachings could still prevent or permit people to follow Jesus.⁶⁷ In that sense, their attitudes and behaviours towards the populace truly affect the commoner's spiritual life.

The second woe (v. 15) – Since the Pharisees misuse of their role, their few proselytes became sons of hell rather than sons of the kingdom. According to Nolland, "a proselyte is the resident alien in Israel. Since the resident alien was expected to live in accord with the Mosaic law, the term came to mean 'convert to Judaism,' which for males would include having themselves circumcised."⁶⁸ Although Justin's *Dialogue with Trypho* 121–122 provides some reference to a Jewish mission to the gentiles after 70 CE,⁶⁹ M. Goodman refutes the idea that there was any such mission.⁷⁰ He claims that it would be hard for any gentiles to consider abandoning ancestral worship, because "he or she in effect left gentile society. For it would be an act of extraordinary folly" in a historical situation where even the Jews found themselves lost because of the destruction of the Holy temple.⁷¹ He further argues that there was no active Jewish proselytizing attitudes toward gentiles in first-century Judaism. Such a notion developed within Judaism later in antiquity alongside with the growth of Christianity.⁷²

Goodman is right to some extent. As he says, the situation of the Pharisees post-70 CE did not support a proselyte mission. For they were in a situation

---

66. J. Nolland, *NIGTC: The Gospel of Matthew* (Grand Rapids, MI: Eerdmans, 2005), 933.

67. Newport, *Sources and Sitz im Leban*, 134; προσήλυτος is one that has arrived at a place, stranger or sojourner (Exod 12:49). Or one who has come to Judaism, convert, proselyte. See further in LSJ the online Liddell-Scott-Jones Greek Lexicon, http://stephanus.tlg.uci.edu/lsj/#eid=91932&context=search (accessed 29 March 2016)

68. Nolland, *NIGTC: The Gospel of Matthew*, 933.

69. Harrington, *Gospel of Matthew*, 325.

70. See further discussion in Goodman, *Mission and Conversion*.

71. Goodman, 54.

72. Goodman, 88–89.

where they had to settle down first at Yavneh. Nevertheless, a proselyte mission was not new in the first-century period. For within the ancient context, there are sources that talk about how the Jews encouraged their neighbours to join their communities. Thus, it would be wrong to understand the Jewish proselyting mission in modern methods of conversion in a contemporary Christian context.[73] More specifically, a proselyte mission did not begin after 70 CE, but much earlier in OT times. For instance, Exodus 12:48 states that any "stranger" who desired to keep the Passover should be circumcised. References to foreigners joining the Israelites can also found in Isaiah 14:1; 56:3, 6 and Ruth 2:11–12. Furthermore, Rabbinic literature,[74] the NT, and Josephus[75] also inform us about proselytes who feared God and followed the Judaic way of life.[76] The Pharisees argued that "God-fearing" gentiles had to become full converts to Judaism and observe the Pharisaic tradition.[77] The point here is that Jesus did not dispute the Pharisees' role and authority, but he does criticize their attitudes towards the gentiles who wished to be God's children, claiming that they placed unnecessary extra burdens on them that were hard to bear.[78] These unnecessary burdens might also refer to extra ritual obligations imposed on Jews. Much of the purity ritual was practiced in the temple rather than at home, whereas the Pharisees urged that it should be practiced there too.

The third woe (vv. 16–22) attacks the Pharisees' hair-splitting distinctions on oaths and vows. In ancient society, people took oaths and vows. They debated what were valid and what were invalid. The OT shows that people used oaths and vows judicially and socially to prove their sincerity. However, using God's name in oaths is allowed only when one has to fulfil his justice

---

73. A. Runesson, "Was There a Christian Mission before the Fourth Century? Problematizing Common Ideas about Early Christianity and the Beginnings of Modern Mission," in *The Making of Christianity*, eds. M. Zetterholm and S. Byrskog (Winona Lake, IN: Eisenbrauns, 2012), 229.

74. m.Pe'ah 4.6; m.*Demai* 6.10; m.*Hallah* 3.6 see Danby, *Mishnah*.

75. Josephus, *Apion* 2.282; *Ant.* 14.9

76. Newport, *Sources and Sitz im Leban*, 99.

77. S. McKnight, *A Light among the Gentiles: Jewish Missionary Activity in the Second Temple Period* (Minneapolis: Fortress, 1991), 106–108.

78. D. Instone-Brewer, *Traditions of the Rabbis from the Era of the New Testament*, vol. 2a (Grand Rapids, MI: Eerdmans, 2011), 31.

and righteousness. Otherwise, it is prohibited as taking the name of the Lord God in vain (Exod 20:7, 16; Deut 5:11, 20; 6:13; 10:20; Num 30:3).[79]

Thus, warnings against false or excessive swearing were common in Jewish society. The covenant of Damascus warns that God's name is not to be used in certain oaths (CD 15:1) but allows a solemn oath (15:5). The Temple Scroll legalizes some vows and orders the public to keep its vows.[80] According to Josephus, the Essenes refused to take any public vows. Vows could only be sworn within their own group. For that reason, even Herod the Great exempted them from taking oaths during his reign.[81] Jesus is not condemning the Pharisees for taking oaths and vows. What he condemns is their hair-splitting. The Pharisees teach that, "The Temple gold and the altar gift were binding as part of an oath because they were connected with the term *Korban* (consecrating/offering), while the Temple and the altar, though holy objects, were illegitimate substitutes in an oath formula."[82] In Jesus's eyes, such fine distinctions were a way of deceiving others. For that reason, Jesus finds all this irrelevant.[83] Jesus considered all oaths valid, but it was best not to use an oath at all and simply and honestly say "yes" or "no" (5:34–37).

The fourth woe (vv. 23–24) – The fourth woe is a criticism of tithing. It was the Pharisees' way of fulfilling the law of Moses according to Leviticus 27:30 and Deuteronomy 14:22–23. Leviticus 27:30 requires tithing "the seed of the land or of the fruit of the trees" and "the tithe of herds and flocks." Similarly, Deuteronomy 14:22 commands that, "you shall tithe all the yield of your seed, which comes forth from the field year by year." The commands of God show us that ancient Jewish society was an agrarian society and they gave one-tenth of their produce for the care of the Levites and priests, the landless and the poor every third year (Num 18:21–29).[84] Since tithing is an ordinance of God to obey, the point of Jesus's criticism is not on the Pharisees' insistence on tithing spices, but on "the *halakhic*

---

79. Saldarini, *Matthew's Christian-Jewish Community*, 152.
80. Saldarini, 152.
81. Josephus, *Ant.* 2.135; *Ant.* 15:371.
82. Garland, *Intention of Matthew 23*, 135.
83. Hagner, *Matthew 14–28*, 669.
84. Keener, *Gospel of Matthew*, 550.

matter of weightier versus lighter matter," as France rightly says.[85] Since they observed all religious duties regarding agricultural taboos and rules,[86] they instructed even to tithe mint, dill and cumin (23–24) which are herbs used for cooking. They are tithable according to the Pharisees although the law does not require them for tithing.

In fact, Jesus's criticism is not against tithing itself. His point is that this focus on petty detail gets in the way off more important matters, such as mercy and justice. He makes the point vividly and metaphorically when he describes the Pharisees straining out gnats, but swallowing camels. According to Levitical law 11:4, 41, both creatures are unclean. Water into which a gnat had fallen or which a camel had drunk from was considered unclean (Lev 11:32–35). Perhaps the Pharisees actually strained gnats out of water before the fall of the temple. For there is no indication of the practice after 70 CE.[87] Even in the Mishnah, the rabbi mentioned the practice of straining learned from their predecessors. The m.*Shabbat* 20.2 writes, "They may pour water over wine-dregs to dilute them, and strain wine through a napkin or Egyptian basket."[88] The practice of straining wine through a "napkin" or "basket" is presumably understood to prevent impurities. The caution of impurities is also seen in b.*Horayot* 11a and b.*Aboddah Zarah* 26b where it states that eating a flea or a gnat caused offence to the law.[89] Jesus points out that gnat-straining observes the Levitical requirement for purity. However, it is a big mistake to swallow the camel, which is big enough and also an unclean creature. Jesus appears to use this literal and metaphorical image from an Aramaic word play between *qalma* (gnat) and *gamla* (camel).[90] In Jesus's eyes, the misconduct of the Pharisees was that while embracing and fulfilling the minutest biblical requirement they neglected the greatest commandment – justice, mercy and faith.

Jesus attacks them for being obsessed with tithe minutiae while ignoring the greater commands to show mercy, to be just and faithful. If the Pharisees

---

85. France, *NICNT*, 872; Hagner, *Matthew 14–28*, 670.
86. Neusner, "Pharisaic Law in New Testament Times," 331.
87. Newport, *Sources and Sitz im Leban*, 105.
88. m.*Shabbat* 20.2 in Danby, *The Mishnah*, 117.
89. b.*Horayot* 11a; b.*Aboddah Zarah* 26b; Neusner, *Babylonian Talmud*, 2009.
90. France, *NICNT*, 874.

had not neglected these greater matters, Jesus might not have criticized their practice. The words of Jesus here echo Isaiah 6:6 and Micah 6:6–8. His whole concern was that religious rituals should be performed with love, justice, and mercy toward others.[91]

The fifth and sixth woes (vv. 25–28) – These two woes are about the Pharisees' obsession with outer purity and their neglect of inner purity.[92] Jesus picks out cleaning utensils as an example. He says this is like whitewashing a tomb: it may be clean on the outside, but it is unclean inside. According to biblical law, dead bodies, human bones and graves were unclean. Anyone who touched them had to undergo a purification ritual (Num 6:6–7; 19:11–22; Lev 21:1–11), for Mosaic law was very strict about this.[93] According to the Pharisees' quest, they have extended traditional observances of the priestly purity to non-priests and also to their utensils using. Their concern of ritual purity became central in Jewish society at Jesus's time, particularly for the Pharisees who wanted to live a pious life,[94] in a state of priestly purity.[95] It was not the Pharisees' fear of uncleanness Jesus was attacking but their show-off piety and their obsession with cup and plate cleaning and neglect of internal purity. They were just like a whitewashed tomb. France states that Jesus here drew on the imagery of Ezekiel 13:10–16, in which the prophet used the language of "whitewashing" to attack the leaders' failure.[96]

However, it does appear that the practice of whitewashing (tombs and so on) was a normal maintenance practice to make decaying things look things better, a practice that flourished especially after the success of rabbinic Judaism after 70 CE. Since the apostle Paul mentions a "whitewashed wall" in (Acts 23:3), it seems possible that such a custom was not new in Jesus's time.[97] Jesus here uses vivid images to illustrate his point.

---

91. Turner, "Jesus' Denunciation of the Jewish Leaders," 70.
92. Turner, 70.
93. France, *NICNT*, 875.
94. Saldarini, *Matthew's Christian-Jewish Community*, 135.
95. Marshall, *Portrayals of the Pharisees*, 46.
96. France, *NICNT*, 876.
97. Instone-Brewer, *Traditions of the Rabbis*, 208.

Like other cases, Jesus was not attacking the Pharisees' practices as part of biblical law, but he strongly opposed their excessive outer concern while being full of hypocrisy and lawlessness.[98] According to Jesus, internal cleanness is what counts, for the root cause of unrighteousness, hypocrisy, iniquity and wickedness is inward impurity. Therefore, internal purity has precedence over external purity.[99] Only bothering about outward purity is like furnishing a rotten corpse with a whitewashed tomb.

The seventh woe (vv. 29–36) – The seventh of Jesus woe is the contrast between "the descendants of the prophets vs. descendants of those who killed them."[100] This seventh woe would make most sense in Palestine where there were graves of prophets and righteous ones. As Theissen says, "the hearer must be acquainted with local customs about the graves and the veneration of holy persons."[101] Newport considers that with this seven woe, Matthew's target shifts from a specific group to the general audience – not only to the Pharisees but also to all the descendants of Abraham – who were involved in the killing and rejection of the prophets in the past as well as in the present.[102] However, for Matthew's Jesus, his focus does not shift. He continues to blame the Pharisees and those who associate with them for the future destruction of the temple and the disaster that will befall the Jews who would suffer from it. The destruction of the temple is also an image for the killing of God's sent prophet, Jesus. According to Jewish tradition, the Jews know that their ancestors had killed the prophets and the righteous,[103] for their leaders built memorial tombs for those that their ancestors had rejected and killed. According to Senior, such memorial tombs were constructed and furnished at the time of Jesus.[104]

What Jesus challenges here is the hypocrisy of the Pharisees, who honour the prophets by caring for their tombs, yet repeat their ancestors' crime by

---

98. Turner, *Israel's Last Prophet*, 323; Saldarini, *Matthew's Christian-Jewish Community*, 134.
99. Hagner, *WBC: Matthew 14–28*, 672.
100. Keener, *Gospel of Matthew*, 554.
101. Theissen, *Gospels in Context*, 52–53.
102. Newport, *Sources and Sitz im Leban*, 148.
103. Keener, *Gospel of Matthew*, 554.
104. Senior, *Matthew*, 262.

doing the same to the prophet God has sent them.[105] Jesus points out that the Pharisees confess that the ones who killed God's messengers are their ancestors, for they are their physical and moral descendants.[106] Garland stated that the seventh woe has no particular application.[107] However, in this temple setting, the rejection of God's messenger is the key issue Jesus confronts the Pharisees with.

The historic rejection of the prophets is also recorded in the Second Temple literature, *The Book of Jubilees*, which probably dates from around 150 BCE, and predicts that Israel will be judged for rejecting and killing the prophets (1:12–14). *The Lives of the Prophets*, a Jewish work of the first century CE, mentions the death of twenty-three prophets (1–3; 6–7; 15; 23). The *Book of Tobit* (14:3–7) describes the authenticity of God's word through the prophet Jonas. Jonas appears to predict the fall of the Second Temple, the scattering of the people, and the final restoration of God.[108] Qumran literature also recounts the rejection of the prophets. The document 4Q166 f1ii1–6, which comments on Hosea 2:10, recounts that the people rejected God's messengers but followed the gods of false prophets. Similarly, the document 4Q266 f3ii18–19 says that Israel shunned the words of the prophets and describes the violent things they will do to God's prophets in the future (4Q390 f2i5).[109] All these writers say that Israel will reject God's prophets and fail to listen to God's messengers, thus bringing misfortune on the nation.[110] Jesus reminds them of the innocent blood shed from the time of Abel to Zechariah.[111] The shedding of innocent blood (v. 35) is then the cause of the disaster to come that is the fall of the temple.

By recalling this, Jesus draws a parallel with the Pharisees' rejection of his ministry (10:41–42; 25:35–45). Jesus points out that they were the descendants of those who killed the prophets even though the Pharisees distance themselves from the persecution of the prophets.[112] Jesus means

---

105. Keener, *Gospel of Matthew*, 554.
106. Turner, *Israel's Last Prophet*, 323.
107. Garland, *Intention of Matthew 23*, 164–166.
108. Turner, "Jesus' Denunciation of the Jewish Leaders," 75–76.
109. Turner, 76.
110. Turner, 74.
111. According to 2 Chr 24:20–22, he was stoned to death in the temple.
112. Theissen, *Gospels in Context*, 52–53.

that the Pharisees are not the spiritual successors of the prophets but rather the descendants of those who rejected and killed God's true messengers to the nation. Therefore, they will reap their ancestors' judgments if they follow in their footsteps.[113] Consequently, the destruction of the temple will affect the whole generation, not only of those who would cause its fall, but also the disciples themselves will suffer as a consequence of the apocalyptic catastrophe caused by the Pharisees (23:36–24:2).[114]

The two pronouncements (vv. 37–39) – in these verses Jesus's accusation turns into a lament. The temple will be destroyed because of the Pharisees' hypocrisy and Jerusalem's rejection of God's messengers. The second pronouncement is prediction of the future coming of his glory, at time Jerusalem will confess, "Blessed is he who comes in the name of the lord."[115] Jesus addresses his audience both as a prophet and wisdom sent from God.[116] From the seventh woe until the end, although no specific time is mentioned for the killing and rejection of the prophets, the core point is that Jerusalem is the central place that rejected, persecuted and killed God's messengers.[117] Consequently, she will face desolation and abandonment in the near future, yet it will be turning into blessing and joy because of God's mercy and grace.[118]

4.3. The Traditional Materials in Matthew 23

As we have seen, the disputes in Matthew 23 are very much based on Pharisaic traditions at the time of Jesus. The following sections discuss the most notable Pharisaic traditions dating before 70 CE.

4.3.1. The Seat of Moses

The seat of Moses represents the authority of the Pharisees at Jesus's time both literally and metaphorically. Jesus sees the Pharisees as the most devoted and authoritative interpreters of the Mosaic laws of the time.[119] In that sense

---

113. Keener, *Gospel of Matthew*, 554.
114. Runesson, "Purity, Holiness, and the Kingdom," 171.
115. Newport, *Sources and Sitz im Leban*, 153.
116. Harrington, *Gospel of Matthew*, 330.
117. Theissen, *Gospels in Context*, 229.
118. Turner, *Israel's Last Prophet*, 328.
119. Flusser, *Jewish Sources in Early Christianity*, 30.

Jesus sees them as the heirs of the Mosaic law. For within Judaism, there were other groups such as the Essenes and the Qumran community who preferred to live undisturbed lives and therefore abstained from public affairs.[120] The Sadducees, on the other hand, were interested in working with the elites. The Priests themselves collaborated with both the Herodians and the Romans. The Zealots wanted to expel the Romans from the land. The only group who could influence the Jewish social-religious community through the teaching of Mosaic law in Jesus's time was the Pharisees. Their primary interest was the law of Moses in whose name and authority they worked. Among them the Houses of Shammai and Hillel were the most powerful groups who were popular in society because of their way of life,[121] their emphasis on the oral law, and their pious life. Although the priests performed animal sacrifices, it was the Pharisees who controlled the animals sacrificed, so that even the priests and Sadducees had to live by their *halakhic* principles.[122]

Among the Pharisaic community, the Shammaic Pharisees attempted to dominate over the Hillelites until the fall of the temple.[123] Indeed, from about 20 BCE to 70 CE the Shammaic Pharisees outnumbered their rivals in the Jerusalem Sanhedrin.[124] The following text describes how the Shammaites controlled what animals could be sacrifice in the temple and their conflicts with the Hillelites:

> An incident occurred involving Hillel the elder, who brought his whole offering into the Temple courtyard on a festival day to lay hands on it.[125] The disciples of Shammai the elder ganged up on him. They said to him, "What sort of animal is it?" He

---

120. Josephus, *War* 2.124.

121. Culbertson, "Changing Christian Images of the Pharisees," 542. Their ways of living included valuing the traditions of the fathers alongside with the laws of Moses, ritual purity, tithing, and various kinds of Sabbath observance. See Harrington, *Gospel of Matthew*, 323.

122. See also in b.*Yoma*.19b.

123. Culbertson, "Changing Christian Images of the Pharisees," 540; McNamara, *Palestinian Judaism*, 163.

124. Falk, "Jesus the Pharisees," cited in D. J. Harrington, "The Jewishness of Jesus: Facing Some Problems," 126.

125. The laying on of hands mean giving authority (e.g. Gen 27; 48:18–20; Num 27:18–20; Acts 6:6). Laying hands in the context of the sacrifice is that, before one slit the throat of the animal in sacrifice to God, he was required to lay his hands on its head and confess sins (Exod 29:10; Lev 16:21; Num 8:12). See further in James, *The Laying on of*

said to them, "It is a female (which cannot be a whole offering), and I brought it as a peace offering!" (Hillel) swung its tail at them (to indicate it was a female) and they walked off. On that same day the House of Shammai got the upper hand, and they desired to fix the law according to their (opinion, that one does not lay on hands at festivals). (b.*Betzah* 20a.1.7)[126]

There occurred another incident involving one of the disciples of the House of Hillel who brought his whole offering to the Temple courtyard in order to lay hands on it. One of the disciples of Shammai found him (there). [The Shammaite] said to him, "What's this laying on of hands?" [The Hillelites] answered him, "What about shutting up"! [The Hillelite thus] silenced him with a rebuke, and [the Shammaite] walked away. (b.*Besah* 20b.1.8)[127]

These are some of the laws which they have stated in the upper room of Hananiah b.Hezekiah b.Gurion when they went up to visit him. They took a vote, and the House of Shammai outnumbered the House of Hillel. And eighteen rules did they decree on that day. (b.*Shabbat* 13b. 1:4)[128]

The rule of the house of Shammaite also reflects through Eliezer the follower. He says, "People may not go from one Sukkah[129] to another, and they may not erect a sukkah to begin with on the intermediate days of the festival." (b.*Sukkah* 37b)[130]

The above references give us a glimpse of the situation among the Pharisees at Jesus's time. Most likely the Shammaic Pharisees primarily controlled the seat of Moses. Jesus instructed the crowd and his disciple to

---

Hands-S'mikhah, https://thinkhebrew.wordpress.com/2009/12/07/the-laying-on-of-hands-smikhah/ (accessed 2 November 2015).

126. Neusner, *The Babylonian Talmud: A Translation and Commentary* (Peabody, MA: Hendrickson, 2009).

127. Neusner.

128. Neusner.

129. Sukkah means the feast of Tabernacles.

130. Neusner, *Babylonian Talmud*.

follow the Pharisees' teaching just because they were the best option of his day and their *halakha* flourished at the time. Hengel and Deines also state,

> There is now more evidence that the Pharisaic *Halakah* flourished in Judaism prior to 70 CE in the synagogue. The use of stone vessels to prevent the transmission of cultic impurity, and the reburial of bones in ossuaries all attest to the fact that Jewish religious life was dominated by Pharisaic rules and teachings in Jesus' days.[131]

It is possible that Jesus, like any other Jew, recognized the Pharisees' legitimate social-religious role concerning Mosaic law without being a member of the group, while pointedly criticizing their conducts.[132] Jesus not only recognizes the Pharisees' role and authority, but also instructs the crowd and his disciples to follow and obey their teachings, not because of the Pharisees' intellectual arrogance but because they were the best authority in his day. In short, the Pharisees were the most legitimate scholars of Jesus's days, and the Shammaic Pharisees principles dominated in the social-religious sphere as well as over the Hillelite Pharisees.

4.3.2. Phylacteries

Jews did not start wearing Phylacteries after the post-70 CE period. Although the practices of wearing phylacteries or *tefillin* appeared to be part of Jewish religious life in Jesus's time, there was no fixed rules regarding the principles of the phylacteries and tassels. This fact is seen through the two Pharisaic houses disagreed about how often they needed to check the phylacteries, in accordance with Exodus 13:10. Melkhilta de.R.Ishmael, Pisha 17:209–216 says,

> Another interpretation of . . . "from year to year (Exod 13:10)" says that a man needs to examine the phylacteries once in twelve months. "Here it says from year to year, and below it says for a full year shall he have the right of redemption (Lev 25:29).

---

131. M. Hengel and R. Deines, "'Common Judaism,' Jesus, and the Pharisees," *JTS* 46 (1995): 34.
132. Mason, "Pharisaic Dominance," 379.

Just as year there means fully twelve months, so here it also means fully twelve months" the words of the House of Hillel.

The House of Shammai says, "He never needs to examine them." Shammai the Elder said, "These are the phylacteries of my mother's father."[133]

From this statement, one can see that the House of Hillel examined their phylacteries once a year in order to make it right according to the commandment of God. However, the House of Shammai felt they did not have to be examined, and even kept on wearing the phylacteries of their grandfather.[134] In rabbinic sources which reflect Hillel's attitudes, the identical accusation of Pharisaic hypocrisy for making the phylacteries broad is also seen. In the testimony of R. Hai Gaon:[135]

> It was the custom in the academy for the students to make their phylacteries small, not higher than a finger ... whereas the great rabbis would make theirs some three fingers high, so that the students should not be equal to them.

This indication points out that the successors of Hillel condemned an ostentatious sign of status in their academy. The Mishnah recorded various references to φυλακτήριον – phylacteries, and gives rulings about exemptions and liabilities. For instance,

> Women and slaves and minors are exempt from reciting the Shema and from wearing phylacteries, but they are not exempt from saying the *tefillin*, from the law of the *Mezuzah*[136] or from saying the Benediction after meals (m.*Berakhot*.3:3).[137]

---

133. Melkhilta de.R. Ishmael, Pisha 17:209–216; see, J. Neusner, *The Rabbinic Traditions about the Pharisees before 70: Part 2 The Houses* (Atlanta, GA: Scholars Press, 1999), 6.

134. Samuel A. Berman, *Midrash Tanuma-Yelammedenu* (Hoboken, NJ: KTAV Publishing, 1996), 408.

135. Weinfeld, "Misunderstanding of Judaism," 69–70.

136. *Mizuzah* is a capsule. The capsule contains the following texts written on parchment: Deut 6:4–9; 11:13–21. This is also another sign of the covenant between God and Israel. Another reminder of the covenant is the kitchen and the food. Mezuzah is used in almost every room. Class lecture handout by Dr Goran Larsson at LTS Hong Kong, 2015 October.

137. m.*Berakhot* 3.3, in Danby, *Mishnah*.

According to this, although women, slaves and minors were exempt from wearing phylacteries on the forehead, they were still required to recite the biblical verses inside the phylacteries. Thus, wearing the phylacteries was already practised among the Pharisees and also in the Qumran community (cave 8Q) in the time of Jesus.

4.3.3. Tassels

Like the phylacteries, the custom of wearing tassels is traditional. In Jesus's day, the followers of two houses disputed a number of details, like the number of threads in each tassel and their length.[138] According to b.*Menahot* 41b, the debate was about:

> 1. "How many threads does one put into the hole of the corner, to form the fringes?"
>
> The House of Shammai says, "Four." And the House of Hillel says, "Three."
>
> 2. "And how far must the threads hang down beyond the hem?"
>
> The House of Shammai says, "four fingerbreadths." The House of Hillel says, "three finger breadths." And the three fingerbreadths of which the House of Hillel have spoken are measured as one fingerbreadth out of four to a handbreadth of any person (b.*Menahot* 41b).[139]

The House of Shammai favoured inserting four threads into the whole of each corner of the garment and four fingerbreadths of thread left after it had been winded and knotted, whereas the House of Hillel instructed three threads at each corner of the garment and three fingerbreadths for the length.[140] The House of Shammai prescribed longer tassels than the House of Hillel.[141] Babylonian Talmud *Menahot* 41b describes the points of the debate in detail:

---

138. France, *NICNT*, 862.
139. b.*Menahot* 41b, in Neusner, *Babylonian Talmud.*
140. b.*Menahot* 41b, in Neusner, *Babylonian Talmud.*
141. France, *NICNT*, 862; Bruner, *Church Book Matthew 13–28*, 435.

> 1. Said R. Huna, "four threads are to be inserted in the garment within the distance of four fingerbreadths from the corner, and they must hang down for four fingerbreadths."
>
> 2. R. Judah says, "Three within three, and they must hang down three."
>
> 3. Said R. Papa, "The decided law is that there must be four threads inserted within three fingerbreadths of the corner and they must hang down for four fingerbreadths."
>
> 4. Show fringes (Num 15:38) – The sense of the word means only that something must protrude, and the word implies that any length whatsoever suffices.
>
> 5. In point of the fact the elders of the House of Shammai and the elders of the House of Hillel went up to the upper room of Yohanan b. Batera and they said, "There is no fixed measurement attaching to show fringes." (b.*Menahot* 41b)[142]

From this we can conclude that although wearing tassels was practiced among the Pharisees, there were no fixed rulings over the measurement and length of the tassels in Jesus's time.

4.3.4. Proselytes

As we have seen in the exegesis on the proselytes, such customs already existed during Jesus's time. For proselyting began even in biblical times and continued in the Second Temple period. Although the NT does not provide a clear picture of how the Pharisees dealt with proselytes, the rabbinic literature gives information on the principles of the two Pharisaic masters – Hillel and Shammai – and the way they dealt with a proselyte who wanted to become a God-fearer. The b.*Shabbat* 31a demonstrates the contrasting attitudes of Hillel and Shammai to the three proselytes who wanted to come under God's wings.[143] A proselyte asked Shammai to teach him only the written Torah. Shammai told him sharply to leave, whereas Hillel was able to teach the proselyte the two-fold Torah. On another occasion, a gentile

---

142. b. *Menahot* 41b, in Neusner, *Babylonian Talmud*.

143. I have already mentioned detailed events on the two masters' teachings on proselytes in section 2.3.3.

asked Shammai to teach him the whole Torah while standing on one foot. Hearing this outlandish condition, Shammai chased him out the door with a stick. Hillel, by contrast, summarized the whole Torah in one sentence: "What is hateful to you, do not do it to others." Another gentile came to Shammai and said that he would become a proselyte only if Shammai appointed him the high priest. Shammai chased him out of the house with a stick and ordered others to follow in their exact footsteps regardless. Hillel, however, patiently enlightened the gentile about God's command concerning the high priest.[144]

When the tree proselytes meet, the proselytes concluded that Shammai, with his strict rules, irritability and impatience, had blocked the door on their becoming God's sons, whereas Hillel, with his acceptance and gentleness, brought them under the wing of God's divine presence. Thus, we may fairly conclude that the tradition of proselyzing does not origin after post-70 CE. It was already practiced among the Pharisaic community before 70 CE.

4.3.5. Oaths and Vows

Oaths and vows attached to the temple belong to pre-70 Pharisaic tradition. At the time of Jesus, the two Pharisaic houses disagreed about the validity of oath formulas.

> 1. If a man saw others eating (his) figs and said, "May they be *Korban*[145] to you!" and they were found to be his father and brothers and others with them. The House of Shammai say: "For them the vow is not binding, but for the others with them it is binding." And the House of Hillel says: "The vow is binding for neither of them."[146]
>
> 2. Men may vow to murderers, robbers, or tax-gatherers that what they have is heave offering, even though it is not heave offering; or that they belong to the king's household even though they do not belong to the king's household. The House of Shammai says: "They may vow in any form of words save in

---

144. b.*Shabbat* 31a, Neusner, *Babylonian Talmud*.

145. *Korban* – an offering or consecration. Korban is considered as valid oath for which is associated with divine name.

146. m.*Nedarim* 3.2, in Danby, *Mishnah*, 266.

the form of an oath."[147] And the House of Hillel says: "Even in the form of an oath."

The House of Shammai say: "A man should not be first with a vow (but he should vow only under constraint)." And the House of Hillel says: "Even in a matter over which a vow is imposed." And the House of Hillel says: "He may even be first with a vow."

The House of Shammai says: "Only in a matter over which a vow is imposed," and the House of Hillel says: "Even in a matter over which no vow is imposed." Thus, if they had said to him, "Say, *Konam*[148] be any benefit my wife has of me!" and he said, "*Konam* be any benefit my wife and my children have of me!" The House of Shammai say: "His wife is permitted to him and his children are forbidden." And the House of Hillel says: "Both are forbidden."[149]

According to this, the two Pharisaic houses gave differing guidelines about vows and oaths. The question of the first case was: "Is a vow made under a false supposition valid?", because a person swore it without knowing his father and brothers was among others who ate his figs. The House of Shammai said the oath was valid for others but invalid for his own family. Whereas the house of Hillel taught that the vow was binding for neither of them. The second dispute was over vows made under constraint. The House of Shammai said that one may use any sort of vow, except for the oath – *Korban* because it is associated with a divine name. It was a standard oath formula in Jesus's milieu, for the word *Korban* indicated a property devoted to the temple treasury.[150] But the House of Hillel maintained that all forms of vows are either permitted or forbidden.[151]

---

147. Oath is more like swearing and vow is making a promise, but the two are sometime used interchangeably.
148. Konam or Konah or Konas are substitutes for Korban, an offering or consecration.
149. m.*Nedarim* 3.4, in Danby, *Mishnah*, 267.
150. Saldarini, *Matthew's Christian-Jewish Community*, 154.
151. Neusner, *Rabbinic Traditions about the Pharisees, Part 2*, 213.

These indications show that the House of Hillel did not make such fine distinctions as the House of Shammai between binding and not-binding oaths. Although no mention is made of swearing by the temple or the altar, the two Pharisaic houses could have debated the issue. For the later rabbi's teaching in the *Tannaitic* period reflected what the Shammaites claimed: oaths associated with the Divine Name or "*Korban*"[152] were considered to be the most valid.

> If a man said, "I adjure you," or "I command you," or "I bind you," they are liable. But if he said, "By heaven and by earth," they are exempt. If he adjured them "by Aleph-Daleth" or "by Yod-He" or "by Shaddai" or "by Sabaoth" or "by the Merciful and Gracious" or "by him that is long-suffering and of great kindness," or by any substituted name, they are liable. If a man cursed by any of these he is liable. So R. Meier. But the Sages say: "He is exempt."[153]

Here, R. Meier, a follower of Shammai, agrees that an oath is valid when sworn by any name associated with divinity, but it is exempt when sworn by heaven and earth. Whereas the Sages represented the view of Hillel, who discouraged separating oaths into valid and exempt. Mishnah. *Nedarim* 1.3 also provides such distinctions. It says,

> If [a man] vowed by any of the utensils of the Altar, although he did not utter the word *Korban, an offering*,[154] it is a vow as binding as if he had uttered the word *Korban*. R. Judah says: If he said, "May it be Jerusalem!" He has said naught.[155]

A similar example is also found in b.*Nedarim* 14b, where it says a vow by the Torah is considered invalid. However, it becomes valid when one takes oath by the contents of the Torah.[156] The Shammaites' standpoint is also reflected in the Damascus codex, where it says, "oaths by God or by the

---

152. Consecrating.
153. m.*Shebuoth* 4.13, in Danby, *Mishnah*, 415.
154. "A thing as forbidden to him for common use as a Temple offering." See Danby, *Mishnah*, 264.
155. m.*Nedarim* 1.3, in Danby, *Mishnah*, 264.
156. France, *NICNT*, 871.

Mosaic law cannot be broken, while certain other oaths can" (CD 15:1–5).[157] Thus, oaths and vows associated with God, the temple and its treasury were widely practiced by both Pharisaic houses at Jesus's time. Although the Shammaic Pharisees maintained binding and non-binding oath formulas, Jesus forbade such differentiated oath formulas and the misuse of oaths, but encouraged simple truthfulness.[158]

4.3.6. Utensils Cleaning

Ritual purity outside the temple was the Pharisees' primary commitment before 70 CE. According to Neusner and rabbinic literature, with the rise of the House of Hillel and Shammai, during the reign of Herod the great, the Pharisees' focus shifted to ritual purity, and purity laws dominated the Pharisaic way of life. Neusner writes, "The primary mark of Pharisaic commitment was the observance of the laws of ritual purity outside of the temple, where everyone kept them. Eating one's secular (that is, unconsecrated) food in a state of ritual purity, as if one were a temple priest in the cult."[159] Since the hallmark of the Pharisees' commitment was to observe a sanctified life, they made sure to have rules and regulations to keep their utensils clean. Jesus uses the image of cleaning the outside but not the inside of a cup. Cleaning utensils was an issue discussed among his contemporaries,[160] but there appeared to be no fixed rules about it. The m.*Berahkot* 8:2–4 states:

> The House of Shammai says: "They wash the hands and then mix the cup." And the House of Hillel says: "They mix the cup and then wash the hands."[161]

The House of Shammai meant that one should wash the hands first so that the uncleanness of one's hand may not make the outer side of the cup unclean. For them if the outer part is unclean, it could contaminate the inside. In contrast, the House of Hillel taught that there is no reason to protect the outer cup from the hand's uncleanness. The outer side of the cup does

---

157. Fornberg, "Matthew and the School of Shammai," 23.
158. Saldarini, *Matthew's Christian-Jewish Community*, 151.
159. Neusner, "Pharisaic Law in New Testament Times," 331.
160. Keener, *Gospel of Matthew*, 552.
161. m.*Berahkot* 8.2–4, in Danby, *Mishnah*, 8–9.

not contaminate the inside. For the Hillelites, what mattered was that the inside was clean.[162]

Even after 70 CE the two houses' rulings are mirrored in their followers' discussion. Kelim 25:1, 7–8 informs us that the rabbis divided a container into three parts – the inside, the outside, and the handle, and it states, "In all utensils an outer and an inner part are distinguished,[163] as in mattresses, pillows, sacks, and packing bags. So R. Judah (m.*Kelim* 25:1)." Dissimilar opinions over purity continued as:

> If the outer part of the flagon[164] containing the sin-offering water became unclean, its inner part becomes unclean also, and it conveys uncleanness to another flagon, and this to another, even though they be a hundred (m.*Parah* 12:8).[165]

> A utensil, the outer part of which have been made unclean with liquids – the outer part is unclean. Its inside, its rims, hangers and handles are clean. If its inside is made unclean, the whole is unclean (m.*Kelim* 25:6).[166]

> If the outer parts of vessels were rendered unclean by a liquid, R. Eliezer (the Shammaite) says: "They render liquids unclean, but they do not render foodstuffs invalid." R. Joshua says: "They render liquids unclean and foodstuffs invalid (m.*Tohar.* 8:7)."[167]

> For it has been taught on Tannaitic authority: As to the status of glassware that was repaired[168] and mended with molten lead. Said Rabban Simeon b.Gamaliel, "R. Meir declares it

---

162. Saldarini, *Matthew's Christian-Jewish Community*, 140.

163. "If the inner part is rendered unclean by an unclean liquid the outside becomes unclean also: But if the outer part is rendered unclean by an unclean liquid the inner part remains clean." See Danby, *Mishnah*, 640.

164. It was wood or metal. See Danby, *Mishnah*, 713.

165. m.*Parah* 12:8, in Danby, *Mishnah*, 713.

166. Neusner, *Mishnah*.

167. m.*Tohar* 8.7, in Danby, *Mishnah*, 728.

168. For stylistic translation, I use repaired rather than performed as mention in Neusner.

susceptible to uncleanness." And "Sages declare it insusceptible." (b.*Shabbat* 15b)[169]

From the above, two different rulings on utensil cleaning emerge – one house-ruling stressed the importance of cleaning the outside while the other insisted on cleaning the inside first. There seemed to be no fixed rules about cleaning utensils among the Pharisees in Jesus's time. Jesus's remarks about cleaning the outside and not the inside fit well with the Pharisees' practises in his time. Thus, as Neusner rightly points out, "the two Pharisaic houses' debate over the practices of utensil cleaning and the division of utensils into 'inner' and 'outer' parts predates the fall of the temple."[170] In addition, Wild states that Matthew tells us about the Pharisees' utensil cleaning which normal Jews would not generally have observed. It was only the practice among the Pharisaic houses – the House of Shammai and the House of Hillel – in the Palestine of Jesus's time.[171]

4.3.7. Tithing

Tithing was the second major commitment of the Pharisees until the fall of the temple. The rabbinic literature provides us with the legal judgements and disputes of the House of Shammai and the House of Hillel before 70 CE. In m.*Ma'as.* 4.5, Rabbi Eliezer, the follower of Shammai, stated that "from dill the seeds, plants, and pods, must be tithed." However, the Sages (who shared the views of Hillel) disagreed on this point.[172] The House of Shammai's emphasis on tithing is also seen in m.*Demai* 1.3, where it says, "Sweet oil, the House of Shammai declare liable, but the House of Hillel declare it exempt." Cumin is mentioned in m.*Demai* 2.1 and it says, "tithe must everywhere be given from these things as being *demai* (produce); fig-cake, dates, carobs, rice and cumin; but whosoever uses rice from outside the Land of Israel is exempt."[173] The debate over tithing of black cumin is mentioned in the Mishnah *Eduyyot*.5.3: "The House of Shammai declared

---

169. Neusner, *Babylonian Talmud*.
170. J. Neusner, "'First Cleanse the Inside': The 'Halakhic' Background of a Controversy Saying," *NTS* 22 (1976): 486–495.
171. R. A. Wild, "The Encounter between Pharisees and Christian Judaism: Some Early Gospel Evidence," *Novum Testamentum* 27, no. 2 (1985): 116.
172. m.*Ma'as* 4.5, in Danby, *Mishnah*, 72.
173. m.*Demai* 1.3; 2.1, in Danby, *Mishnah*, 21.

[it] insusceptible to uncleanness and thought that it was not liable to tithing. The House of Hillel, on the other hand, thought black cumin both susceptible to uncleanness and subject to tithe law."[174] All this makes clear that there was disagreement over tithing and debate among the Pharisees in Jesus's day.

Matthew 23:23–24 reflects the practices of both Pharisaic houses following the commands and rules of tithing and their other *halakhic* matters on tithable species. In general, the House of Shammai, was stricter than the House of Hillel. Jesus's criticism on the Pharisees' detailed prescriptions on tithing fits into a Jewish and Palestine context[175] at the time of Jesus. For it was the Levites and priests in Jerusalem who consumed the tithes.[176] This is why the Levitical commands were enforced in Palestine but not outside the Holy Land. Thus, the Pharisees and their tithing custom is traditional.

4.3.8. The House-Criticism Languages

The use of polemical language in Matthew 23 does not origin in post-70 CE. Rather, it was Jewish traditional rhetoric for dealing with opponents. Although the denunciations – hypocrites, blind guides, and a brood of vipers – sound hash to modern ears, the polemic language Jesus used was common in the debates among different sects in the early first century. According to Overman, such usage was known as "the language of sectarianism,"[177] and simply a rhetoric of ancient polemics as Johnson states.[178] The OT provides examples of this in designating the failure of Jewish leaders and false prophets. We find similar denunciations in the prophets Amos (5:18–20; 6:1–7), Isaiah (5:8–10, 11–14, 18–24; 10:1–3; 28:1–4; 29:1–4, 15–21; 30:1–3; 31:1–4) and Micah 2:1–4.[179] These denunciations are usually addressed to leaders who misused their roles. Isaiah 29:1–2, 7, 10, 13–15,

---

174. Newport, *Sources and Sitz im Leban*, 102.
175. Newport, 103.
176. Neusner, "Pharisaic Law in New Testament Times," 332.
177. J. A. Overman, *Matthew's Gospel and Formative Judaism* (Minneapolis, MN: Fortress, 1990), 16.
178. L. T. Johnson, "The New Testament's Anti-Jewish Slander and the Conventions of Ancient Polemic," *JBL* 108, no. 3 (1989): 419–441.
179. Harrington, *Gospel of Matthew*, 327

20–21 criticized them for their hypocrisy.[180] The prophets denounced their evil deeds and predicted a harsh judgement.[181] Therefore, Meier says that the idea of dealing politely with opponents is a modern phenomenon alien to the ancient Mediterranean world.[182] As we have seen, a fierce rhetorical polemical tradition flourished from the prophets Amos and Hosea onwards: in this context Jesus's denunciations in Matthew 23 are not anti-Judaic. In short, they are part of a vigorous Jewish tradition in which the prophets castigate the leaders' failures and the sins of the people that can only end in the downfall of the nation.

During Second Temple Judaism, various sects savagely attacked each another through harsh languages.[183] The contrast between "lawless" and "righteous" was part of the sectarian rhetoric. 4 *Ezra* depicted his own community as the righteous and faithful who will inherit the promise of God. Their community is surrounded by an unfaithful, lawless and unrighteous majority. Ezra's righteous community is contrasted with that of the wicked and ungodly. Ezra's aim is to point out that "the righteous are few, but the ungodly abound (7:17, 51; 9:14ff; 7:48; 8:48; 15:23).[184] A similar motif is also seen in 2 *Baruch* 14 where the author talks about the reward of the righteous. The author implicitly depicts his own community as the righteous community which God has gathered and who will be rewarded with the gift of resurrection (15:8; 85:3–5; 49:1–52:7).[185]

Qumran literature before 70 CE contains attacks against the unrighteous and wicked, contrasting the wicked and the righteous in terms similar to the woe sayings. Some are addressed to the wicked sinners, and some to Jerusalem and its leaders for their misconduct (*1 Enoch* 94:6–95:7; 96:4–8; 98:9–99:2; 100:7–9).[186] In *2 Enoch* 52 alternative curses and blessings make rhetorical contrasts.[187] Curses fall on the wicked for trusting only in their

---

180. Turner, "Jesus' Denunciation of the Jewish Leaders," 73.
181. Harrington, *Gospel of Matthew*, 327.
182. Meier, *Marginal Jew*, 338–339.
183. Meier, 338–339.
184. Overman, *Matthew's Gospel and Formative Judaism*, 17.
185. Overman.
186. Turner, "Jesus' Denunciation of the Jewish Leaders," 72; Overman, *Matthew's Gospel and Formative Judaism*, 17.
187. Turner, "Jesus' Denunciation of the Jewish Leaders," 72.

wealth and for persecuting the righteous (*1 Enoch* 95:6; 103:11–12). Evildoers will be charged on judgment day, and will have no share in eternal life (99:10; 94:11; 100:1).[188] The *Psalms of Solomon* 4, which may date around the first century BCE, criticize the hypocritical religious and political leaders as lawless sinners. The author wishes them to die without having a proper burial (4:18–22). He charges them as profaners whose hearts do not please God. What they do and think contradicts their public show of a virtuous life.[189] What they do is only to impress others. He wishes such sinners to perish for all time (15:13) and claims "they will be driven out from their inheritance" (17:23).[190] All these writings have one thing in common – their denunciation of hypocritical leaders. In the Qumran texts, the Pharisees are the community's adversaries and sharply criticized. They are called as "seekers after smooth things."[191] In the Damascus Document (CD) 8:12; 19:25, the community addressed the Pharisees as "the whitewashed."[192] According to Fitzmyer, the Qumran community attacked the Pharisees "because of their alleged insistence on *halakhot* – regulations of conduct."[193] Thus, the Qumran texts are evidence of the internal Jewish dispute in the first century BCE,[194] and it has continued until the fall of Jerusalem.

Consequently, the use of polemical language can be understood as sort of "a philosophical tradition" as Johnson[195] rightly puts it, or "sectarian language[s]," as Overman states. It is a rhetoric tool used to respond to opponents. The outsider might find it strange and unbearable, but it was normal in this Jewish context. The debate between the House of Hillel and the House of Shammai shows that such slander was common among rivals. Josephus also informs us that the Jews of the early first century and the Diaspora Jews were often fanatically and violently divided. Josephus

---

188. Overman, *Matthew's Gospel and Formative Judaism*, 17.

189. G. W. E. Nickelsburg, *Ancient Judaism and Christian Origins* (Minneapolis, MN: Fortress, 2003), 43.

190. Overman, *Matthew's Gospel and Formative Judaism*, 17.

191. See J. Wellhausen, *The Pharisees and Sadducees* (Macon, GA: Mercer University Press, 2001), 99–103.

192. CD 8:12; 19:25 in Flusser, *Jesus*, 69.

193. J. A. Fitzmyer, *The Dead Sea Scrolls and Christian Origins* (Cambridge, UK: Eerdmans, 2000), 251.

194. Wellhausen, *Pharisees and Sadducees*, 99.

195. Johnson, "New Testament's Anti-Jewish Slander," 429.

himself charges the Pharisees, especially those who were members of the aristocratic elite, with being hypocrites and mere pretenders. Josephus charges the Pharisees with being more interested in politics than God's law. He saw this as preparing the way for the downfall of the Hasmonean descendants and the nation.[196] Although Josephus criticizes the Pharisees and dislikes their misbehaviour, he still stands wholly within Judaism.[197] Thus, Jesus's attacks are only characteristic of the intra-Jewish debate which we can see in the Bible and in extracanonical Jewish texts of ancient traditions. It was simply the ancient rhetorical way of dealing with opponents.[198]

If this is the case, there is no reason why Jesus should not follow the rhetorical tradition when he saw the Pharisees pervert core biblical commands with certain excessive *halakhot* traditions. The view that the polemical language in Matthew 23 reflects only a growing opposition to Judaism within the Matthean community rather than the situation at the time of Jesus is then unjustifiable. It is not something Matthew made up because of the situation of his community. As Carson says:

> To read Matthew 23 as little more than Matthew's pique about AD 85 is not only without adequate historical and literary justification, but also fails dismally to understand the historical Jesus, who not only taught his followers to love their enemies but proclaimed that he came not to bring peace but a sword (10:34) and presented himself as eschatological judge.[199]

Therefore, we can conclude that Matthew 23 fits the setting of Palestine before 70 CE. Not only that, it fits the long tradition of Jewish intra-mural disputes with its typical rhetoric. Indeed, Matthew stresses the Jewishness of Jesus's attacks. They are clearly made by an insider.

---

196. Mason, *Josephus and The New Testament*, 144.
197. Mason, 145.
198. For instance, Ael.Arist. *Plat.Disc.*307.6. See Keener, *Gospel of Matthew*, 536.
199. Cited in Osborne, *Exegetical Commentary on the New Testament*, 832.

4.4. The Pharisees and Jesus as Reflected in Matthew 23

The literary analysis of Matthew 23 shows that materials we see in the chapter describe the traditional practices of the Pharisees until the fall of the temple, and do not originate after 70 CE. The practices found in Matthew 23 are: the flourishing of the Pharisees' *halakha* (Moses's seat); tithing and oaths attached to the temple; no agreed rules about wearing phylacteries and tassels; utensil cleaning; and making proselytes observe the religious traditions and customs of pre-70 Pharisaism. The analysis of Matthew 23 affirms that most of the traditions and practices described in the text are the customs of the Pharisees until the fall of the temple. The Mishnah records three hundred and sixteen disputes between the House of Shammai and the House of Hillel before 70; six disagreements over their practises are found in Matthew 23.

Most important, although Jesus criticizes the Pharisees in general, his attack is addressed only to the negative types of Pharisees.[200] The attack (woes) Jesus made in the temple (Matt 23 and Matthew in general) is more related to the Shammaic practices. This indicates that the Pharisees in Matthew 23 reflect the time of Jesus, because most of the Shammai had perished in the war. The Shammaic Pharisees that survived joined the group at Yavneh, which the Hillelites of Matthew's time led. If, as some claim, Jesus's attack on the Pharisees in Matthew 23, is an invention only to fit the needs of his community, would not Matthew have attacked the Hillelites, who now had the leading role? However, it is clear that Jesus's attacks mostly fit the Shammaites and not the Hillelites. This strongly suggests that the attacks refer back to the time of Jesus rather than being a later fiction.

If Matthew was solely concerned with the situation of his community and making up the attack on Pharisaism because it suited its needs, why would he bother using so much Shammaite tradition and why would he center his attack so much around the temple (Matt 23:16; Matt 23:18), when neither the Shammaites nor the temple existed anymore? It makes much more sense that what Matthew writes in 23 is about the actual situation during Jesus's ministry.

---

200. Flusser, *Jewish Sources in Early Christianity*, 30.

Second, Matthew 23 affirms the Pharisaic *halakha* which flourished until the fall of the temple. It reveals that Jesus engaged in the struggle between the House of Shammai and the House of Hillel, by and large sharing the views of the Hillelites and criticizing the Shammaic Pharisees.[201] His attack fits the Shammaites' excessive traditions and practices, their failure to give priority to the weightier biblical commands of *justice, mercy and faith*. They are boastful and insincere in their piety.[202] As for Jesus, hypocrisy is a form of inner absurdity. "It is making pronouncements about what is right while not practicing them (23:3c); and it is appearing outwardly to be righteous while being inwardly full of lawlessness."[203] They wish to impress others with their outer piety and excessive practices they have established which are hard for others to follow. Two of the conflicts of the Pharisees we see in Matthew support my contention that the context is pre-70 and Jesus encountered the Shammaic Pharisees primarily.

Sabbath Observance: There are two occasions on which the Pharisees criticize the conduct of Jesus and his disciples on the Sabbath. The first dispute is about the disciples plucking the heads of grain on the Sabbath (12:1–8), and the second is about healing a man on the Sabbath (12:9–14). The biblical commandment only instructs the Israelites to observe the Sabbath – "Six days they shall labour, and do all their work but no work is to be done by persons or animals on the Sabbath" (Exod 20:9–10; Deut 5:14) – but it does not tell in detail how far a person should observe the Sabbath law. For this, the oral traditions of the Pharisees fill the gap. According to m.*Shabbat* 7.2, the Pharisees forbid the thirty-nine types[204] of labour on the Sabbath. The

---

201. As for Falk, what got Jesus into trouble with the regnant Shammaites was his desire to establish a religion for gentiles on the basis of the seven Noahide commandments (prohibitions against idolatry, blasphemy, killing, stealing, sexual sins, and eating a limb from a living animal, as well as the obligation to establish courts of justice) in D. J. Harrington, "The Jewishness of Jesus," 127.

202. Marshall, *Portrayal of the Pharisees*, 118–119.

203. Kingsbury, "Developing Conflict between Jesus," 61.

204. m.*Shabbat* 7:2 has mentioned the 39 types of forbidden labor on a Sabbath. They are – sowing, ploughing, reaping, binding sheaves, threshing, winnowing; cleaning crops, grinding, sifting, kneading, baking, shearing wool, washing or beating or dyeing it, and spinning, weaving, making two loops, weaving two treads, separating two threads, tying a knot, loosening a knot, sewing two stitches, tearing in order to sew two stitches, hunting a gazelle, slaughtering or flaying or salting it or curing its skin, scraping it or cutting it up, writing two letters, erasing in order to write two letters, building, pulling down, putting out

two Sabbath disputes between Jesus and the Pharisees reflect inner Jewish disagreement over the Sabbath rules and regulations before 70 CE. The two Pharisaic houses had much discussion and disagreement about the Sabbath rulings and observances such as, "carrying, reaping, dying, lifting, tying, lighting the Sabbath lamp, cultic acts, rescuing from danger and healing."[205] Generally, the House of Shammai had stricter rules and regulations than the House of Hillel. The two houses' disputes and teachings on the Sabbath are seen below:

> 1. May the labour of the weekdays extend itself into the Sabbath?
>
> The House of Shammai say, "Six days shall you labour and do all your work (Exod 20:9) – (meaning) that all your work should be completed by the eve of the Shabbat." And the House of Hillel say, "Six days shall you labour – work is what you should do all six days (t.Shabbat 1.21b)."[206]
>
> The House of Shammai say, "They do not [on Friday afternoon] soak ink, dyestuffs, or vetches, unless there is sufficient time for them to be [fully] soaked while it is still day." And the House of Hillel permits.
>
> The House of Shammai say, "They do not put bundles of [wet] flax into the oven, unless there is time for them to steam off while it is still day." "And [they do not put] wool into the cauldron, unless there is sufficient time for it to absorb the colour [while it is still day]." And the house of Hillel permits.
>
> The House of Shammai say, "They do not spread out nets for wild beasts, fowl, or fish, unless there is sufficient time for them to be caught while it is still day." And the House of Hillel permits.

---

a fire, lighting a fire, striking with a hammer and taking out aught from one domain into another, These are the main classes of work: forty save one. Danby, *Mishnah*, 106. This list may presumably complete over the time.

205. Instone-Brewer, *Traditions of the Rabbis*, 82.
206. Neusner, *Tosefta*,

The House of Shammai says, "They do not give hides to a [gentile] tanner, or clothing to a gentile laundryman, unless there is sufficient time for them to be done while it is still day." And in the case of all of them, the House of Hillel permits, while the sun is still shinning (m.Shabbat 1:5–6, 8).[207]

From the above teachings and rulings, the Shammaites said that no work should be started unless it is finished by the Sabbath evening. However, if someone started a process which continued by itself, then the Hillelites tended to permit it, as long as no one had to take an active role. Although they both cited "Six days you shall work and do all your labour," they interpreted this differently in practice. The Shammaites were more restrictive than the Hillelites, for the Hillelites maintained that the Sabbath did not apply to the work but only to the people.[208] The Shammaites' rulings on the Sabbath were described to be stricter than the Hillelites.

Accordingly, it might be the stringent Shammaic Pharisees Jesus meets in Matthew 12:1–7. Perhaps they regard "plucking the heads of grain" as coming under the forbidden category of reaping, winnowing and cleaning. However, Jesus replies that even though David and the priests in the temple profane the Sabbath, they are guiltless. Jesus appears to say that satisfying hunger is preserving human life. By recalling the example of David and his men who ate the consecrated bread in the temple, which was not lawful for them to do on the Sabbath, Jesus can claim that the Sabbath was made for man, not the other way around. Aqiba, a follower of Hillel, argues that priests are obliged to perform their temple service even on a Sabbath, and that concern for the safety of a life also overrules observing the Sabbath:

> Said R. Yose, "How do we know that danger to life overrides the restrictions of the Sabbath? Since it says, 'You shall keep my Sabbath'" (Exod 31:13). R. Aqiba said, "For the Temple service overrides [the prohibitions of] the Sabbath, and the Sabbath does not override it [requirement, that the temple service be conducted on that day as on all others] . . . now if the Temple service overrides the Sabbath and a matter of doubt concerning

---

207. Neusner, *Mishnah*.
208. Instone-Brewer, *Traditions of the Rabbis*, 82.

the safety of life override it, the Sabbath, which the temple service overrides – all the more so should matters of doubt concerning the saving of life override it. Thus you have learned that a matter of doubt concerning the saving of life overrides the Sabbath. (t.*Shabbat* 15:16)

Since Jesus and his disciples were living in a Jewish world where some of the rules about Sabbath observance were controversial, Jesus counters Pharisaic criticism with arguments from this controversy. According to Tosefta *Betzah*1.20, to satisfy hunger with a handful of grain was permissible and it says;

He who rubs ears of corn on the eve of the Sabbath which coincides with a festival sifts them by hand and eats them. But he does not put them into a basket or into a dish . . . He who rubs ears of corn on the Sabbath does so by hand and eats them.[209]

Although this teaching is anonymous, it represented the Hillelites at the time. For them, what the disciples did was permissible, whereas for the Shammaites, it was not; for them rubbing ears of corn to get out the grain to eat was work in line with reaping, winnowing and cleaning, and therefore not allowed on the Sabbath.[210]

Similarly, in the second Sabbath conflict after Jesus healed a man (12:9–14). Jesus asks rhetorically: "What man of you, if he has one sheep and it falls into a pit on the Sabbath, will not lay hold of it and lift it out? Of how much more value is a man than a sheep! So it is lawful to do good on the Sabbath." Jesus's question reflects the teachings of his contemporaries. For instance, the Qumran community forbade bringing up an animal from a pit on the Sabbath, whereas the Pharisees not only allow it but even permit bringing it to the altar for sacrificing as long as the animal is unblemished. This early ruling is reflected in later rabbis' teaching in m. *Betsa* 3:4 as:

A first born [animal] which fell into a pit: R. Judah says: "An expert must go down and look at it." If it has a blemish on it

---

209. t.*Yom Tob* (Besah) 1:20 trans. by Neusner, *Tosefta*, vol. 1.
210. Instone-Brewer, *Traditions of the Rabbis*, 15.

> [so it cannot be sacrificed] he may bring it up and slaughter it [as food] and if not, he must not slaughter." (m.*Betsa* 3:4)

Although the Pharisees have no problem allowing an animal to be brought up from a pit, the Shammaites' Sabbath rulings restricted healing or saving life. They apparently forbade all kinds of work, including charitable activities, healing or praying for the sick on the Sabbath.

> The House of Shammai say: "One should not distribute charity to the poor on the Sabbath in the house of assembly, even to marry an orphan to an orphan-girl, and one should not negotiate (betrothal) between a man and his (future) wife. And one should not pray for the sick on the Sabbath. But the House of Hillel permits (t.*Shabbat* 16.22).[211]

A similar motif is described in Talmud *Shabbat* 12a:

> It has been taught on Tannaite authority: "They don't kill vermin on the Shabbat," the words of the House of Shammai. And the house of Hillel permits."
>
> On the Shabbat they don't negotiate terms for a daughter's betrothal, nor for teaching reading to a child, nor for teaching him a trade, nor do they comfort mourners, nor do they visit the sick," the words of the House of Shammai. And the House of Hillel permits." (b.*Shabbat* 12a)[212]

According to this indication, only the House of Hillel allowed the performance of charitable activities and praying for the sick on the Sabbath.[213] The Shammaites' further restriction of the healing, such as straightening a limb or an act of washing which was more than normal is seen as:

> They may anoint or rub their stomach but not have themselves kneaded or scraped. They may not go down to Kordima – *a muddy wresting ground*, and they may not use artificial emetics; they may not straighten a [deformed] child's body or set a broken limb. If a man's hand or foot is dislocated he may

---

211. Neusner, *Toselfta*, vol. 1.
212. Neusner, *Babylonian Talmud*.
213. Instone-Brewer, *Traditions of the Rabbis*, 70–71.

not pour cold water over it, but he may wash it after his usual fashion, and if he is healed, he is healed. (m.*Shabbat* 22:6)[214]

He may drink purgative water to quench his thirst, and he may anoint himself with root-oil if it is not used for healing. If his teeth pain him he may not suck vinegar through them but he may take vinegar after his usual fashion, and if he is healed he is healed. If his loins pain him he may not rub thereon wine or vinegar, yet he may anoint them with oil but not with rose-oil. One may drink palm-tree water [to quench] his thirst. And one anoints with root oil, not for healing . . . he who [is] concerned about his loins [which give him pain], he may not anoint them with wine or vinegar.) and later even included taking normal food or drink. (m.*Shabbat* 14:3–4)[215]

Subsequently, Jesus's healing activities on the second Sabbath may well have provoked the anger of the Shammaic Pharisees. Thus, the Shammaic Pharisees' *halakhic* principles reflect in the two Sabbath accounts.

Divorce: Jesus meets them again in Matthew 19:2–12. The laws relating to betrothal, marriage, and divorce are an area of major dispute among the Pharisees before 70 CE.[216] The issue of divorce is found twice, once in 5:31–32, and again in 19:3–9. They reveal Jesus's attitude toward divorce. According to Deuteronomy 21:1–4, a man could divorce his wife by issuing her with a certificate of divorce. The two Pharisaic houses disagree on the issue. The House of Shammai say: "A man may not divorce his wife unless he has found unchastity in her, for it is written, 'Because he hath found in her indecency in anything.'" And the House of Hillel say: "He may divorce her even if she spoiled a dish for him, for it is written, 'Because he hath found in her indecency in anything' (m.*Gittin* 9:10)." The House of Shammai was strict about divorce and permitted it only in cases of sexual immorality, whereas the House of Hillel allowed a man to divorce his wife for any cause, even if he did not like her cooking.

---

214. Danby, *Mishnah*.
215. Danby, *Mishnah*.
216. Grabbe, *Introduction to Second Temple Judaism*, 53.

According to the narrative, the Shammaic Pharisees are the ones intent on testing Jesus about this. Their question "Is it lawful to divorce one's wife for any cause?" could well refer to their disagreement with the House of Hillel. Jesus answers that except on the ground of "πορνεία – *Porneia*" divorce is not allowed. There is another term "μοιχεῖαι" used for adultery. Matthew would have used μοιχεῖαι rather than πορνεία if he wanted to state the exception was "adultery" for the meaning of πορνεία is ambiguous.[217] If πορνεία means adultery Jesus agrees with the Shammaic Pharisees and against Hillel, and if it means incest,[218] Jesus was far stricter than almost all Jews.

Some commentators consider that the word "πορνεία" refers to fornication and adultery.[219] Other commentators view "πορνεία" as the specific problem of incestuous marriage.[220] For they consider that there are indications that πορνεία refers to incest. In Acts 15:20, 29, four things are forbidden for gentiles Christians and "to fall victim to πορνεία-incest" (unlawful sexual intercourse) is one of them. For them Leviticus 17–18 is the background to understand "πορνεία" as incestuous marriage. Fornberg also considers "πορνεία" as incest and states, "such marriage, according to Jesus seemed to be no marriage at all therefore it can be dissolved without even the possibility of being able to speak of adultery,"[221] whereas Jesus absolute restricts any real possibility to divorce in a proper marriage.[222] However, the question remains, if an incestuous marriage is not recognized as legal marriage, why is it necessary to talk about divorce? No marriage means no need for divorce at all.[223] Here, Jesus intends πορνεία as a broader term that can be used to

---

217. The word "μοιχεῖαι" is unfaithfulness and adultery. Whereas the word, "πορνεία" is "a selling off of sexual purity" or illicit sex or incest. πορνεία, Strong's Greek Lexicon Number: http://studybible.info/strongs/G4202 (accessed 29 November 2015). In a broader term, "πορνεία" means "fornication and unchastity." See LSJ the online Liddell-Scot Jones Greek-English Lexicon: http://stephanus.tlg.uci.edu/lsj/#eid=88317&context=search (accessed 23 March 2016).

218. Sexual relationship between kinsmen and close siblings.

219. For instance, R. T. France, *NICNT*, 720; U. Luz, *Matthew 8–20* (Minneapolis, MN: Fortress, 2001), 494; Davies and Allison, *Matthew*, vol. 3, 16; R. Gundry, *Matthew*, 381; Keener, *Gospel of Matthew*.

220. For instance, Fornberg, "Matthew and the School of Shammai," 18; J. P. Meier, *Matthew* (Wilmington, DE: Michael Glazier, 1986), 216.

221. Fornberg, "Matthew and the School of Shammai," 19.

222. Fornberg, 19.

223. P. Sigal, *Halakah of Jesus of Nazareth*, 124.

refer to adultery and fornication.²²⁴ According to him, the right to divorce is solely limited to πορνεία.²²⁵

Although Jesus allows divorce on grounds of adultery, his emphatic words, "ὃ οὖν ὁ θεὸς συνέζευξεν ἄνθρωπος μὴ χωριζέτω" (v. 6) reveals his radical demands for marriage goes back to the principle in Genesis. In that sense, he is the antithesis to Deuteronomy 24:1.²²⁶ Jesus points out that, according to divine will, marriage is a permanent union. Because of human sinfulness and hard-heartedness, divorce is exceptionally allowed in cases of "πορνεία." Otherwise, whoever divorces his wife and marries another commits adultery. Jesus does not create a new law for married life, but restores Jewish high ethical standards in marriage based on Genesis.²²⁷ He does this by recalling the creation story and establishing a proper understanding of God's purpose for marriage: God's will is that the union of two persons is meant to be permanent.²²⁸ For this reason, his disciples were shocked and said that if they could not divorce their wives they had better not marry. Thus, this dispute shows intramural debates between the Pharisaic houses. On the topic of divorce, Jesus was closer to the Shammaites, demanding a return to higher standards. From these two debates on Sabbath and divorce, we see that Jesus's conflicts with the Pharisees are about traditional *halakha* that flourished before the fall the temple.

Jesus knows them well because he lived in a Jewish world where the twofold laws – the written and oral laws – of the Pharisees flourished and every first-century Jew lived by the oral law²²⁹ alongside with the written law. Jesus appeared to be familiar with Mosaic law and the *halakhic* debates among the Pharisees. Jesus could have "felt closer to the Pharisees than to any other group in contemporary Judaism, precisely because they were more in earnest about the will of God."²³⁰ Since Pharisees sat on the seat of Moses,

---

224. Hagner, *WBC: Matthew 1–13*, vol. 33a (Dallas: Word, 1993), 124–125.
225. Sigal, *Halakah of Jesus of Nazareth*, 115.
226. Hagner, *WBC: Matthew 14–28*, vol. 33b, 549; Hagner, *WBC: Matthew 1–13*, 25.
227. W. R. Nicoll, *The Expositor's Greek Testament*, vol. 1 (Grand Rapids, MI: Eerdmans, 1951), 110.
228. Saldarini, *Matthew's Christian-Jewish Community*, 149.
229. E. P. Sanders, *Jewish Law from Jesus to the Mishnah* (London: SCM, 1990), 97.
230. B. Viviano, "Study as Worship," *SJLA* 26 (Leiden: Brill, 1978), 171.

and their rulings were binding on him and his disciples, he criticized them for not practising what they preached.[231]

Jesus was also keen on keeping the Jewish commandments, particularly focusing on the core biblical demands and value of love, justice and mercy. Jesus's position on Mosaic laws and the practices of Jewish oral traditions was closer to that of the Hillelites. Like the Hillelites, Jesus asserts that inward, not outward, purity counts. Moreover, Jesus emphasizes the humanitarian side of Judaism.[232] For him, what counts is not so much ritual observance as the love of justice, mercy and faith that God's desires.[233] Jesus, like many members of the House of Hillel, gave the Torah a humanitarian interpretation, at the same time taking the view that love, justice and faith weighed as heavily as the greatest.[234] Jesus also discourages any hair-splitting when it comes to marital relationship. On divorce, he was as strict as the House of Shammai (19:3–9). He opposed the standpoint of the House of Hillel, which sided exclusively with the husband.[235] Thus, any claims that Jesus only emphasized the written law is insupportable. Jesus appears to act as a channel between the positions of the Houses of Hillel and Shammai yet his primary teaching was drawn from biblical demands and values. Jesus was painted as a nonconforming Jewish teacher because of his freedom *vis-à-vis* the law and the tradition.[236] Jesus brings back the core biblical message of the Torah and believes that the Torah must be interpreted and practised in the light of two greatest commands – love for God and love for neighbour.

Chapter Findings

First, it is in the temple that a turning point occurs in Jesus's ministry. It is there Jesus makes known the frauds of the Pharisees, who have been following him, listening and criticising everything he says. His main charge against

---

231. Flusser, *Jewish Sources in Early Christianity*, 30.

232. Flusser, 24.

233. Marshall, *Portrayal of the Pharisees*, 97; Flusser, *Jewish Sources in Early Christianity*, 24.

234. Flusser, *Jewish Sources in Early Christianity*, 24.

235. Flusser, 23.

236. J. P. Meier, "Reflections on Jesus-of-History Research Today," in *Jesus' Jewishness*, vol. 2, ed., J. H. Charlesworth (New York: Crossroad, 1991), 96.

them is that they replace God's core commandment with their dubious and excessive traditions and practices. They abuse their control and authority as interpreters of Mosaic law and reject what he says. He reminds them of what they neglect, the call for justice, mercy and faith. Mosaic law demands inner purity, they exact outer purity.

Second, Jesus's attack on the Pharisees' religious role and practices do not have their origin in the post-70 CE situation. Matthew 23 reflects the flourishing *halakha* of the Pharisees at Jesus's time. All the details in the text – the chair of Moses, making proselytes, tithing, taking oaths and vows, wearing phylacteries and tassels, utensil cleaning, and the polemic languages used to deal with opponents – reflect normal practices and debate between the two Pharisaic houses in the time of Jesus. Thus, Jesus's criticism perfectly makes sense in terms of pre-70 BC Pharisaism.

Third, Matthew 23 focuses on the doom of the nation and the fall of the temple as consequences of the Pharisees' hypocrisy and misconduct. Since the Pharisees' and Jerusalem rejected him as God's messenger, Jesus's laments come as much out of grief as anger.[237] It was in the temple setting that Jesus foretold the fall of the temple in the near future and his returning as a blessing to the nation.

---

237. Turner, "Jesus' Denunciation of the Jewish Leaders," 72.

CHAPTER 5

Understanding Matthew 23 in the Historical Context of the Relationship between the Matthean Community and Judaism

Introduction

How are we to understand Matthew 23? Many scholars claim we can only understand Jesus's condemnation of the Pharisees in the context of the conflicts between the Matthean community and early rabbinic Judaism. However, as we have seen in previous chapters, the charges of hypocrisy that Jesus makes fit the practices of the House of Shammai in Jesus's own lifetime, that is before 70 CE. On a historical level, Jesus attacks only the excessive demands and practices of the Shammaic Pharisees. If the practices and traditions of the Pharisees in Matthew 23 reflect the time of Jesus on the historical level, why did Matthew use this material for his post-70 CE community? What was the situation of the Matthean community? Had the Matthean community separated from parent Judaism and formed a distinct community? These are the questions I hope to answer in this chapter.

5.1 The Suggested Community

5.1.1 Jewish or Gentile Community?

The social setting of the Matthean community creates endless debate in Matthean studies. Early on it was believed that the author was a Hebrew, called Matthew, and he wrote within his own Jewish circle. Irenaeus quoted papyri, and stated that Matthew wrote his gospel to the Hebrew community in their own language, more specifically for the Jews in Palestine. Eusebius, following the same tradition, wrote:

> Among all those who were companions of the Lord only Matthew and John have left us their memoirs and tradition has it that it was through force of circumstances that they turned to writing. For Matthew had preached at first to Hebrews, but when he was about to go off to others he handed on to them in writing the gospel according to his version, in his native language, and so by means of his writing made up for the lack of his own presence with those from whom he was being sent.[1]

The early church father, Jerome, also repeated this tradition, saying,

> Matthew, who is also called Levi, a former tax-collector then an apostle, first composed a gospel of Christ in Judea, for the sake of those who had come to faith out of the circumcision, in Hebrew letters and words; who subsequently translated it into Greek is not known for sure. The Hebrew text itself is still preserved to this day in the library at Caesarea.[2]

He also considers that the Matthew quotations from the OT closely followed the Hebrew Bible rather than the Septuagint.[3] Arguing against such views, there are scholars who notice anti-Jewishness in the Matthew gospel, and therefore consider the Matthean author to be a gentile Christian writing for a gentile community. This view was advanced by Clark, who said that the final form of the Matthew Gospel comes from a gentile Christian community and was written by a gentile Christian author.[4] He argues that a later redaction altered the essentially Jewish character of the Matthew narrative by adding the theme that the Jews had rejected Christ and that the gospel

---

1. Eusebius, *Ecclesiastical History III*. 24.5–6, C. F. Cruse trans. (Peabody, MA: Hendrickson, 1998).
2. Jerome, *De Viris Illustribus* 3. Cited from R. T. France, *Matthew Evangelist and Preacher* (Downers Grove, IL: InterVarsity Press, 1989), 62.
3. France, *Matthew*, 62.
4. Clark, "The Gentile Bias in Matthew," 165–172.

was now addressed to the gentiles; that is the theme of the gentile Great Commission. The gentiles have replaced the Jews as the children of God. This comes across clearly in the language Matthew uses: "The children of the kingdom will be cast out" (8:12); "In his name will the gentiles trust" (12:21); "The kingdom of God will be taken away from you, and given to a people producing the fruits of the kingdom" (21:43); "Go and make disciples of all the gentile peoples (τα ἔθνη) . . . teaching them to obey all the commands I have laid on you." Clark was also convinced that Matthew's way of presenting the greatest commandments of Jesus in 22:37–40 as the centre of the laws and prophets emphasizes this gentile bias. Matthew declares in 22:41–46 that the Messiah does not have to be a descendant of David for he was superior even to King David. Matthew makes a series of denunciation in the following chapter.[5] Matthew repeats that as they have rejected Christ, they are no longer the true Israel of God.[6]

Similarly, Brown, Davies and Allison point out that the virgin birth account in Matthew 1:18–25 has no parallel in Jewish literature, and therefore, could not have come from a Jewish writer.[7] Additionally, Gaston in his article states that Jesus came to Israel as their Messiah, as a prophecy fulfilment; however, the Jews rejected him so that this Messiah became a teacher of the gentiles and a blessing to them. For Gaston, Matthew's gospel is the good news aimed at a gentile community.[8]

Hare[9], Meier[10] and Menninger[11] hold the same view. They base their arguments on the gentile traits in Matthew 1:3, 5, 6; 2:1–12; 4:15–16; 8:5–12; 15:24–28; 22:9. Not only that, but the gospel is aimed at the world (13:38a) and all nations (24:14; 28:18–20). In addition, the gospel

---

5. Clark, 167.

6. Clark, 166.

7. R. Brown, *The Birth of the Messiah* (New York: Doubleday, 1977), 143–164; W. D. Davies and D. Allison, *The Gospel According to St. Matthew*, 2 vols. (T&T Clark, 1988).

8. L. Gaston, "The Messiah of Israel as Teacher of the Gentiles," *Interpretation* 29 (1975): 24–40.

9. D. R. F. Hare, *The Themes of Jewish Persecution of Christians in the Gospel According to St. Matthew* (Cambridge: Cambridge University Press, 1967), 86.

10. J. P. Meier, *Vision of Matthew: Christ Church, and morality in the First Gospel* (New York: Paulist, 1979), 17–25.

11. R. E. Menninger, *Israel and the Church*, American University Studies 7, Theology and Religions 162, (New York: Lang, 1993), 36.

distinguishes Jewish institutions (their/your synagogues and scribes) 4:23; 9:35; 13:54; 23:34; 7:29). It also contains Jesus's attack on Jewish practices and leaders (23:13–39; 15:1–20; 21:45), and his interpretation of the law. Consequently, they conclude that the community of Matthew was a gentile-Christian community that had no longer any relation or link with Judaism. For this reason, Matthew concludes his gospel with the instruction of the Great Commission (28:16–20) in favour of gentile Christians.[12]

5.1.2. Extra-Muros Community

In recent Matthean studies on the community of Matthew, the emphasis and focus has been on the relationship between the Matthean community and Judaism. Most scholars today are convinced that the Matthean community was composed largely of Jewish believers and gentile Christians did not form the majority.[13] The issue these scholars were concerned about, was whether the Matthean community was extra-muros (outside the wall) or intra-muros (within the wall) of Judaism.[14]

Stendahl appears to see the community of Matthew as both extra-muros and with mostly gentile members.[15] Stendahl finds little evidence of intra-Christian polemic in Matthew. For him, the community was largely composed of gentiles, the polemic was between gentile Christians versus conformist Jews. He is convinced that Matthew's purpose was to present "Christian ethics as superior to that of Judaism."[16] Moreover, for the Christians this was a period of transition from being a predominantly Jewish to being an increasingly gentile constituency. At this stage, according to Stendhal, it was a community that suffered neither persecution, nor much opposition from or tension with Judaism; there was though a sharp contrast between the two. Stendahl understands that there was a Matthean School

---

12. Hare, *Themes of Jewish Persecution*, 86; Menninger, *Israel and the Church*, 36; Meier, *Vision of Matthew*, 17–25.

13. This view is held by both extra-muros and intra-muros scholars. We will see their arguments in the followings.

14. A. O. Ewherido, *Matthew's Gospel and Judaism in the Late First Century C.E*, SBL Series 91 (New York: Lang, 2006), 21.

15. I classify scholars who see the Matthean community as outsiders or outside the wall of Judaism under extra-muros position.

16. K. Stendahl, *The School of St. Matthew and Its use of the Old Testament*, 2nd ed (Philadelphia: Fortress, 1968), xii.

behind the composition of the gospel of Matthew. The author, who could have been a Jewish scribe and trained in Palestine before the war, was now in the Matthean scribal community and part of a Hellenistic Christian community.[17] For Stendahl, the transition from a Jewish to an increasingly gentile community of believers was quite peaceful.

In contrast, Stanton's extra-muros Matthean community suffered a lot of mistreatment and oppression by mainstream Judaism. He argues that the author of Matthew was pained by Israel's continued rejection of Jesus, and their ill-treatment of whoever was proclaiming Jesus's as the fulfilment of Israel's hope. By the time the author composed his gospel, the Matthean community had been rejected by mainstream Judaism, and was living as a separate body. In such a situation, the author still suffered from the trauma of separation from and torment by Judaism when he was writing to a Jewish Christian community. For the community at the time was already represented as a legalistic sect which had been cut off from Judaism.[18] Thus, for Stanton, the gospel of Matthew marks the parting of the ways by encouraging polemics against Jewish leaders while stressing a mission to the gentiles. In so doing, Matthew portrays the church as the true heir and interpreter of the Scriptures.[19]

Luz is another important Matthean scholar who considers that the Matthean community comes from "a Judaism that already is distanced from a Pharisaic and scribal Judaism." For Luz, Matthew's words, such as "their" "your" synagogues and "your scribes" in 4:23, 7:29, 10:17, 13:54 and 23:34 are clues to understanding this separation.[20] He believes that although the Matthean community was separated from Judaism, the members still lived, followed and practiced according to traditional Jewish law. However, they based their practice on the teaching of their only teacher, Jesus. A teacher who was not a Pharisee, nor a scribe, which means that the community conducted purity laws with more focus on inner purity as Jesus taught, rather than outer purity (15:11).[21] For Luz, the Matthean community kept

---

17. Stendahl, *School of St. Matthew*, xiii.
18. G. Stanton, *A Gospel for a New People* (Edinburgh: T&T Clark, 1992), 157.
19. Stanton, 169
20. Luz, *Theology of the Gospel of Matthew*, 14.
21. Luz, 15.

the entire law, not because they belonged to Judaism but because they were instructed to do so by Jesus (5:17–18).²²

In contrast, Schnackenburg states that the Matthean community was a mixed society, consisting of Jews, Greeks, and other gentiles in a large city.²³ He thinks that Matthew composed his gospel after the destruction of the Jerusalem temple, when the Pharisaic leadership was in a triumphant position. The Matthean community had already broken with mainstream Judaism because of the strict leadership of the Pharisaic scribes and the tension they had created in Matthew 27:25 and 23:34. For this reason, Matthew emphasized the church as the true heir and its members as the true people of God through Jesus Christ (21:43).²⁴ However, this does not mean that the Matthean community abandoned mainstream Judaism, for they respected it as the original home from which the Messiah had descended.²⁵

Like Schnackenburg, Gundry presumes that the Matthean church was a large community with members from all nations. However, unlike Schnackenburg, Gundry is convinced that the conflict and subsequent separation between Judaism and the Matthean community took place even before the fall of Jerusalem. For the persecution came not from the Romans, but from the Jewish religious leaders of Jerusalem itself right from the beginning. Gundry views that many passages (such as 5:10–12; 13:24–30, 36–43, 47–50; 22:11–14; 25:1–13) point out the fact that the persecution of the Jews distinguished true disciples from false disciples.²⁶ The church's early separation from Judaism could be seen in the book of Acts and the Pauline letters (e.g. Phlm 3:5–6; Acts 8:3; 9:1–2, 13–14, 21; 22:3–5, 19; 26:9–11; 1 Cor 15:9; Gal 1:13; 1 Thess 2:13–16; 1 Tim 1:13). Thus, he argued that it was not necessary to date the separation between the two after 70. For the opposition of the Pharisees to Christ's followers was there from the beginning. For him, the Pharisees' dominance before 70 CE was the key to understanding the potential they had to create conflicts and tensions. Thus,

---

22. Luz, *Matthew 1–7*, 48.

23. R. Schnackenburg, *The Gospel of Matthew*, trans. Robert R. Barr (Grand Rapids, MI: Eerdmans, 2002), 5.

24. Schnackenburg, 6.

25. Schnackenburg, 7.

26. Gundry, *Matthew*, 5. However, I do not think all these passages support Gundry's contention that they are about Jewish persecution of Christians.

as for Gundry, the 70-event was not the turning point for the separation, for the Matthean church had become a counterpart to Judaism even before the destruction of the Jerusalem temple.[27]

5.1.3. Intra-Muros Community

Intra-muros scholars[28] hold that the Matthean community remained within Judaism despite the fierce clashes they had with the mainstream. Four scholars' views on this position are worth mentioning. Bornkamm was the first to argue this. He thinks that the Matthean community did not view themselves as a separate group from the synagogue environment. He states that the Matthean community actually responded to two different opposing groups – "to antinomian tendencies in some Christian groups and to non-Christian Jews who had rejected the group's claims about the Messiahship of Jesus, but Matthew failed to name them explicitly."[29] Bornkamm does not name the non-Christian Jews who had rejected Jesus's Messiahship, but in referring to non-Christian Jews he is probably addressing the formative rabbinic Judaism of the time. Nonetheless, Bornkamm is firmly convinced that, in large part, the conflict between the Matthean community and its opponents was a sibling fight within Judaism.[30]

Overman is more explicit about the Matthean community's existence within the sphere of the synagogue life. Through his sociological analysis, he firmly states that the conflicts, tensions and problems of the Matthean community should be seen within the period of formative Judaism. The Matthean community did not separate from Judaism in that period, but had a struggle characteristic of sectarian communities in the post-70 period within Judaism. The fiercest rival the Mattheans encountered was formative-rabbinic Judaism; their quarrel was not with the whole body of the Jewish

---

27. Gundry, *Matthew*, 601.

28. I classify the scholars who see the Matthean community as insider of the Judaism under the Intra-muros position. According to D. A. Carson, the term "intra-muros" was first used by G. Bornkamm in his article. See G. Bornkamm, "End-Expectation and Church in Matthew," in *Tradition and Interpretation in Matthew* (London: SCM, 1963), 15–51.

29. P. Foster, *Community, Law and Mission in Matthew's Gospel* (Tubingen: Mohr Siebeck, 2004), 24–25.

30. Bornkamm thinks that "the struggle with Israel is still a struggle within its walls." See G. Bornkamm, "End-Expectation and Church in Matthew," 15–51; Foster, *Community, Law and Mission*, 24–25.

community. Like several other communities in this period, particularly formative Judaism, the Matthean community claimed and legalized themselves as the true Israel, the only faithful body, and the fulfillers of the divine plan and law.[31] Besides, Overman argues that Matthean community did not consider themselves as Christians at this point but still as true Jews.[32]

Saldarini is another scholar who believes in the intra-muros position. Through a socio-rhetorical approach, he agrees with Overman's argument that the Matthean community is "a deviant" group within a wider Jewish world in greater Syria.[33] He thinks that the community's faith in Jesus caused conflicts with the leaders of mainstream Judaism, who were more influential than the Matthean community, at least in Matthew's city. Matthew uses Jesus's polemics to undermine their authority.[34] Besides, Saldarini points out that the practice of the law played an important role in the Matthean community. Saldarini is convinced that Matthew's interpretation of the law is a part of the attempt to legitimize his community against the opponents.[35] For Saldarini then, the community can be seen as one of the reformist Jewish sects with its own stance within the body of Judaism. Moreover, the author's Jewishness could be seen through the gospel's polemics, disputes, and conflicts with the Jewish leaders.[36] For him, the dispute is a family quarrel.

Similarly, Sim believes that the war against the Romans in 70 CE was a decisive moment for both formative Judaism and the Matthean community. The war caused problems between the two and it created a new way of dealing with the gentile community for the Matthean community. After the war and the fall of the Jerusalem temple, the Pharisees attempted to unify the remaining Jews in Yavneh for the continuation of the Jewish nation.[37] This was also the time for a new beginning for them, as the group later became

---

31. Overman, *Matthew's Gospel and Formative Judaism*, 148–149.

32. Overman, 4–5.

33. Saldarini, *Matthew's Christian-Jewish Community*, 124–164, 198. Saldarini, however, suggests in his article that the Matthean community lived in a Galilean city where the rabbinic Judaism was influential or else in a Syrian city. See Saldarini, "Delegitimation of Leaders in Matthew 23," 663–664.

34. See Saldarini, "Delegitimation of Leaders in Matthew 23," 663–664.

35. Saldarini, *Matthew's Christian-Jewish Community*, 124.

36. Saldarini, 198.

37. D. C. Sim, *The Gospel of Matthew and Christian Judaism* (Edinburgh: T&T Clark, 1998),300.

formative rabbinic Judaism. At the same time, a group of Jews existed who believed in Jesus, "within the confines of the Jewish faith."[38] While believing in Jesus as the coming Messiah, they practiced circumcision and tithing, followed the purity rules and Sabbath observance. Sim considers that these people were the Matthean community. They were one of many Jewish sects who survived the destruction of Jerusalem.[39]

What happened next was that the formative Judaism adherents clashed with the Mattheans. Although the Matthean Jewish believers had some clashes with formative Judaism, their main problem came not from the rabbinic Judaism but mainly from the gentile Christians who did not practise Jewish laws. In Sim's view, the Matthean community was firmly opposed to the Pauline churches, which consisted mainly of gentile believers. The Matthean community believed that Christianity meant being both Jews and believing in Christ. For Sim, anti-gentile motifs are found in Matthew 5:46–7; 6:7–8, 31–32; 7:8; 18:15–17 so that the gospel is not so much anti-Judaic as anti-Pauline.[40] Thus, Sim concludes that the Matthean community was a Jewish sect within Judaism that opposed the Pauline gentile churches. The main conflicts the community had were with the law-free community of Pauline Christianity. Sim's understanding of Matthean's opponents is in line with Bornkamm's first type of opponents – the ones with antinomian tendencies.

As we have seen above, there have been two extreme positions about the Matthean community – the first was that a Hebrew gospel was written by Matthew, a tax collector, to a Jewish community, and the second was that Matthew was a gentile Christian who was writing to gentile Christians, declaring that God has now chosen gentile believers in Jesus as the true heirs of Abraham. Then in the last two decades the debate has arisen over whether the Matthean community was extra-muros or intra-muros. This debate has continued. Scholars who favour an extra-muros position believe that the gospel contains so many anti-Judaic sentiments that the Matthean

---

38. D. C. Sim, "The Social Setting of the Matthean Community," *HTS* 57 no. 1 & 2 (2001): 274, 280.

39. Sim, *Gospel of Matthew and Christian Judaism*, 300–301.

40. Sim, "Social Setting of the Matthean Community," 278.

community must have been a gentile community, or at least a community distinct from Judaism.

On the contrary, intra-muros scholars say that the parting never actually took place in the first century, although there was conflict within the sphere of Judaism. Intra-muros scholars believe that Matthew's community was basically composed of a Jewish believers' community, a sect within the synagogue network and Judaism.[41] Matthew's knowledge of Hebrew scriptural typology, citations, fulfilment formulas, imagery and practices (15:1–20), as well as his use of untranslated Hebrew terms (10:25; 1:23; 27:33, 46) and some parables like the parable of the Tares (13:30a) as an encouragement to his fellow community to remain within Judaism, indicate that the Matthean community remained within Judaism.[42]

5.2 The Matthean Community

5.2.1. Intra-Jewish Community

The Matthean community, as Sim states, is much more complex then we realize. It is extremely hard to understand and difficult to come up with a specific Matthean community and its relationship with the rest of the body of Judaism. However, I tend to be more in line with scholars who see the Matthean community as an intra-Jewish community. It is undeniable that early after the fall of the temple, the existence of the Jewish believers and the rise of Pharisaic Judaism may have created a new situation, causing both Jewish believers in Jesus and non-Jewish believers to adapt new stances. However, that does not mean that this new situation led to a total separation. Rather, the Matthean community appeared to be one particular form of Judaism that claimed its own special understanding of the Torah.

We see this fact from the work of Chilton and Neusner, who shed some light on understanding the connection between the early Jewish Christian community and Judaism. According to them,

---

41. S. Safrai, "The Synagogue," in *The Jewish People in the First Century: Historical Geography, Political History, Social, Cultural, and Religious Life and Institutions*, 2 vols, eds. S. Safrai and M. Stern (Philadelphia: Fortress, 1976), 908–944.

42. This view is also held by Keener. See Keener, *Commentary on the Gospel of Matthew*, 390.

In the setting of the diversity of social groups and their viewpoints in ancient Israel, the New Testament cannot be treated as a foreign body, asking about how an alien religion played its part in the formation of that body. We rather see a variety of Judaic religious groups as equally representative of Judaism, all of them heirs to the same scripture, every one of them insisting on the unique truth it alone possessed."[43]

They say that we need to be aware of religious diversity within Judaism and that the diversity could have been expressed in different forms. For this reason, it is essential to read and understand the New Testament in the context of a diverse Judaism, since the response to messianic prophecy was diverse, and the New Testament is only one of the responses.[44] It allows us to understand that, within the sphere of Judaism itself, there is no normative group, nor single Israel and its single interpretation of the Torah, nor agreement that unites all the various sects. As Goodman correctly states, "if uniformity was to be found in any area at all, it should perhaps best be sought in the publicly observable of the Sabbath and basic food laws, rather than in theology."[45] Different writers work on different premises and address different audiences.[46]

Consequently, the gospels can be understood as one way of interpreting the meaning of the Torah, and the prophecy of messianic hope.[47] Thus, Stanton and other extra-muros scholars seem to have been too hasty in making a judgment about the parting of the ways. Although Gundry rightly points out the early conflicts Christ's followers encountered with the dominant Pharisaic religious leaders, it is still too early to conclude there was a total separation of the two groups. Rather, the Matthean community at this stage could best be understood as one form of Judaism, a Judaism that portrayed itself in different ways.

As Chilton and Neusner point out, recent studies have begun to lead to the awareness that in the first century Palestine there was no monolithic

---

43. B. Chilton and J. Neusner, *Judaism in the NT* (London: Routledge, 1995), 8.
44. Chilton and Neusner, *Judaism in the NT*, 9.
45. Goodman, *Mission and Conversion*, 39.
46. Chilton and Neusner, *Judaism in the NT*, 5–6.
47. Chilton and Neusner, 5.

but rather a diverse Judaism with tension and conflicts among sects. Dunn made another important contribution to the debate, which we need to discuss.[48] Dunn says that there is no evidence in the text itself that would lead us to conclude that there was a parting of the ways as extra-muros scholars would have us believe. Many of the extra-muros scholars mention formative rabbinic Judaism after 70 as the cause of this parting of two polarized communities. They believe that the Pharisaic-rabbinic leadership took over Judaism, and that this led to persecution and problems for the Matthean community, which finally caused them to leave mainstream Judaism.

Nonetheless, we need to reconsider these views logically and historically.[49] In the first place, it is true that the Matthean community could have co-existed with a new form of rabbinic Judaism after post-70 CE. Because the remaining Pharisees who were not involved in the war were allowed to found a rabbinical school at Yaveh, a Judean city on the Mediterranean coast, first under the leadership of Yohanan ben Zakkai, and then Gamaliel II after the fall of Jerusalem. With the loss of the temple and all the turmoil they have gone through recently, the Pharisaic-rabbinic group would have fewer chances of persecuting others or creating problems as this might have led the Romans to regard them as troublemakers. Because their lives were totally in the hands of the Romans, it would have been very risky to create conflicts and tension within what remained of the Jewish nation.[50] As they now had to live without a physical temple, their sole focus was on how to live in the light of the Torah's teaching. They began to interpret the Torah and its law in the absence of the temple so as to transmit their early traditions. To do this they developed the *halakha*, by which they believed Israel should live.[51] Their re-interpretation of the Torah in the absence of the temple caused the creation of the Mishnah in 200 CE, which in turn became a source for the Talmud. At this point, what we need to realize is that the Yavneans at the beginning of post-70 CE were not in a position to impose their views on all the Jews. It was only after the fourth century that the Yavneans gained

---

48. J. D. G. Dunn, *The Partings of the Ways*, 2nd ed (London: SCM, 2006).

49. Dunn's argument on these facts is reasonable. See further in Dunn, *Partings of the Ways*, 303–309.

50. Baumgarten, *Flourishing of Jewish*,195.

51. Dunn, *Partings of the Ways*, 303.

influence over Palestine and the Diaspora Jewish community. The Yavneans themselves in the late first century were struggling to organize the system and the principles within their new and own academy.[52] In other words, the Yavneans at this point of post-70 history were too busy with their own issues to have the time to ill-treat or persecute other communities, although they may have had some conflicts of opinion. It is also important to note that "there is not a single accusation of hypocrisy was levelled" in the early church Fathers' work. This can be as Flusser rightly says because hypocritical Pharisees disappeared with the victory of the house of Hillelites at Yavneh.[53]

Second, as rabbinic Judaism was taking time to establish its stance, the view that the early Christian community at this point was largely composed of gentile Christians is unconvincing. Even though the early church father Eusebius says that the Jewish Christians of Jerusalem fled to the city of Pella in Tran Jordan, many Jewish followers of Jesus remained in the land of Palestine who were also firmly loyal to the law. We must not assume that the Jewish believers disappeared altogether within a day, and the gentile Christians took over. Like the followers of post-70 rabbinic Judaism, post-70 Jewish Christians struggled to survive within mainstream Judaism and by putting their faith in Jesus.[54] Third, there were other forms of Judaism that also attempted to claim and redefine the heritage of Second Temple Judaism. These other forms of Judaism can be seen through two Jewish apocalypses – IV Ezra and II Baruch. These classic pieces of literature, written during this period, expressed the hope that Jerusalem would be restored in the future. As such, the spectrum of post-70 was not confined only to the Yavneans and Jewish Christians.[55] Finally, non-rabbinic texts provide evidence that Jewish Christians remained within Judaism and continued to be associated with other forms of Judaism. It was not the rabbis but Christian Jews who preserved texts such as *the Psalms of Solomon, Testament of Moses, Sibylline Oracles, IV Ezra and II Baruch*.[56] It was not Jewish Christians who confined

---

52. Dunn, 303–304.
53. Flusser, *Jewish Sources in Early Christianity*, 31.
54. Dunn, *Partings of the Ways*, 305–306.
55. Dunn, 306.
56. Goodman, *Mission and Conversion*, 39; Dunn, *Partings of the Ways*, 309.

themselves to live within their particular circle, it was the rabbinic Jews who limited their contact with the *minim* (Jewish Christians).[57]

Moreover, Matthew's references to the use of "their/your synagogues (s)," are not a reflection of the community considering itself extra-mural. According to A. Runesson,[58] the term "synagogue" refers to two basic types of institutions. In Palestine, the term refers to a public village or town assembly. This type of institution is for public Torah reading on the Sabbath. The one who is in charge of this type of assembly can be anyone and any group or individual can use this institution for the conceptualization of their own understanding of traditional practices and Jewish law. The second type of synagogue refers to a voluntary association type (e.g. Acts 6:9). This sort of synagogue is "a non-, or semi-public, institutional setting in which groups could maintain their specific religious and/ or other identities."[59] According to such an understanding then, the synagogue which Matthew indicates as "their" possibly belongs to the assembly of the Pharisees, and "Jesus intentionally seeks out and relates to Pharisees in their own assembly building."[60] Thus, the term "their/your/synagogue" appears not an indication supporting the separation of the Jewish believers and Pharisaic-rabbinic Judaism, but was just a clue to understanding the split structure of the synagogue, even when the temple was still standing.[61] Therefore, it is too hasty to conclude that there was a clear-cut separation between the two communities at this point. As Zetterholm rightly points out, the early Christ-centred Jewish community was portrayed as "one of a number of competing Jewish groups and the followers of Jesus as a group within Judaism."[62] Consequently, at the time, the Matthean community still existed within the walls of Judaism.

---

57. t.*Hullin* 2.20–21 Neusner, *Tosefta*, 1379.

58. Runesson, "Rethinking Early Jewish-Christian Relations," 112.

59. According to Philo, Essenes (*Prob.* 81), the Pharisees and other Jewish groups would have their own synagogues (Philo, *De Vita Contemplativa*). Runesson, "Rethinking Early Jewish-Christian Relations," 112.

60. Runesson, 121.

61. Runesson, 113.

62. K. H. Zetterholm, "Alternate Visions of Judaism and Their Impact on the Foundation of Rabbinic Judaism," *JJMS* no. 1 (2014): 134.

5.2.2. Palestine Located Community

As I have discussed in the previous section, the parting of the ways is not the point of Matthew's presentation, rather the Matthean Jewish believers are still part of the Jewish community and do not live separately at this stage. Although we cannot know for sure the specific nature of the Matthean community,[63] it seems that, since the Pharisees are far more harshly criticized in Matthew than in the other gospels, the author and his addresses must have been closely involved with Pharisaic communities.[64] Matthew's audience appears to be Jewish believers of Palestinian origin, many of whom knew Judaism well and were familiar with the Pharisaic way of life. If the Matthean community lived alongside formative rabbinic Judaism, the community would have been located in the land of Palestine, more specifically in Galilee,[65] where formative rabbinic Judaism had settled. Matthew tells the story of Jesus's relations with the Pharisees in a Palestinian setting comprising mostly Jewish believers; probably even including some Pharisees who believed in Jesus[66] and who were familiar with the land and Pharisaic traditions and practices. Otherwise, there would not have been any reason for Matthew to warn people so intensely against the Pharisees.[67]

Besides, there is no clear and firm historical evidence that this Palestinian-based Matthew community faced persecution from the Yavneans. It is unconvincing that the polemic against the Pharisees is a reflection of post-70 CE rivalry. As Shaye Cohen[68] and Baumgarten[69] point out, the Yavneans have reached a point where they have no choice but to practise mutual tolerance, and agree to disagree. As we have seen in chapter 2, the situation of

---

63. As we have seen in section 5.1 of this chapter, the Matthew community was defined by the scholars as – Jewish community; gentiles community; and a mixed community of Jews and gentiles. Runesson identifies the community of Matthew as Pharisaic communities. He argues that according to Acts 15:5, there were many Pharisees who became Jesus believers without abandoning their identity in the first century. Although Paul became a Jesus believer, he always regarded himself as a Pharisee. For him, Matthew is telling about an "inner-Jewish parting of the ways, specifically an inner-Pharisaic split between groups." See further discussion by Runesson, "Early Jewish-Christians Relations," 95–132, 131–132.
64. Skype discussion with Runesson (11.3.2016).
65. Saldarini, "Delegitimation of Leaders in Matthew 23," 663–664.
66. Runesson, "Rethinking Early Jewish-Christian Relations," 132.
67. Skype discussion with Runesson (11.3.2016).
68. Cohen, "Significance of Yavneh," 27–54.
69. Baumgarten, *Flourishing of Jewish Sects*, 195.

formative-Pharisaic rabbi Yavneans had taught them to accept differences in such critical situations. This is to say that the conflict between Pharisaism and Jesus's followers does not have to date to a post-Yavnean era. The gospel makes it clear that from the beginning the intense conflicts between the Pharisees and Jesus and his followers came from Jewish leaders in Jerusalem itself. Such conflicts are also seen in other writings of the New Testament (Phlm 3:5–6; Acts 8:3; 9:1–2, 13–14, 21; 22:3–5, 19; 26:9–11; 1 Cor 15:9; Gal 1:13; 1 Thess 2:13–16; 1 Tim 1:13). Since the Qumran community was distanced from the Jewish community and the elite Sadducees lived above the masses and did not associate so much with the populace, it was the Pharisees who controlled the access to Torah, and they exerted more influence over the populace, and became the main opponents of both Jesus and his followers.[70] The book of Acts also informs us that Paul, as a zealous Pharisee, was active in the early 30s in persecuting the followers of Jesus (Acts 8).[71]

At the same time, the community was in a period of transition. The Matthean community at this point was not only serious about maintaining the connection with their ancestral practices and faith but also began to be concerned about their future in the light of Jesus's teachings about gentile believers. The gospel itself makes obvious the dual stands of the community (e.g. 10:5–6; 15:21–28; 21:43; 28:18–20). They appeared to be in a situation where they have to remain faithful to their Jewish roots but where it was also necessary to mingle with gentile believers, because Jesus had told them to do so. Thus, from Matthew's point of view, Jesus and his mission ensured the community of Matthew should retain its roots and yet it should have a new direction for the future.[72]

The faith that the Matthean's community put in Jesus as both Messiah and the Son of God and in practising Jesus's teachings might pull them in a different direction from the dominant Jewish community.[73] However, the Matthean community's divergent perspective on Messiahship and Jesus as the fulfiller did not mean that Mathew's Jewish believers had separated from Judaism in the late first century. They were a deviant group who still lived

---

70. Gundry, *Matthew*, 601.
71. Theissen, *Gospels in Context*, 231.
72. Senior, *Matthew*, 24.
73. Senior, 24.

within the boundaries of Judaism, but held views not supported by majority of the remaining Jews. At the same time, they were attempting to claim their legitimacy in the face of the rise of rabbinic Judaism.[74]

5.3 The Function of Matthew 23

If the practices and traditions of Matthew 23 reflect the time of Jesus on the historical level, why did Matthew use this material for his post-70 intramural community? Is the purpose of Matthew 23 to delegitimize the leaders of Judaism at the time and to promote Jesus-centred Judaism as Saldarini claimed? Or is Garland right that Matthew compose an "anti-Judaic" text to warn Christian leaders within his own community so they would escape the condemnation that the Pharisees had fallen under? Or is Marshall right that Matthew's polemics are a response to opposition faced by the evangelist and his community after 70? Did Matthew write Matthew 23 to argue for a replacement theology?

In my view, Matthew 23 is a response to the destruction of the temple. As Runesson points out, Matthew puts "the blame for the destruction of the temple is laid squarely at the feet of the Pharisees"[75] and establishes Jesus as a new temple. That fits in with the way Matthew focuses the Pharisees in his gospel and with my historical analysis. The temple that had been so important to all Jews was now lost. Matthew 23 insinuates that part of the reason for the loss of the temple was the hypocrisy of the Pharisees. The use of the traditional material in Matthew 23 fits well with Matthew's attack on the Pharisees in general at this point as a response to the destruction of the temple.

Apparently, the historical context of the Matthean time is after the fall of the second temple. The Jewish the revolt against the Romans brought only national chaos, calamity and failures throughout the land (66–70 CE). The remaining Jews had reached a point where they had to establish a new social and religious framework for the continuation and survival of their

---

74. Saldarini, *Matthew's Christian-Jewish Community*, 124–164, 198; Senior, *Matthew*, 23.

75. Runesson, "Purity, Holiness, and the Kingdom," 150.

identity,[76] in a situation where Jews were widely dispersed and where there was no temple. At this historically decisive moment, the nation was suffering from national turmoil and despair. Left behind were probably the two main groups – Jewish believers in Jesus and a new form of Judaism at Yaveh led by the Hillelite Pharisees (plus other remaining groups).

Matthew's response to the disastrous situation is that the Pharisees were part of the reason for what happened. The Pharisees in Matthew 23 are related to the temple-centred motif and its destruction. Matthew links Jesus's criticism of the Pharisees with the destruction of the temple.[77] He blames the loss of the temple on the Pharisees' hypocrisy. He uses arguments that are likely to convince the Jews – the *halakhic* matters of the Pharisees and the debates they had with Jesus. He condemns them as a "brood of vipers," "hypocrites," and "blind guides," arguing against them even in the temple itself for misusing the "seat of Moses," in other words, their authority. As for Matthew, the Pharisees were impure and defiled the holy temple by ignoring the weightier commandments – justice, mercy, and faith.[78] Matthew's Jesus exposes the frauds of the Pharisees in the temple and the loss of the temple as its consequence.

Second, through Matthew 23, Matthew weakens and delegalizes the Pharisaic leadership who were beginning to be influential at Yavneh. Neither group (Jewish believers in Jesus or a new form of Judaism led by the Pharisees) has influence over the Jewish nation as a whole yet. However, Matthew sees that the Pharisees at Yavneh have begun to be influential over the Jewish community at least in the area where they settled. To counteract this influence, Matthew claims that Jesus is the only true teacher; his teachings surpass those of the Pharisees' teachings. For Jesus brings back the core biblical value of Mosaic law which the Pharisees neglect. Matthew shows us that during Jesus's mission on earth he clashed with the Pharisees over the interpretation and practices of Mosaic laws. No matter how hard the Pharisees tried to entrap Jesus in these *halakhic* debates, Jesus emerged victorious. For

---

76. Gafni, "*Historical Background*," 14.
77. Runesson, "Purity, Holiness, and the Kingdom," 150.
78. Runesson, 160.

Matthew, Jesus alone deserves the title of teacher.[79] This is why Matthew makes more of the conflicts with the Pharisees than does Mark.

Therefore, Matthew claims that Jesus is far above the Pharisees of Jesus's time and the leading Pharisees at Yavneh. Indeed, he is the only true teacher who can heal the loss of the temple. As the Pharisaic-rabbis at Yavneh focused Torah studies as a replacement of the temple, Matthew encourages his community to put its hope in Jesus, whom he considers the promised Messiah who replaces the temple. For Jesus comes as the one who fulfils the promise to Abraham and the prophets. We see this at the beginning of his gospel as he carefully traces the family lineage of Jesus back to the Davidic house and presents Bethlehem as Jesus's birthplace. In this way he meets the criteria of the Jews at the time for the expected Messiah.[80] Matthew even extended Jesus's lineage back to Abraham and ended with Jesus's commandment to go to all nations, which indeed was similar with the Abrahamic calling. Matthew presents the fact that Jesus fulfils two of God's promises – to Abraham to bless all nations and to the people of Israel to give them a Messiah.

By embracing Jesus as the Messiah and following his teachings alongside the observance of the Mosaic law, Matthew legitimizes that they were the only faithful and loyal community compared to the other Jews and the Pharisees at Yavneh who did not respond to Jesus. There is no doubt that the community considered the Hebrew Bible as their primary Scripture, following all the commands of the Torah. The only new perspective and revelation they had was that they saw Jesus as Messiah, the fulfiller of the OT prophecy. Such an understanding is described at the beginning of Jesus's Sermon on the Mount: "Do not think that I have come to abolish the law or the prophets; I have come not to abolish but to fulfil (5:17)." They believed that the arrival of Jesus and his ministry had brought the fulfilment of God's promise to Israel in history.[81] While they were embracing both "Jesus and Torah," the other remaining Jews and the Pharisees at Yavneh, were not adequately

---

79. C. Keith, *Jesus against the Scribal Elite: The Origin of the Conflict* (Grand Rapids, MI: Baker Academic, 2014), 5.

80. D. Flusser, "Jesus, His Ancestry, and the Commandment of Love," in *Jesus' Jewishness*, ed. J. H. Charlesworth (New York: Crossroad, 1991), 163–176, 159.

81. Senior, *Matthew*, 24.

responding to both. It is like a sibling fight and a competition about who are the true Jews in terms of observing the Torah and responding to prophecy.

One might wonder if Matthew 23 reflects the historical practices of Shammaites, why does Matthew provide such a text for the Matthean community when the Hillelites were in the majority at Yavneh. However, Matthew's attack is on the Pharisees in general at this point for a certain purpose. Matthew does not seem to distinguish Shammai from Hillel or even know which argument and interpretation belong to whom. What he realized was probably the fact that the Pharisees at Yavneh had begun to exert a dominant influence over the Jewish community at least in their surroundings. In order to convince the Matthean community and other Jews who remained within the teaching and leadership of the Pharisaic-rabbis, Matthew argues that while the Pharisees' frauds had caused the loss of the temple, Jesus is a healing. Because Jesus is the only true interpreter and teacher who fulfilled a prophecy, Matthew establishes that Jesus and his teachings were the only way to heal the Matthean community in a disastrous situation.

Therefore, following Jesus's teaching is far better than following Pharisaic teachings at Yaveh. By retelling the stories of the disputes between Jesus and the Pharisees, Matthew encourages his community to stand firm in their faith in Jesus in faced with the rise and coming domination of Pharisaic-rabbinic Judaism. They are encouraged by the example of Jesus himself, who is the true teacher and Messiah. Matthew and his community attempted to legitimize their understanding of the common Jewish heritage based on the Torah and Messianic prophecy while delegitimizing the Pharisaic-rabbis at Yavheh. Through his assertion of the authority of Jesus, Matthew is telling not that the Jews will be replaced, but that, through Jesus, Jews and non-Jews can be the people of God.[82]

Chapter Findings

First, this chapter has shown that events after 70 did not cause persecution and did not yet separate Matthean Jewish believers from Judaism. The Matthean community was composed largely of Jewish believers in Jesus, and

---

82. Judaism has opened the possible way for non-Jews to be part of the children of the God of Israel. See A. Runesson, "Was There a Christian Mission," 211.

they still lived within the main body of Judaism, living side by side with the Pharisaic community in the land of Palestine. As formative-rabbinic Judaism struggled to survive and legitimize its position after 70 as the defender of a continued Jewish nation, the Matthean community also tried to legitimize its faith and identity. Their faith and Jewish identity was in Jesus, which they legitimized by giving a new understanding and meaning to the Messianic prophecy. They saw the prophecy fulfilled in Jesus, and they followed his teachings by being loyal and faithful to Judaism.

Second, Matthew 23 is a response to the destruction of the temple. Through the stories of conflict between Jesus and the Pharisees, particularly in Matthew 23, he establishes that the loss of the temple was partly because of the Pharisees misled the Jews and abused their authority. The Pharisees' impurity has brought disaster on the nation. In contrast, Matthew presents Jesus as the one who surpasses the Pharisees' teachings. He alone is the true teacher. Matthew encourages the Matthean community to see Jesus as one who can heal the nation, because Jesus replaces the temple. The Pharisees, in contrast, only brought misfortune on the nation. For Matthew, only Jesus could restore the core values of the biblical message. Jesus had understood this message correctly, while the Pharisees had got it wrong by putting all the weight on ritual minutiae.

Finally, the function of Matthew 23 is to persuade his community to be firm in Jesus while facing the challenge of Pharisaic-rabbis' authority at Yavneh. By narrating the conflicts Jesus had with the Pharisees and his condemnation of them, Matthew is encouraging his community to stand firm by their faith in Jesus at a time when rabbinic Judaism is becoming more and more dominant among the surviving Jews, at least in their area. Matthew's community is experiencing a period of transition, experiencing challenges from rabbinic Judaism and struggling to survive as a Jewish Christian community.

CHAPTER 6

Conclusion

In this final chapter, I will give the finding of the thesis after summarizing the conclusions of each chapter. The thesis begins with the topic "The Pharisees in Matthew 23 reconsidered." Since a majority of scholars view Matthew 23 as a fictional piece born out of the post-70 CE period, the main concern is to examine whether the Pharisees and materials we find in Matthew 23 reflect the time of Jesus or the post-70 CE rabbinic period.

Accordingly, chapter 2 sets out to examine briefly historical Pharisaism from the Second Temple period to the late first century with an emphasis on the Pharisees of Jesus's time. A brief historical survey of the Pharisees showed that the Pharisees already existed before the Maccabean revolt in the Hellenistic period in opposition to the Sadducees. They accepted both the Oral and Written Torah and encouraged the common Jews to build up a holy Jewish community and a universal priesthood through their *halahkic* purity prescriptions.

However, they became both religious and political advisers for the Hasmonean rulers who were both kings and priests in the Hasmonean period. A patron-client relationship maintained the interests of both groups. Queen Salome Alexandra placed political authority in their hands. Now the most powerful group, they began to misuse their position. When the Herodians came to power, the Pharisees still retained some influence but no longer had the same power as during Salome Alexandra's reign. As a result, the Pharisees focused more on the study of the Torah and began to conceptualize the oral traditions in the synagogues, strictly following priestly ritual rules and tithing in their daily lives. It was also the time when the two Pharisaic Houses (Shammai and Hillel) *halakha* flourished in Palestine.

Although the two Pharisaic Houses existed under Herodian rule, the Shammaic Pharisees supported a strict attitude towards the gentiles and dominated until the fall of Jerusalem. After post-70 CE, it was the Hillelite Yohannan ben Zakkai who founded a new form of inclusive religious society focusing on Torah studies, performing loving-kindness and good deeds for the continuation of Judaism at Yavneh. The work and the practice of the community revealed that the Yavneh community (including surviving Shamaic Pharisees) preserved the Pharisaic traditions of their predecessors.

After historical analysis of the Pharisees, I examine the picture of the Pharisees in Matthew literary setting in chapter 3. The finding shows that Matthew focuses on the Pharisees as bad examples. He presents more conflicts between Jesus and the Pharisees than Mark and Luke do. The conflicts are about Sabbath observance, table fellowship, observing the tradition of the fathers regarding hand washing, the issue of divorce, paying taxes, and the interpretation of Mosaic law. Matthew appears to present the Pharisees as the most legitimate dialogue partners of Jesus on Mosaic law at the time. Matthew has more material on the Pharisees than the other gospels and he is more determined to present them as unclean creatures: "brood of vipers," "hypocrites," and "blind."

Chapter 4 makes a literary analysis of chapter 23. The setting is in the temple context and the chapter contains climax of Jesus's conflict with the Pharisees. It is in the temple setting that Jesus denounces their hypocrisy, their rejection of him and the fall of the temple as the consequence. The Pharisees have been following him, listening and criticizing everything he says throughout his ministry. He now turns on them in the temple itself. They claim to be the people's religious leaders and yet they have misunderstood and misled the people. They have misread the Scriptures. They are only concerned with tradition and outer show. Jesus, in contrast, calls for justice, mercy and faith for Mosaic law demands inner purity.

The first part of chapter 4 demonstrates Matthew's literary strategy in building up to a climax of the conflict between Jesus and the Pharisees. The second part of the chapter illustrates that the Pharisees Jesus attacks in Matthew 23 are very much the Pharisees of Jesus's own times. The detail matches the *halakha* that then flourished already pre-70 of Pharisaic tradition.

In chapter 5, I examine the function of Matthew 23 in the historical context of Matthean community and formative-rabbinic Judaism. The findings show that the early post-70 events did not yet separate Matthean Jewish believers from Judaism. Although the Matthean community had different views on the prophecy of Messiah than other Jewish groups, they still considered themselves Jewish. It was an intra-mural conflict. It was in a situation where the Jews were still mourning for the loss of the temple. Matthew 23 is a response to the destruction of the temple.

From the above chapter findings, the thesis claims that Matthew 23 reflects the Pharisees and their practices pre-70. The thesis further contends that the Matthew 23 functions also as an attack against post-70 the Yavnean Pharisees. Historically, the material used in 23 dates to Pharisaic tradition before 70, and Jesus's criticisms best match Shammaic practices. The historical study of the Herodian period (ch. 2) and chapter 4 fit this analysis. Therefore, previous scholarly claims that Matthew 23 material cannot be explained if one does not assume a post-70 CE date for them are unconvincing. On the contrary, materials in Matthew 23 in fact not only make sense before 70 CE, but even in most cases seem to require a pre-70 setting. Otherwise, why did Matthew bother so much about the holy temple, the altar, sacred and the things associated with it in a situation where there was no temple at all? Matthew devotes more attention than the other gospels to this group, giving us precise accounts of pre-70 Pharisaic traditions. The function of Matthew 23 is to lay the blame for the loss of the holy temple on the Pharisees. Their misguided leadership and misconduct defiled the holy temple so that God finally abandoned them. It was vital for him to emphasize that his community should remain true to Jesus's teaching – that inner purity was what counted, not outer practice. For Matthew, lack of mercy, justice and faith led to hypocrisy and conceit. To argue his case Matthew did not need to invent new material. It was already there before 70. Now, Matthew says that the consequence of the Pharisees' misconduct is the loss of the temple, the heart of all Jews. But there is salvation.

Matthew claims that Jesus replaces the temple. He legitimizes Jesus's authority above the Pharisees. Through the narration of Jesus's conflicts with the Pharisees, Matthew encourages his community to stand firm faced with the disastrous situation and the rise of rabbinic Judaism. "Put your faith," he urges, "in the only teacher and Messiah who is the new temple."

Scholars have paid lot of attention is given to the gospel writer's intention in writing for his community. However, this should not distract us from acknowledging that the materials may contain authentic materials. In fact, as I have argued, Matthew 23 has a double function – it both reflects disputes between Jesus and the Pharisees of his time, and it serves the purpose of warning the Matthean community to stand fast by their faith in Jesus. If the arguments of this study are correct, namely that Matthew 23 does contain authentic material, should this not have implications for research on the historical Jesus?

Bibliography

1. Primary Source and Translation

Josephus, F. *The Jewish Antiques: Books 15–17: Loeb Classical Library.* Translated by R. Marcus and A. Wikgren. London: William Heinemann, 1963.

Josephus, F. *The Jewish Antiques: Books 12–14: Loeb Classical Library.* Translated by R. Marcus. London: William Heinemann, 1961.

Josephus, F. *The Jewish Antiques: Books 18–20: Loeb Classical Library.* Translated by L. H. Feldman and R. Marcus. London: William Heinemann, 1965.

Josephus, F. *The Jewish War: Books I–III: Loeb Classical Library.* Translated by H. S. T. J. Thackeray. London: William Heinemann, 1961.

Josephus, F. *The Life against Apion: Loeb Classical Library.* Translated by H. S. T. J. Thackeray. London: William Heinemann, 1926.

The Mishnah: A New Translation. Translated by J. Neusner. Yale University, 1988.

The Mishnah. Translated by H. Danby. London: Oxford University Press, 1964.

The Talmud: The Selected Writings. Translated by Bokser, Ben Zion. New York: Paulist, 1989.

The Tosefta, vol 1. Translated by J. Neusner. Peabody, MA: Hendrickson, 2002.

2. Books, Articles, and Online Resources

πορνεία. Strong's Greek Lexicon Number. http://studybible.info/strongs/G4202. Accessed 29 November 2015.

Abrami, L. M. "Were All the Pharisees 'Hypocrites'?" *Journal of Ecumenical Studies* 47, no. 3 (Summer 2013): 427–435.

Albright, W. F., and C. S. Mann. *Matthew: The Anchor Bible*, vol. 26. London: Doubleday, 1971.

Anderson, J. C. *Matthew's Narrative Web.* Sheffield: JSOT Press, 1994.

Bacon, B. W. "'The Five Books' of Matthew against the Jews." *Expositor* 15 (1918): 56–66.

———. "Jesus and the Law: A Study of the First Five 'Books' of Matthew (Mt. 3–7)." *JBL* 47 (1928): 203–231.

Bauer, D. R. *The Structure of Matthew's Gospel*. Sheffield: Almond Press, 1988.

Baumgarten, Albert I. *The Flourishing of Jewish Sects in the Maccabean Era*, vol. 55. Atlanta: SBL Press, 1997.

Beckwith, R. "The Pre-History and Relationship of the Pharisees, Sadducees and Essenes: A Tentative Reconstruction." *RQ* 11 (1982): 3–46.

Bellinzoni, A. J., ed. *The Two-Source Hypothesis: A Critical Appraisal*. Macon, GA: Mercer University Press, 1985.

Berman, Samuel A. *Midrash Tanuma-Yelammedenu*. Brooklyn, NY: KTAV Publishing, 1996.

Bokser, Ben Zion, trans. *The Talmud: The Selected Writings*. New York: Paulist, 1989.

Borchardt, F. *The Torah in 1 Maccabees: A Literary Critical Approach to the Text*, vol. 19. Berlin: de Gruyter, 2014.

Bornkamm, G. "End-Expectation and Church in Matthew." In *Tradition and Interpretation in Matthew*, edited by G. Bornkamm, 15–51. London: SCM, 1963.

Brown, R. *The Birth of the Messiah*. New York: Doubleday, 1977, 1993.

Bruner, F. D. *The Church Book Matthew 13–28*, vol. 2. Grand Rapids, MI: Eerdmans, 1990.

Bultmann, R. *The History of the Synoptic Tradition*. Translated by J. Marsh. Oxford: Blackwell, 1963.

Buxbaum, Y. *The Life and Teaching of Hillel*. New York: Rowman & Littlefield, 1994.

Carson, D. A. "The Jewish Leaders in Matthew's Gospel: Reappraisal." *JETS* 25, no. 2 (June 1982): 161–174.

Charlesworth, J. H., ed. *Jesus' Jewishness*, vol. 2. New York: Crossroad, 1991.

Charlesworth, J. H., and L. L. John, eds. *Hillel and Jesus*. Minneapolis, MN: Fortress, 1997.

Chilton, B., and J. Neusner. *Judaism in the NT*. London: Routledge, 1995.

Clark, K. "The Gentile Bias in Matthew." *JBL* 66 (1947): 165–172.

Clarke, H. *The Gospel of Matthew and Its Readers*. Bloomington, IN: Indiana University Press, 2003.

Cohen, S. J. "The Significance of Yavneh: Pharisees, Rabbis, and the End of Jewish Sectarianism." *Hebrew Union College Annual* 55 (1984): 27–53.

Cohen, S. J. D. *From the Maccabees to the Mishnah*. Philadelphia, PA: Westminster, 1987.

Cook, D. E. "A Gospel Portrait of the Pharisees." *Review & Expositor* 84, no. 2 (Spring 1987): 221–133.

Cook, M. J. *Mark's Treatment of the Jewish Leaders*. Leiden: Brill, 1978.

Culbertson, P. "Changing Christian Images of the Pharisees." *ATR* 64, no.4 (1982): 539–561.
Davies, W. D. *The Setting of the Sermon on the Mount.* Cambridge: Cambridge University Press, 1964.
Davies, W. D., and D. Allison. *The Gospel According to St. Matthew*, 2 vols. Edinburgh: T&T Clark, 1988, 1991.
———. *Matthew*, vol. 3. Edinburgh: T&T Clark, 1997.
———. *Matthew*. London: T&T Clark, 2004.
Dunn, J. D. G. *The Partings of the Ways.* 2nd edition. London: SCM, 2006.
Evans, O. E. "Synoptic Criticism Since Streeter." *ET* 72 (1961): 295–299.
Eusebius, *Ecclesiastical History III.* 24.5–6, translated by C. F. Cruse. Peabody, MA: Hendrickson, 1998.
Ewherido, A. O. *Matthew's Gospel and Judaism in the Late First Century C.E.* SBL 91. New York: Lang, 2006.
Falk, H. *Jesus the Pharisee: A New Look at the Jewishness of Jesus.* New York: Paulist, 1985.
Farmer, W. R. *The Synoptic Problem: A Critical Analysis.* Dillsboro, NC: Western North Carolina Press, 1976.
Finkelstein, L. "The Origin of the Pharisees Reconsidered." *Conservative Judaism*, (Winter 1969): 25.
———. "The Pharisaic Leadership after the Great Synagogue (170 B.C.E-135 C.E)." In *The Cambridge History of Judaism*, vol. 2, edited by W. D. Davies and Louis Finkelstein, 245–277. Cambridge: Cambridge University Press, 1989.
Fitzmyer, J. A. *The Dead Sea Scrolls and Christian Origins.* Cambridge, UK: Eerdmans, 2000.
———. "The Priority." In *The Two-Source Hypothesis: A Critical Appraisal*, edited by A. J. Bellinzoni, 37–52. Macon, GA: Mercer University Press, 1985.
Flusser, D. "Hillel and Jesus: Two Ways of Self-Awareness." In *Hillel and Jesus*, edited by J. H. Charleswort and L. L. Johns, 71–107. Minneapolis, MN: Fortress, 1997.
———. "Jesus, His Ancestry, and the Commandment of Love." In *Jesus' Jewishness*, edited by J. H. Charlesworth, 163–176. New York: Crossroad, 1991.
———. *Jesus.* The Hebrew University. Jerusalem: Magnes, 1998.
———. *Jewish Sources in Early Christianity.* Tel-Aviv, Israel: MOD, 1993.
———. *Judaism of the Second Temple Period*, vol. 2. Translated by Azzan Tadin. Jerusalem: Hebrew University Press, 2002.
Fornberg, T. "Matthew and the School of Shammai: A Study in the Matthean Antithesis." *Theology and Life* (Hong Kong) 7 (1984): 35–59.

Foster, P. *Community, Law and Mission in Matthew's Gospel*. Tubingen: Mohr Siebeck, 2004.
France, R. T. *Matthew Evangelist and Preacher*. Downers Grove, IL: InterVarsity Press, 1989.
———. *NICNT: The Gospel of Matthew*. Grand Rapids, MI: Eerdmans, 2007.
Gafni, I. M. "The Historical Background." In *The Literature of the Sages*, edited by S. Safrai and P. J. Tomson, 1–34. Philadelphia, PA: Fortress, 1987.
Garland, D. E. *The Intention of Matthew 23*. NovTSup, 52. Leiden: Brill, 1979.
Gaston, L. "The Messiah of Israel as Teacher of the Gentiles." *Interpretation* 29 (1975): 24–40.
Goodman, M. *Mission and Conversion*. Oxford: Clarendon, 2001.
Gottlieb, B. "Yohanan Ben Zakkai." In *The Oxford Dictionary of the Jewish Religion*, edited by R. J. Zwi Werblowsky and Geoffrey Wigoder. Oxford: University Press, 1997.
Gowan, D. G. *Bridge between the Testaments*. 3rd edition. Allison Park, PA: Pickwick, 1986.
Grabbe, L. L. *An Introduction to First Century Judaism, History and Religion of the Jews in the Time of Nehemiah, the Maccabees, Hillel and Jesus*. Edinburgh: T&T Clark, 1996.
———. *Introduction to Second Temple Judaism, History and Religion of the Jews in the Time of Nehemiah, the Maccabees, Hillel and Jesus*. London: T&T Clark, 2010.
Graetz, H. *History of the Jews, vol. 2: From the Reign of Hyrcanus (135 B.C.E) to the Completion of the Babylonian Talmud 500 C.E.* New York: Cosimoclassic, 2009.
Gundry, R. *Matthew*. 2nd edition. Grand Rapids, MI: Eerdmans, 1994.
Hagner, D. A. *WBC: Matthew 1–13*, vol. 33a. Dallas, TX: Word, 1993.
———. *WBC: Matthew 14–28*, vol. 33b. Dallas, TX: Word, 1995.
Hare, D. R. A. *The Themes of Jewish Persecution of Christians in the Gospel according to St. Matthew*. Cambridge: Cambridge University Press, 1967.
Hare, D. R. A., and D. J. Harrington. "Make Disciples of All the Gentiles (Mt. 28.19)." *CBQ* 37(1975): 359–369.
Harrington, D. J. *The Gospel of Matthew: Sacra Pagina Series*, vol. 1. Collegeville, MN: Liturgical Press, 1991.
———. "The Jewishness of Jesus: Facing Some Problems." In *Jesus' Jewishness*, vol. 2, edited by J. H. Charlesworth, 123–152. New York: Crossroad, 1991.
Hengel, M., and R. Deines. "'Common Judaism,' Jesus, and the Pharisees." *JTS* 46 (1995).
Herford, R. T. *The Pharisees*. Boston, MA: Beacon, 1962.
Horbury, W., and W. D. Davies. eds. *The Cambridge History of Judaism*, vol. 3. Cambridge: Cambridge University Press, 1999.

Instone-Brewer, D. *Traditions of the Rabbis from the Era of the New Testament*, vol. 2a. Grand Rapids, MI: Eerdmans, 2011.
James. "The Laying on of Hands-S'mikhah." https://thinkhebrew.wordpress.com/2009/12/07/the-laying-on-of-hands-smikhah/. Accessed 2 November 2015.
Jastrow, Marcus and S. Mendelsohn. "Bet Hillel and Bet Shammai." http://www.jewishencyclopedia.com/articles/3190-bet-hillel-and-bet-shammai. Accessed12 October 2015.
Jeremias, J. *Jerusalem in the Time of Jesus*. Philadelphia, PA: Fortress, 1969.
———. *Jerusalem in the Time of Jesus: An Investigation into Economic and Social Conditions during the New Testament Period*. Translated by F. H. and C. H. Cave. Philadelphia, PA: Fortress, 1967.
Jewish Encyclopaedia: School of Shammai and Hillel.
Johnson, L. T. "The New Testament's Anti-Jewish Slander and the Conventions of Ancient Polemic." *JBL* 108, no. 3 (1989): 419–441.
Kampen, J. *LXX: The Hasideans and the Origin of Pharisaim*. Atlanta, GA: Scholar Press, 1988.
Karesh, S. E., and Mitchell M. Hurvitz. *Encyclopaedia of Judaism*. New York: Facts on File, 2006.
Keener, C. S. *A Commentary on the Gospel of Matthew*. Grand Rapids, MI: Eerdmans, 1999.
———. *The Gospel of Matthew*. Grand Rapids, MI: Eerdmans, 2009.
Keith, C. *Jesus against the Scribal Elite: The Origin of the Conflict*. Grand Rapids, MI: Baker Academic,2014.
Kingsbury, J. D. "The Developing Conflicts between Jesus and the Jewish Leaders in Matthew's Gospel: A Literary-Critical Study," *CBQ* 49 (1987), 57–73.
Kloppenborg, J. S. ed., *Q and the Earliest Gospel*. London: John Knox, 2008.
———. *The Shape of Q*. Minneapolis, MN: Fortress, 1994.
Koester, H. *History, Culture, and Religion of the Hellenistic Age*, vol. 1. Philadelphia, PA: Fortress, 1982.
———. *Introduction to the NT*, vol. 1. Philadelphia: Fortress, 1982.
Kummel, W. G. *Introduction to the New Testament*. London: SCM, 1975.
———. "In Support of Markan Priority." In *The Two-Source Hypothesis: A Critical Appraisal*, edited by A. J. Bellinzoni, 53–84. Macon, GA: Mercer University Press, 1985.
Levine, L. I. *The Ancient Synagogue: The First Thousand Years*. New Haven: Yale University Press, 2000.
Lohse, E. *The NT Environment*. Nashville, TN: Abingdon, 1976.
LSJ the online Liddell-Scott-Jones Greek Lexicon. http://stephanus.tlg.uci.edu/lsj/#eid=91932&context=search. Accessed 29 March 2016.

Luz, U. *Matthew 1–7*. Minneapolis, MN: Fortress, 2007.
———. *Matthew 8–20*. Minneapolis, MN: Fortress, 2001.
———. *Matthew 21–28: A Commentary*. Minneapolis, MN: Fortress, 2005.
———. *The Theology of the Gospel of Matthew*. Cambridge: Cambridge University Press, 1995.
Magness, J. *Stone and Dung, Oil and Spit: Jewish Daily Life in the Time of Jesus*. Grand Rapids, MI: Eerdmans, 2011.
Marshall, M. *The Portrayals of the Pharisees in the Gospels and Acts*, vol. 254. Gottingen: Vandenhoeck & Ruprecht, 2015.
Mason, S. *Josephus and the New Testament*. Peabody, MA: Hendrickson, 1992.
———. "Pharisaic Dominance before 70CE and the Gospels' Hypocrisy Charge (Matt 23:2–3)," *HTR* 83, no. 4 (1990), 363–381.
McKnight, S. *A Light among the Gentiles: Jewish Missionary Activity in the Second Temple Period*. Minneapolis, MN: Fortress, 1991.
McNamara, M. *Palestinian Judaism and the New Testament*, vol. 4. Wilmington, DE: Glazier, 1983.
Meier, J. P. *A Marginal Jew*, vol. 3. New York: Doubleday, 2001.
———. "Nations or Gentiles in Matthew 28:19?" *CBQ* 39 (1977): 94–102.
———. "Reflections on Jesus-of-History Research Today." In *Jesus' Jewishness*, vol. 2, edited by J. H. Charlesworth, 84–107. New York: Crossroad, 1991.
———. *Vision of Matthew: Christ Church, and Morality in the First Gospel*. New York: Paulist Press, 1979.
Menninger, R. E. *Israel and the Church*. American University Studies, 7: Theology and Religions, 162: New York: Lang, 1993.
Murphy, F. J. "Second Temple Judaism." In *The Blackwell Companion to Judaism*, edited by Jacob Neusner and Alan J. Avery-Peck, 58–77. Oxford, UK: Blackwell, 2003.
Neusner, J. *The Babylonian Talmud: A Translation and Commentary*. Peabody, MA: Hendrickson, 2009.
———. "'First Cleanse the Inside': The 'Halakhic' Background of a Controversy Saying." *NTS* 22 (1976): 486–495.
———. *From Politics to Piety: The Emergence of the Pharisaic Judaism*. Englewood Cliffs, NJ: Prentice Hall, 1973.
———. *History of Religions*. NTS 19 (1972–73): 271–287.
———. *Origins of Judaism*, vol. 2: Part II. New York; London: Garland, 1990.
———. "Pharisaic Law in New Testament Times." *Union Seminary Quarterly Review* 24 (1971): 331–340.
———. *The Rabbinic Traditions about the Pharisees before 70: Part 1, The Masters*. Atlanta, GA: Scholars Press, 1999.
———. *The Rabbinic Traditions about the Pharisees before 70: Part 2, The Houses*. Atlanta, GA: Scholars Press, 1999.

Neusner, J., ed. *Dictionary of Ancient Rabbis: Selections from the Jewish Encyclopaedia*. Peabody, MA: Hendrickson, 2003.

———, ed. *Dictionary of Judaism in the Biblical Period: 450 B.C.E to 600 C.E.* Peabody, MA: Hendrickson, 1999.

Newport, K. G. C. "A Note on the 'Seat of Moses.'" *AUSS* (1990): 53–58.

———. *The Sources and Sitz im Leben of Matthew 23*. Sheffield: Sheffield Academic, 1995.

Nickelsburg, G. W. E. *Ancient Judaism and Christian Origins*. Minneapolis, MN: Fortress, 2003.

Nicoll, W. R. *The Expositor's Greek Testament*, vol. 1. Grand Rapids, MI: Eerdmans, 1951.

Nolland, J. *NIGTC: The Gospel of Matthew*. Grand Rapids, MI: Eerdmans, 2005.

Osborne, G. R. *Exegetical Commentary on the New Testament*. Grand Rapids, MI: Zondervan, 2009.

Overman, J. A. *Matthew's Gospel and Formative Judaism*. Minneapolis, MN: Fortress, 1990.

Pickup, M. "Matthew and Mark's Pharisees." In *Quest of the Historical Pharisees*, edited by J. Neusner and B. D. Chilton, 67–112. Waco, TX: Baylor University Press, 2007.

Pixner, B. "Jesus and His Community: Between Essenes and Pharisees." In *Jesus' Jewishness*, vol. 2, edited by J. H. Charlesworth, 193–224. New York: Crossroad, 1991.

Powell, M. "Do and Keep What Moses Says (Matthew 23:2–7)." *JBL* 114 (1995): 419–35.

Rabbinowitz, N. S. "Matthew 23:2–4: Does Jesus Recognize the Authority of the Pharisees and Does He Endorse Their Halakah?" *JETS* 46, no. 3 (September 2003): 42–447.

Rahmni, L. Y. "Stone Synagogue Chairs: Their Identification, Use and Significance." *International Endodontic Journal* 40 (1990): 192–214.

Repschinski, B. *The Controversy Stories in the Gospel of Matthew*. Gottingen: Vandenhoeck & Ruprecht, 2000.

Richardson, P. *Herod*. Minneapolis, MN: Fortress, 1999.

Rivkin, E. "Defining the Pharisees: the Tannatic Sources." In *Origins of Judaism*, vol. 2 part 2, edited by Jacob Neusner, 173–217. New York & London: Garland, 1990.

———. *A Hidden Revolution*. Nashville, TN: Abingdon, 1978.

———. "Scribes, Pharisees, Lawyers, Hypocrites: A Study in Synonymity." *HUCA* 49 (1978): 135–142.

Roth, C. "The 'Chair of Moses' and Its Survivals," *Palestine Exploration Quarterly* 81 (1949): 100–111.

———. "The Pharisees in the Jewish Revolution of 66–73." In *Origins of Judaism*, vol. 2, edited by J. Neusner, 255–272. London: Garland, 1990.

Runesson, A. "The Origins of the Synagogue in Past and Present Research." *Studia Theologica* 57 (2003): 60–76.

———. *The Origins of the Synagogue: A Socio-Historical Study*. Stockholm: Almqvist & Wiksell, 2001.

———. "Purity, Holiness, and the Kingdom of Heaven in Matthew's Narrative World." In *Purity, Holiness, and Identity in Judaism and Christianity: Essays in Memory of Susan Baber*, edited by C. S. Ehrlich, A. Runesson and E. Schuller, 144–180. Tubingen: Mohr Siebeck, 2013.

———. "Rethinking of Early Jewish-Christian Relations: Matthean Community History as Pharisaic Intragroup Conflict." *JBL* 127, no. 1 (2008): 95–132.

———. "Was There a Christian Mission before the Fourth Century? Problematizing Common Ideas about Early Christianity and the Beginnings of Modern Mission." In *The Making of Christianity*, edited by M. Zetterholm and S. Byrskog, 205–247. Winona Lake, IN: Eisenbrauns, 2012.

Safrai, S. "The Synagogue." In *In the Jewish People in the First Century: Historical Geography, Political History, Social, Cultural, and Religious Life and Institutions*, 2 vols., edited by S. Safrai and M. Stern, 908–944. Philadelphia: Fortress, 1976.

Saldarini, A. J. "Delegitimation of Leaders in Matthew 23." *CBQ* 54 (1992): 659–680.

———. *Matthew's Christian-Jewish Community*. Chicago, IL: University of Chicago Press, 1994.

———. *Pharisees, Scribes, and Sadducees in Palestinian Society*. Grand Rapids, MI: Eerdmans, 2001.

———. "Reading Matthew without Anti-Semitism." In *The Gospel of Matthew in Current Study*, edited by David E. Aune, 166–184. Cambridge: Eerdmans, 2001.

Sanders, E. P. *Jewish Law from Jesus to the Mishnah*. London: SCM, 1990.

———. *Judaism: Practice and Belief 63 BCE–66 CE*. London: SCM, 1992.

Schaper, J. "The Pharisees." In *The Cambridge History of Judaism*, vol. 3, edited by W. Horbury and W. D. Davies, 402–427. Cambridge: Cambridge University Press, 1999.

Schiffman, L. H. "Beit Hillel and Beith Shammai." In *The Oxford Dictionary of the Jewish Religion*, edited by R. J. Zwi Werblowsky and Geoffrey Wigoder. Oxford: Oxford University Press, 1997.

Schnackenburg, R. *The Gospel of Matthew*. Translated by R. R. Barr. Grand Rapids, MI: Eerdmans, 2002.

Schweizer, E. *The Good News according to Matthew*. Translated by D. E. Green. London: SPCK, 1975.

Senior, D. *The Gospel of Matthew*. Nashville, TN: Abingdon, 1997.
———. *Matthew*. Nashville, TN: Abingdon Press, 1998.
Sigal, P. *The Halakah of Jesus of Nazareth according to the Gospel of Matthew*. Leiden: Brill, 2008.
Sim, D. C. *The Gospel of Matthew and Christian Judaism*. Edinburgh: T&T Clark, 1998.
———. "The Social Setting of the Matthean Community." *HTS* 57, no. 1 & 2 (2001): 268–280.
Simmons, Rabbi Shraga. http://www.aish.com/jl/m/pb/48969816.html. Accessed 5 October 2015.
Simmonds, A. R. "Woe to You . . . Hypocrites! Re-Reading Matthew 23:13–36." *Bibliotheca Sacra* 166 (July-Sep 2009): 336–349.
Smith, F. "A Study of the Zadokite High Priesthood within the Graeco-Roman Age: From Simon the Just to the High Priests appointed by Herod the Great." Dissertation, Harvard, 1961.
Smith, M. "The Troublemakers." In *The Cambridge History of Judaism*, vol. 3, edited by W. Horbury and W. D. Davies, 501–568. Cambridge: Cambridge University Press, 1999.
Stanton, G. *A Gospel for a New People*. Edinburgh: T&T Clark, 1992.
Stemberger, G. *Introduction to the Talmud and Midrash*. Translated and edited by Markus Bockmuehl, 2nd edition. Edinburgh: T&T Clark, 1996.
———. *Jewish Contemporaries of Jesus*. Minneapolis, MN: Fortress, 1995.
Stendahl, K. *The School of St. Matthew and Its Use of the Old Testament*, 2nd edition. Philadelphia, PA: Fortress, 1968.
Stock, A. *The Method and Message of Matthew*. Collegeville, MN: Liturgical Press, 1994.
Streeter, B. H. "The Priority of Mark." In *The Two-Source Hypothesis: A Critical Appraisal*, edited by A. J. Bellinzoni, 23–36. Macon, GA: Mercer University Press, 1985.
Theissen, G. *The Gospels in Context*. Translated by L. M. Maloney. Minneapolis, MN: Fortress, 1991.
Throckmorton, B. H., ed. *Gospel Parallels: A Synopsis of the First Three Gospels*. Nashville, TN: Nelson, 1967.
Tommasino, A. J. *Judaism before Jesus*. Leicester: InterVarsity Press, 2003.
Tuckett, C. M. *Q and the History of Early Christianity*. Edinburgh: T&T Clark, 1996.
———. "Synoptic Problem." In *The Anchor Bible Dictionary*, edited by D. N. Freedman, 6:263–270. New York: Doubleday, 1992.
Turner, D. L. *Israel's Last Prophet: Jesus and the Jewish Leaders in Matthew 23*. Minneapolis, MN: Fortress, 2015.

———. "Jesus' Denunciation of the Jewish Leaders in Matthew 23, and Witness to Religious Jews Today." In *To the Jew First,* edited byDarrell L. Bock and Mitch Glaser, 66–77. Grand Rapids, MI: Kregel, 2008.

Vermes, G. *The Dead Sea Scrolls*. Philadelphia, PA: Fortress, 1981.

Viviano, B. "Study as Worship." *SJLA* 26. Leiden: Brill, 1978.

Weinfeld, M. "Hillel and the Misunderstanding of Judaism in Modern Scholarship." In *Hillel and Jesus*, edited by J. H. Charlesworth, and L. L. John, 56–70. Minneapolis, MN: Fortress, 1997.

Wellhausen, J. *The Pharisees and Sadducees*. Macon, GA: Mercer University Press, 2001.

Wigoder, G., ed. *The New Encyclopaedia of Judaism*. 1989.

Wild, R. A. "The Encounter between Pharisees and Christian Judaism: Some Early Gospel Evidence." *Novum Testamentum* 27, no. 2 (1985): 105–124.

Zeitlin, S. "The Origin of the Pharisees Reaffirmed." In *Origins of Judaism: The Pharisees and Other Sects*, vol. 2, part 2, edited by Jacob Neusner and William Scott Green, 471–483. New York & London: Garland, 1990.

Zeller, D. "Redactional Process and Changing Setting." In *The Shape of Q,* edited by J. S. Kloppenborg, 116–130. Minneapolis, MN: Fortress, 1994.

Zetlin, Irving M. *Jesus and the Judaism of His Time*. Cambridge: Polity Press, 1988.

Zetterholm, K. H. "Alternate Visions of Judaism and Their Impact on the Foundation of Rabbinic Judaism," *JJMS* No 1 (2014): 127–153.

———. *Jewish Interpretation of the Bible*. Philadelphia, PA: Fortress, 2012.

Zwi Werblowsky, R. J., and Geoffrey Wigoder, eds. *The Oxford Dictionary of the Jewish Religion*. Oxford: Oxford University Press, 1997

Langham Literature and its imprints are a ministry of Langham Partnership.

Langham Partnership is a global fellowship working in pursuit of the vision God entrusted to its founder John Stott –

> *to facilitate the growth of the church in maturity and Christ-likeness through raising the standards of biblical preaching and teaching.*

Our vision is to see churches in the majority world equipped for mission and growing to maturity in Christ through the ministry of pastors and leaders who believe, teach and live by the Word of God.

Our mission is to strengthen the ministry of the Word of God through:
- nurturing national movements for biblical preaching
- fostering the creation and distribution of evangelical literature
- enhancing evangelical theological education

especially in countries where churches are under-resourced.

Our ministry

Langham Preaching partners with national leaders to nurture indigenous biblical preaching movements for pastors and lay preachers all around the world. With the support of a team of trainers from many countries, a multi-level programme of seminars provides practical training, and is followed by a programme for training local facilitators. Local preachers' groups and national and regional networks ensure continuity and ongoing development, seeking to build vigorous movements committed to Bible exposition.

Langham Literature provides majority world preachers, scholars and seminary libraries with evangelical books and electronic resources through publishing and distribution, grants and discounts. The programme also fosters the creation of indigenous evangelical books in many languages, through writer's grants, strengthening local evangelical publishing houses, and investment in major regional literature projects, such as one volume Bible commentaries like *The Africa Bible Commentary* and *The South Asia Bible Commentary*.

Langham Scholars provides financial support for evangelical doctoral students from the majority world so that, when they return home, they may train pastors and other Christian leaders with sound, biblical and theological teaching. This programme equips those who equip others. Langham Scholars also works in partnership with majority world seminaries in strengthening evangelical theological education. A growing number of Langham Scholars study in high quality doctoral programmes in the majority world itself. As well as teaching the next generation of pastors, graduated Langham Scholars exercise significant influence through their writing and leadership.

To learn more about Langham Partnership and the work we do visit **langham.org**